FIVE MILES HIGH

PETZOLDT

AVALANCHE ON WEST FACE OF K2

Five Miles High

THE STORY OF AN ATTACK
ON THE SECOND HIGHEST MOUNTAIN
IN THE WORLD BY THE MEMBERS OF THE
FIRST AMERICAN KARAKORAM EXPEDITION

Robert H. Bates · Richard L. Burdsall
William P. House · Charles S. Houston, M.D.
Paul K. Petzoldt · Capt. Norman R. Streatfeild

ILLUSTRATIONS FROM PHOTOGRAPHS
TAKEN BY MEMBERS OF
THE EXPEDITION

The Lyons Press

Originally published in 1939 by Dodd, Mead and Company, Inc.
First Lyons Press edition, 2000
ISBN 1-58574-051-9

10 9 8 7 6 5 4 3 2 1

The Library of Congress Cataloging-in-Publication Data is
available on file.
Printed in Canada

*To our predecessors in the Karakoram
on whose shoulders we climbed*

PRELUDE

Since time immemorial man has longed to go beyond the horizons. Now after centuries of his travels most horizons have been passed, but there are still the unclimbed peaks.

Protected as we are today in our specialized 20th century lives, few have known, even for a short time, a primitive existence or felt the thrill of pitting their strength against the forces of nature. Men who climb mountains go in humility to try their skill and knowledge against wind and cold, great heights and far distances. They know that the contest purges them of artificialities, returning them to their homes refreshed. Having faced life stripped to essentials, they can better appreciate and properly evaluate the luxuries of civilization.

Man is continually struggling to reach a tangible goal, a definite objective. That is why men struggle to the North Pole, the South Pole, toward Mindanao Deep or Everest.

Expeditions to high mountains free man from the trammels of everyday living, pit him against the forces of nature, furnish him one small point to reach. To gain a summit he must strain himself to the utmost; he is on a pilgrimage. With him are men bound on the same pilgrimage, and the kinship of an arduous expedition is deep and lasting. Only a team that thinks and feels as one man can succeed in this quest.

To those who have gone before us in the Karakoram, and especially to Luigi Amedeo, Duke of the Abruzzi, we owe our greatest debt. More personal is our gratitude for the help and inspiration of Ellis Fisher, J. Monroe Thorington, Edward Groth, Harry P. Nichols, William F. Loomis and Oscar Houston.

To Elizabeth Farrand George we are deeply indebted for the drawings in this book.

Ours is the tale of a party of six climbers and six porters who tried as one to climb the second highest mountain in the world. Our story, like our climb, is the work of a team.

One word more. We had originally planned a six-man attack on the mountain, but circumstances forced us to leave two men in support. Streatfeild and Burdsall, on whom fell this duty, contributed fully as much to the work of the team as any man who went higher.

R.H.B.
C.S.H.

CONTENTS

ix

ILLUSTRATIONS

INTRODUCTION

Welcome to *Five Miles High*, Robert H. Bates's and Dr. Charles S. Houston's account of their team's attempt to summit K2. Welcome to 1938, to the last years of western colonialism and to an all-but-forgotten piece of climbing history.

Five Miles High is more than a book about climbing. It is also one of the first adventure-travel books of the previous century. Adventure travel may be a relatively new term, but this book proves that the process itself has American roots that run deep.

What is adventure travel?

Good question. You don't have to be a climber to be an adventure traveler, but you can be. You don't have to leave the country to participate, but you can do that, too. Adventure travel is not easily defined, and that's one reason why those of us who do it like it. As Dr. Houston writes, "Protected as we are today in our 20th century lives, few have known, even for a short time, a primitive existence or felt the thrill of pitting their strength against the force of nature . . . Having faced life stripped to the essentials, they can better appreciate and properly evaluate the luxuries of civilization."

You betcha. That's adventure travel. Part of it, anyway. Anything that takes us away, gets us out of the rut, conflicts with or confounds the bureaucratic status quo. Gathering up six friends and attempting to climb the earth's second highest peak, for instance.

The voice of this book is an anachronistic one that bespeaks old money, colonial imperatives, and a privileged class. Listen to Bates: "Often the natives would give each of us a bouquet of flowers and then beg for the honor of being allowed to help our Sherpas smooth the ground and put up the tents. Several coolies would plead for the privilege of being allowed to blow up the sahib's air mattress . . . Next each Sherpa himself would lay out his sahib's sleeping bag, diary and toilet kit . . . and personally take off his master's marching boots. Such luxury doesn't exist in civilized countries."

Nor will it ever again.

Also of interest are the contrasting voices of this book's two authors. It is interesting because their lives were not dissimilar. Dr. Houston was one of his era's foremost climbers. He was born in New York City in 1913, and by age 11, he was mountaineering in the Alps with his father.

His love of the mountains and climbing never left him.

While still in school, Houston climbed Mount Crillon and Mount Foraker in Alaska. He made several successful climbs in the Alps. In 1936, he went to India and helped organize the Anglo-American expedition to Nanda Devi, a 25,660–foot peak. In 1938, he led the first American expedition to climb K2, which failed. The next year Houston, with a BA from Harvard, graduated from the College of Physicians and Surgeons, Columbia University. He entered the Navy as a lieutenant, just a few months before the Japanese bombed Pearl Harbor.

Robert Bates, born in 1911, also came from a privileged background and developed an early interest in climbing. He began to climb seriously when at Harvard, and spent the winter of 1935 mapping mountainous sections of the Yukon for the National Geographic Society.

In 1941, Bates became a consultant at the War Department and entered World War II as a commissioned officer.

Along with the rest of the free world, Houston and Bates made their lives and their personal passions secondary to the war effort. They could not have known, but the world they wrote about during their expedition of 1938—the world you will find between the covers of this book—would never be the same again.

Capturing a lost world. It's another manifestation of adventure travel.

Randy Wayne White
Pineland, Florida
April 2000

FIVE MILES HIGH

Chapter I

The Idea

Charles S. Houston, M.D.

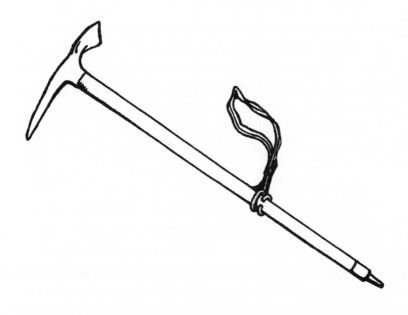

Chapter I   The Idea

BIG things are often done in the small hours.

Bob Bates was just climbing into bed late at night when the telephone rang.

"Is this Philadelphia, Evergreen six-eight-seven-six? New York is calling."

"Yes."

"Hello, Bob, this is Charlie. Sorry to wake you up,

but I want to ask you something."

"What is it?"

"Can you go to the Himalaya this summer?"

"What's that? What do you mean?"

"Well, the club has just received permission to send a small party to K2 and they've asked me if I could get a group together."

"I'll be darned!"

*   *   *   *

This was the beginning of the American Alpine Club Expedition to the second highest mountain in the world.

*   *   *   *

In the northwest end of the mighty Himalaya lies a subsidiary range, the Karakoram, which contains many of the highest and most spectacular peaks in all the world. King of these giants is K2, which rears its head 28,250 feet above sea level, while its only peer, Mount Everest, 29,002 feet high, lies a thousand miles to the south and east.

Since its discovery in 1856 only two expeditions have approached K2 with thoughts of attempting its ascent, and both parties fell far short of its distant top. Many reasons make the climb an outstandingly difficult problem. First: the mountain is over 330 miles from the nearest city, Srinagar, capital of Kashmir, and for only the first 210 miles can pony transport be used. For the final 120 miles all equipment for a climbing group must be carried on men's backs. Second: the walls of this nearly symmetrical four-sided pyramid rise 12,000 feet above its base in exceptionally steep and broken slopes of rock and ice. So formidable are the few approaches to its summit that many climbers have felt the ascent to be impossible, for climbing of such severity is almost prohibitive at great altitudes. In addition, establishing camps at frequent intervals up such precipitous slopes requires much time and labor.

A final factor is the weather. Though the dreaded monsoon, which renders Everest unclimbable for so many months of snow and wind, probably does not penetrate the range of the Karakoram, still there is little definite information available to indicate the best season for climbing there. By reading the scanty literature on the region one finds every opinion. Some writers feel that May and June are the months of choice, claiming that storms begin in July and continue till fall. Others have experienced almost perfect weather till mid-August. Friends in England told us that the fall months are most settled, and that from June till August frequent storms interrupt the climbing weather. In this conflict of opinion we decided to use the two months most convenient for our leaves of absence, and planned our attack for June and July.

Three main ridges lead upward from the base of K2 on its more accessible sides—the northwest, the northeast, and the south. Each of the three has been called the best climbing route by different parties, and the chief result which our group hoped to accomplish was to decide definitely which of the three was the safest and least difficult approach to the summit. Could we determine which route offered most possibility of success, perhaps a later expedition, unhampered by the need of reconnoitering the mountain, might hope to reach the top. Ours then was to be a preliminary attack whose main plan was to find a way for a later party.

To summarize briefly, then, we were to travel halfway round the world, to carry food and equipment for 330 miles into the heart of a great range of mountains, there to work for six weeks above an altitude of 16,000 feet. We were to examine three main ridges, separated by miles of glacier travel, and to decide which of the three would be most likely to furnish a route to the summit. Finally, given time, weather, and the smile of fortune, we were to try to reach that distant point.

Chapter II

Geographical and Historical

Richard L. Burdsall

Chapter II   Geographical and Historical

THE Himalaya, "the abode of the snow, " extend in a great sweep of 1500 miles along the northern frontier of India, a vast system of lofty mountain ranges and deep gorges. While sometimes considered as comprising all of the mountains of central Asia, the true Himalaya are confined to the area enclosed within the arms of the Indus and the Brahmaputra. These two

rivers, the Indus bending around Nanga Parbat in the
northwest and the Brahmaputra flowing through a tremendous gorge around Namcha Barwa at the south-
eastern end of the range, collect the drainage from the
northern slopes and carry it into the Indian Ocean.
Other rivers, also rising on the northern side, cut directly through the range to the plains of India, so that
the Himalaya, the backbone of Asia, though a barrier
in every other sense, do not form the continental divide. It is the Karakoram and lower, almost unknown
ranges extending eastward across Tibet that separate
the rivers flowing southward from those that flow northward to lose themselves in the deserts of Central Asia.

As mountaineers we view the Himalaya much as our
predecessors of 160 years ago viewed the Alps. In 1779
a few of the small peaks had been climbed, but all the
greater ones were still unconquered and the prize
offered by De Saussure for the discovery of a route to
the summit of Mont Blanc (15,782 feet) was not to be
claimed until Dr. Packard and Balmat climbed it in
1786. One by one the proud Alpine summits have
yielded, and now every one of them has been climbed.

For new peaks to conquer, the mountaineer may,
however, turn to Asia and find them in overwhelming
abundance. It seems impossible that all the mountains
that exceed the altitude of Mont Blanc will ever be
climbed. Confining our attention for the moment to
those that exceed it by two miles or more, we find 15

summits over 26,240 feet or 8000 meters in altitude. The names, locations and heights of these mountains are given below. Not one of them has been climbed and only five have been attempted.

Name	Location	Altitude in feet	Altitude in meters
Mount Everest	Nepal Himalaya	29,002	8840
K2	Karakoram	28,250	8610
Kangchenjunga I	Nepal Himalaya	28,146	8579
E1 (Lho Tse)	" "	27,890	8501
Kangchenjunga II	" "	27,803	8474
Makalu	" "	27,790	8470
Dhaulagiri	" "	26,810	8172
Cho Oyu	" "	26,750	8153
Kutang I (Manaslu)	" "	26,658	8125
Nanga Parbat	Punjab Himalaya	26,620	8114
Annapurna I (XXXIX)	Nepal Himalaya	26,504	8078
Gasherbrum I (Hidden Peak)	Karakoram	26,470	8068
Broad Peak	"	26,400	8047
Gasherbrum II	"	26,360	8024
Shisha Pangma (Gosainthan)	Nepal Himalaya	26,291	8013

Everest has been the objective of seven expeditions, two for reconnaissance and five for the purpose of climbing. Thus far the last thousand feet has proved impregnable.

K2, previous to our expedition, had been attempted twice, the highest altitude reached being 21,870 feet at Savoia Pass.

Kangchenjunga has been attempted by three large expeditions and it would be difficult indeed to equal the skill and determination of the parties led by Bauer in 1929 and 1931. The latter reached an altitude of 25,256 feet on the northeast spur, or Bavarian Ridge as it is now known in their honor. Two thousand, eight hundred and ninety feet remain unclimbed.

Gasherbrum I, or Hidden Peak, was attempted by the Dyhrenfurth Expedition in 1934 and by the French Expedition in 1936, the latter reaching an altitude of about 22,960 feet when bad weather forced a retreat.

Nanga Parbat, since it claimed the life of Mummery in 1895, has been the objective of five expeditions, two of which met with the greatest tragedies in mountaineering history. In June, 1934, the advance party was caught in a terrific storm which finally brought death to three climbers and four porters. On the 1937 expedition seven climbers and nine porters, while asleep at Camp IV on the night of July 14, were buried by an avalanche. The highest altitude reached on Nanga Parbat is about the same as that on Kangchenjunga, 25,256 feet, which was attained in 1934 just before the storm, the climbers being within 1400 feet of their goal.

The highest mountain whose summit has been reached is Nanda Devi (25,645 feet) in the central Himalaya of Garhwal, which was conquered by the British-American Himalayan Expedition of 1936, of which Houston was a member. The second highest mountain climbed is Kamet (25,447 feet) 45 miles northwest of Nanda Devi, which yielded to a British expedition led by Smythe.

After this brief review of Himalayan mountaineering in general, let us turn to the Karakoram, the scene of our expedition. This range is located north of the western end of the Himalaya, from which it is separated by the Indus Valley. Starting in the bend of the Shyok River, a large tributary of the Indus, the Great Karakoram extend for a distance of 300 miles to the northwest, ending at the mountain Koz Sar (21,907 feet) and the Chilinji Pass. The main range has been divided into seven groups bearing the name Muztagh (muz = ice, and tagh = mountain); the central group, known as the Baltoro Muztagh, is on the continental divide and culminates in K2. The Karakoram might well be considered the top of Asia, for they surpass even the Himalaya in the number of giant peaks found within a limited area.

Karakoram comes from two words: *kara*, meaning black, and *koram*, meaning fallen rock or gravel. Anyone visiting the mountains will agree that this name is appropriate, for though they themselves are white with snow, millions of tons of *black fallen rock* lie upon their glaciers. The name was extended to the mountains from the Karakoram Pass farther east, over which caravans crossed on their long journey from India, Kashmir and Ladakh to the ancient city of Karakoram in central Asia, the capital of Genghis Khan.

And what of the name K2? It was a provisional desig-

nation given by the Survey of India, K standing for
Karakoram and 2 for the particular peak. K1 was for
Masherbrum and K3, K4, K5 the Gasherbrum peaks,
the numbers being set down according to location, not
altitude. Many other names have been proposed for K2,
Mount Waugh, Mount Albert, Mount Montgomerie,
Mount Godwin-Austen, Mount Akbar, and Mount
Baber. The name Mount Godwin-Austen has been
widely used and is found on many maps. It was given
in honor of the great explorer and Surveyor-General
of India, upon whose grave is the inscription, "He sur-
veyed the Karakoram."

But the Survey of India decided to reject all personal names for mountains, save only that of Everest.
Explorers have tried to discover a native name for K2
and have reported Chiring, Chogori, Lanfafahad, Dap-
sang, and Lamba Pahar. These however have not been
substantiated, and we fall back upon the Survey sym-
bol K2, which is now firmly fixed, and will stand wit-
ness to the fact that this great mountain had no native
name in general use. K2 seems appropriate, for it has
a certain bold, grim flavor characteristic of the mountain which it designates.

"Babu, we have shot the giant," are the words which
Colonel Montgomerie is supposed to have said to his
Indian recorder when he first intersected K2 from
Mount Haramukh in 1856. The altitude of K2 has
been measured from nine stations, distant 59 to 137

miles, with results ranging from 28,218 feet to 28,323 feet, the value finally adopted being 28,250 feet. According to these official figures it is the second highest mountain in the world—752 feet lower than Everest and 104 feet higher than Kangchenjunga. It is still possible however that Kangchenjunga, which is 900 miles southeast of K2, may eventually be found to exceed it in altitude, for the difference is small and present uncertainties of measurement fairly large.

K2 is located about 800 miles north of Delhi, the capital of India, and is almost exactly on the other side of the world from Denver, Colorado. Its latitude is about the same as that of southern California, North Carolina, the Straits of Gibraltar, and Tokio.

There have been thirty expeditions to the Karakoram, as shown by a list in the Appendix, which gives the date, leader, and principal accomplishment of each. Only those which worked in the immediate vicinity of K2 will be noted here.

The Baltoro Glacier, discovered in 1861 by Godwin-Austen, who ascended it as far as the mouth of the Muztagh Glacier, was explored for its whole length in 1892 by a large expedition led by Sir Martin Conway. After mapping the Hispar, Biafo, and Baltoro Glaciers, Conway, with Major Bruce, the guide Zurbriggen, and two Gurkhas, made the ascent of a 22,600-foot summit which he named Pioneer Peak, rising from a ridge of the Golden Throne. The account of this notable expedition is in Conway's book, "Climbing and Exploration in the Karakoram-Himalayas."

The first attempt to climb K2 was made in 1902 by an expedition led by the English mountaineer O. Eckenstein, accompanied by two other Englishmen, A. E. Crowley and G. Knowles, two Austrians, Drs. H. Pfannl and V. Wesseley, and the Swiss doctor, J. J. Guillarmod, who told the story in his book, "Six Mois dans l'Himalaya." This was the first expedition to explore the upper Godwin-Austen Glacier, where they spent six weeks from June 20 to August 2. Camp IX was established a short distance southwest of the foot of the northeast spur of K2, as this was the route by which they had decided to attack the mountain.

On July 10 Wesseley and Guillarmod left this camp at 5:30 A. M. in an attempt to gain the snowy shoulder of the spur. As they approached this point Guillarmod relates that they found a meter of powder snow which had to be brushed away before they could cut steps in the hard, black ice, each step requiring 20 to 30 blows of the ax. They regretted having left their crampons half way from camp. The slope varied from 47° to 50°, as measured by their clinometer, and at 12:45 they turned back when about 150 feet below the shoulder, their aneroid indicating a height of 22,000 feet. (Calculations by the Abruzzi Expedition give an altitude for the shoulder of 21,588 feet, and about 21,400 feet for the point reached by the climbers.)

They decided to wait for the snow to solidify, and during this period Pfannl and Wesseley established Camp XII in the cirque between the northeast spur and Staircase Peak. They attempted to climb a gully on the western wall of this cirque, but were driven back by steep ice and falling stones. Wesseley made a trip to the col at the head of the Godwin-Austen Glacier, the limit of the Baltoro Basin, and Guillarmod named this point Windy Gap. Pfannl became ill and the expedition was brought to a close. They had accomplished a fine piece of work in exploring the upper Godwin-Austen and fixing the continental divide at Windy Gap. Guillarmod still believed in the feasibility of climbing K2 by the northeast ridge.

The second expedition to attempt the ascent of K2 was led by H.R.H. Prince Luigi Amedeo of Savoy, Duke of the Abruzzi, who took with him Dr. Filippo de Filippi, Lieutenant M. F. Negrotto, Vittorio Sella, and seven Italian guides and porters from Courmayeur. Two of these had been in the Karakoram before with Dr. and Mrs. Bullock-Workman, and two had been with Longstaff on expeditions to explore Nanda Devi and climb Trisul. The account of the expedition, written by Filippi, is a magnificent work, entitled "Karakoram and Western Himalaya," with a supplement containing an unexcelled series of photographic panoramas by Sella and maps produced by the photogrammetric survey carried out by Negrotto.

The expedition left Srinagar on April 23, 1909, following the same route traveled by Guillarmod and later by our own expedition, and established a camp at the base of K2 on May 26. After a rapid reconnaissance of the mountain, the Duke decided to attempt the southeast ridge, and left the base camp on May 30, with three guides, four porters, and coolies who carried their own tents and provision of *chupattis*. They climbed the ridge till they came to a rock buttress at the top of a scree slope. There, at 18,245 feet, little levels were made for the two Whymper tents, the coolies camping close by. After a rest the guides and coolies started on. The latter soon turned back, but the guides continued to a narrow saddle less than 1000 feet above the camp, where they left their loads and returned.

Next day, with 25-pound loads, the coolies followed the guides up to the saddle and the latter continued, reaching a height of "certainly 20,000 feet." The following morning they sent six coolies back to the base camp for more provisions. Meanwhile those left on the ridge climbed again to the saddle and on up a *couloir,* with the help of rope fixed the day before. They found the rock broken and crumbling but continued slowly for three hours more toward a reddish rock, where the Duke had hoped to locate a camp.

"The guides finally came to the reluctant conclusion that it was useless to proceed farther, not because they had encountered insurmountable obstacles, but because it was hopeless to think of bringing so long and formidable an ascent to a successful issue, when from the very first steps they had met with such difficulties as made the climb barely possible to guides not hampered by loads, and put out of the question the conveying of luggage necessary to keep one from perishing from cold and exhaustion. They came slowly back, gathering up the rope they had put along the way. The Duke heard their report, and wisely decided to relinquish the attack in that direction."

June 2 found the expedition united at the base camp, and two days later they moved to the northwest, establishing a camp near the western spur of K2 at an elevation of 18,176 feet. On June 7 the Duke set out at 5:30 with three guides in an attempt to reach the col at the head of the glacier. After four hours they crossed the bergschrund at the foot of the steep slope and then spent seven and a half hours cutting steps up this ice wall, finally reaching the ridge at a point to the right and slightly higher than the col at an altitude of 21,870 feet.

"The watershed proved to have on its northern side a broad cornice prolonged to the right in such a way as to cut off completely the view of the northern slope of K2. Below the col to the westward they could just make out the wall descending toward the north and disappearing vertically from view. And that was all. As a reward for his labors the Duke thus saw utterly annihilated the hopes with which he had begun the ascent."

After lingering 15 minutes on the col, they descended and reached the camp at 9:30, having been met on the way by porters with hot drinks and Alpine lanterns. They had performed a remarkable feat which had required 16 hours of exertion. The Duke gave the name Savoia to the glacier and to the pass.

The whole party returned to the base camp and on June 12 commenced an exploration of the upper Godwin-Austen Glacier. A camp was placed just beyond a natural amphitheater on the eastern side of the glacier north of Broad Peak. On the northeast side of this semicircle of mountains is a depression which the Duke named Sella Pass, and to which he climbed with three guides on June 15. It was again visited seven days later by Sella for photographic purposes.

On the way up from the base camp, the Duke discovered articles left by Guillarmod at their Camp X. In the seven years these had moved nearly a mile from the location shown by Guillarmod for Camp X, which would indicate an average daily movement of the glacier of a little less than two feet.

A camp was next established near Windy Gap, from which the Duke attempted the ascent of Staircase Peak (Skyang Kangri), with two guides, reaching 21,650 feet, on June 25, where they were stopped by a huge crevasse. The view of K2 from this point convinced the Duke of the hopelessness of making further efforts to climb it.

Though his exploration of the mountain was finished, he had no intention of ending his campaign but determined to attempt Bride Peak, 20 miles to the south. On July 18, with three guides, he reached an altitude of 24,600 feet, where they became lost in mist and were therefore unable to reach the summit 510 feet above. They had exceeded by 700 feet the highest altitude previously attained by mountaineers, and their record was not surpassed until the Everest expedition of 1922.

The Duke started the return journey on July 20, crossing the Skoro La and the Deosai Plateau, the same route taken by Guillarmod and by our own expedition, and reached Srinagar on August 11.

Twenty years later another large and well-equipped Italian expedition went to the Karakoram under the leadership of Aimone di Savoia-Aosta, Duke of Spoleto. Professor Ardito Desio wrote the account of the expedition, entitled, "La Spedizione Geografica Italiana al Karakoram." Their base of operations was at Urdukas, from which parties went out to map and carry out geological and other scientific work. Of special interest to us was their map of K2 with its ridges, also a photograph of the north side of the mountain.

The next strictly mountaineering expedition was that of Dr. and Mme. Dyhrenfurth, which took place in 1934 and is recounted in their book, "Dämon Hi-

malaya." They succeeded in climbing the Golden
Throne, 23,990 feet, and Queen Mary Peak, 24,350
feet. (Their calculations, giving an altitude of over
25,000 feet for this mountain, have not as yet been accepted.) They also attempted Gasherbrum I, or Hidden
Peak.

This mountain was again attacked by the French Expedition to the Himalaya in 1936. On our way to India
two years later we were cordially entertained in Paris
by members of the French Alpine Club, among them
Pierre Allain, a member of this expedition.

In addition to the leader, Henry de Ségogne, their
large party was composed of nine French Alpinists,
Captain N. R. Streatfeild as liaison and transport officer, 35 Sherpas, 2 shikaris, 2 cooks, a sweeper, and 4
postal couriers. Food and equipment made 510 loads.
They left Srinagar on April 17 and reached their base
camp on May 26. Six hundred and fifty porters had
been required on leaving Askole.

During the following weeks five camps were established on Hidden Peak, and on June 21 they carried
equipment to a site selected for Camp VI at about 22,-
960 feet. Then bad weather set in, the monsoon or
something very like it, and they were forced to abandon
the attempt. They had apparently conquered the most
difficult part of the climb and another week or two of
good weather might well have given them the summit. In descending from Camp II, two Sherpas, slid-

ing on new snow, started an avalanche with which they fell over 2000 feet. Miraculously no bones were broken but the two were terribly bruised and had to be carried all the way back to Srinagar, the journey being made in 18 days, from July 5 to 22.

Such was the record of exploration and mountaineering in the Baltoro Basin up to the spring of 1938. Only two attempts had been made to climb K2, and none for the last 29 years. Clearly this second mountain of the world called for a fresh reconnaissance in the light of modern mountaineering methods and equipment. To accomplish this was the primary purpose of the first American Alpine Club Karakoram Expedition.

Chapter III

Biscuits and Boots

Charles S. Houston, M.D.

Chapter III   Biscuits and Boots

THE American Alpine Club, through its officers
Joel Ellis Fisher and James Rogers, had tried for
several years to obtain the consent of the Government
of Kashmir to send an expedition to the Karakoram.
Finally, due to the invaluable aid of Mr. Edward
Groth, American Consul in Calcutta, permission was
received in the fall of 1937 for a small party accom-

panied by a British liaison officer to enter the province of Baltistan and attempt the ascent of K2. Fritz Wiessner, a well-known climber of the club, was first selected to lead the group, but when he found himself unable to leave New York the permit was handed over to me, and I was given a free hand in organizing a compact expedition.

Then began months of detailed work. The dean of the medical school where I was completing my third year proved most lenient and granted me six weeks of additional vacation to participate in this first American expedition. Bob Bates of Philadelphia was enlisted immediately, and his protests that he must complete his work for his Ph.D. in English were weak and quickly overcome as soon as he was granted leave of absence from his teaching at the University of Pennsylvania. Bates and I were both members in 1933 of a party attempting the ascent of Mount Crillon in Alaska under the leadership of Bradford Washburn, well-known American mountaineer, whose numerous Alaskan ascents are models of small mobile expeditions. Bates had gone again with him to the Yukon for three months in 1935 to engage in survey work and exploration. And in 1936 the two alone had climbed 17,150-foot Mount Lucania and crossed a hundred miles of little known country on their return, one of the great climbing feats in the history of Alaskan mountaineering.

A firm believer in small expeditions, I led the 1934

party which climbed 17,300-foot Mount Foraker in the McKinley Range of Alaska. In 1936, with Loomis, Emmons, and Carter of Boston, I went to Nanda Devi in India with the British climbers, Tilman, Odell, Graham Brown, and Lloyd. This British-American expedition penetrated the strong defenses of the mountain and after several weeks of work reached its 25,600-foot summit, the highest yet climbed. Bates, twenty-seven years old, and I, twenty-five, were both accustomed to the sub-zero temperatures and high winds of Alaska and I in addition had had some Himalayan experience.

Dick Burdsall, forty-two-year-old engineer of Port Chester, New York, was the next to join our group. He had been a member of the small party that in 1932 reached the top of Minya Konka—a 24,900-foot peak in western China. Months had been spent in the long and tedious approach to this unmapped mountain, with many additional weeks of surveying and climbing its steep ridges. Since that time Burdsall had been a perennial agitator for a Himalayan expedition, and each fall, as regularly as Hallowe'en, he approached us to try to plan some trip for the following summer. At last his chance had arrived, but it was only with difficulty that he was able to leave his responsible position and join us. In view of his business experience, his stability, and his patience, he was immediately made expedition treasurer, an involved and unpleasant position he was to fill in long-suffering silence.

Negotiations with the British Foreign Office were opened at once for obtaining a liaison officer. Weeks later we were informed that Captain Norman R. Streatfeild, M.C., R.A., of the Bengal Mountain Artillery, had been granted leave of absence to join us. Though we had never met him, many mutual friends had praised him to us and we were indeed grateful to the Government of India for furnishing us so able and willing an officer and so agreeable a companion. During his 13 years in India he had been numerous times to the Karakoram on shooting and mapping trips, had climbed many peaks over 20,000 feet, and was well versed in dealing with the natives of Baltistan. In 1936 he had served as liaison officer to the huge French Expedition to Hidden Peak, not ten miles from K2. We were to find his ingenuity, his ready wit and his enthusiasm invaluable, and without him our party might never have reached Base Camp.

Letters were written and advice sought in all quarters to fill the two remaining vacancies, for we had decided on six men as the optimum number for the undertaking. Late in February, Bill House, twenty-five-year-old forester from Concord, N. H., was prevailed on to give up his job and join us. He had been climbing for a number of years and had made fine ascents in the Alps and the Rockies. In 1936, with Wiessner, Woolsey, and Wilcox, he had made a brilliant ascent of Mount Waddington, the formidable rock peak in British Columbia which had resisted 16 previous assaults. Though he had had comparatively limited expedition training, his climbing ability was exceptional.

At about the same time Paul Petzoldt of Jackson Hole, Wyoming, joined our ranks. He had spent many summer seasons exploring in the Rockies and had also done considerable climbing during the winter in sub-zero weather. He had made numerous first ascents in the Wyoming Rockies, and in the Alps had one day led the double traverse of the Swiss Matterhorn, a feat of unusual endurance. His great experience with mountain camping, winter weather and climbing of exceptional technical difficulty made him a splendid addition to our group.

To complete our personnel we planned to engage six mountain porters from Darjeeling. These Sherpas are veterans of most of the climbs made in India and Tibet and are almost a *sine qua non* to a party planning an attack on any major peak. They are a mixture of Tibetan, Nepalese, Mongolian and Indian blood, accustomed to rigorous living and hard work. Familiar as they are with expedition technique, they are as indispensable to the Himalayan climber as his ice ax or his boots. Though slight of build, they are strong, willing, and above all filled with enthusiasm for mountaineering. To them an attempt on a high mountain is a pilgrimage and the white climber almost a holy man. No previous expedition has failed to praise them both as climbers and companions. With the kind help of Mrs. Townend, and Mr. Wale of the Himalayan Club, Tilman, leader of the Mount Everest Expedition, selected six veterans for us.

One of our first considerations had been to secure necessary funds for the expedition. The total cost was estimated at about $9000 from New York to New York (which proved substantially correct). Some of us were able to raise our shares of this sum through the generosity of our families, while Loomis in Boston and Fisher in New York made very generous contributions to our treasury. The balance we borrowed on the strength of expected returns from lectures and articles in the coming fall.

The difficult problem of finance settled, we turned our attention to more tangible details. Art Emmons came down from Boston and Bob Bates from Philadelphia and we spent several exhausting days drawing up detailed food and equipment lists. These were based on similar lists of many previous expeditions and were optimistically designed to satisfy all palates. Bates, who was to assume the responsibility for the commissary during the trip, later realized that pleasing everyone was an impossibility.

As soon as the lists were drawn up, dozens of samples of various foods were tested, and here our trusting families served as willing subjects. Many different kinds of meat, chocolate and dried fruits were cooked and served in blindfold tests, until, after many trials and errors, the most satisfactory became the basis of our food supply. One of the big problems was to supply bulk; for, in order to conserve weight and at the same time provide foods with high energy content, it was necessary to take the most concentrated substances. After testing dozens of types of biscuits and hard bread —by dropping them from the second-story window and leaving them out in the rain over night—we finally selected one brand. This biscuit tasted good and resisted moisture, yet needed no sledge hammer to break it. We took almost 100 pounds and found that even this was an inadequate supply.

From Massachusetts we bought a large amount of the famous dried vegetables which had proved so satisfactory on other trips. These are manufactured by a small company through a secret process and are eminently suited to meet the needs of light weight and easy cooking. When properly prepared, they taste almost like fresh vegetables and some can be cooked as high as 25,000 feet, where one can put his hand into boiling water without hurt.

Chocolate was a difficult problem. Some of the party insisted that a sweet chocolate was best. Others demanded unsweetened, bitter chocolate. Still others felt that nuts and honey should be added. Eventually, we compromised and took some of each, but the problem of getting a supply of chocolate through the tropical India heat to Base Camp—without deterioration—had also to be considered.

Dried fruits, likewise prepared by a small company through a secret process, were bought in California. Some very fine cheddar cheeses, tested on former trips, were ordered from Liverpool. A vast supply of malted milk tablets came from Wisconsin, and from Denmark we ordered 50 pounds of pemmican. This is a highly concentrated extract of meat, including rice, sugar, and raisins, which forms the basis of menus used in the Arctic and Antarctic. One pound of this concentrated substance dissolved in several pints of boiling water makes a thick soup, which Bates and I considered more than enough to fill the stomachs of six hungry men. Several hundred rolls of hard candy in the form of fruit drops were ordered. These would be useful for lunches on the mountain to allay high-altitude thirst, and would also delight the natives. Much dried milk was necessary, as this forms a base for many foods used on the mountain. Inevitably, we took 15 pounds of tea. Coffee was omitted because of greater difficulty in preparation. And finally there were numerous little delicacies, such as kippered herring, two tins of caviar and four plum puddings for moments of celebration.

All during the winter months we struggled with the menu—sampling, testing, and reorganizing. Before shipment, all the cereals, the rice, and the macaroni were weighed out in small paraffin bags for safety and convenience in carrying. The dried fruits, the chocolate and the fruit drops also were repacked in watertight bags. Finally the whole food supply was carefully listed, sealed in larger canvas sacks and packed in tea chests for shipment. We took all of our food from this country or from England, so as to become acquainted in advance with the brands we would be using.

The problem of equipment was even more complicated. Our woolen underwear and woolen sweaters occupied the attention of an entire village in the Shetland Isles. Socks and gloves and woolen helmets were ordered in London, after considerable research by David Robertson, an American friend of ours at Cambridge; and special windproof suits of Grenfell Cloth were made by another London firm. These suits were to prove particularly satisfactory. Light-weight sleeping bags of eiderdown were made to order in England. They were composed of two sacks, one inside the other, the inner one lined with flannel blanket, the outer covered with a thin, light, water-repellent material. The two together weighed but 7 pounds and were guaranteed for temperatures of 30° below zero.

Tiny tents modeled after the high-altitude ones used on Everest were also made in England. These measured 7 by 4 feet and weighed 12 pounds complete with collapsible bamboo tent poles and lightweight metal pegs.

We felt sure they would be easy to pitch. Each tent could sleep two men, and we were confident that their tough material and great flexibility would resist the highest winds. In addition, several larger tents and heavier sleeping bags were purchased in New York for use at Base Camp.

The problem of boots was most exasperating. Every climber is firmly convinced that his model boot and his design for the hobnails in the sole are by all odds the best. After long investigation and many hours of futile argument, we decided on an English model of non-freezing leather which seemed better suited to Himalayan climbing than any American boot. Each man designed the scheme of nailing which he thought best. Fitting the boots was a problem, and finally we were forced to send careful measurements to London in the hopes that skilled shoemakers could make a satisfactory boot. In order to climb more safely on steep ice or hard snow, it is necessary to have crampons (climbing irons). These metal spikes strap to the soles of the boots and give the climber a much better foothold on slippery surfaces. These too were bought in England.

Gasoline stoves had to be especially tested for us in decompression chambers to insure satisfactory performance in the rarefied air of our mountain camps. Thirty light-weight plywood boxes were cut in New York to be shipped out piecemeal, and to be assembled in Kashmir. Light-weight cookpots, called *dekshis,* were to be bought in India. Finally came multitudes of small details—matches packed in small waterproof tins, flashlight batteries, scales, pliers, mattress repair kits, sewing kits, notebooks and pencils, shovels and whiskbrooms—all had to be thought of and selected. I collected a complete medical chest, realizing that I should be expected to treat the entire population of each village through which the expedition passed. Dr. Thorington in Philadelphia donated a miniature kit of eye medication. My father presented us with a bottle of potent Demerara rum, brought all the way from Alaska, while other friends added many small details for our comfort. At last the entire mass of material was assembled, carefully listed, and packed. On the first of April, after a strenuous last five days, the shipment was solemnly consigned to a freighter for England, where it would be shipped to the steamer on which the expedition would sail for India.

These innumerable items consumed our entire attention during the winter. Without the help of our many friends and our long-suffering families, it would have been impossible to complete the task of providing for the physical and mental needs of six men for four months away from civilization. At last the final preparations were finished. Passports and tickets were bought. The expedition was ready to sail.

On April 14 a hilarious group of friends and relatives

dined together in New York, and at midnight four men embarked on the great adventure. I was forced to wait over two weeks to complete my medical course; I would then sail for England and fly directly to India, arriving in Kashmir on the same day as the rest of the party. In the last hours before departure the team more fully realized for the first time the magnitude of the task before them. They were preparing to go halfway around the world and spend five months exploring and perhaps attempting the ascent of the second highest summit in the world. To be sure, the party set out primarily to find the best way for the attack, hoping that, if the route could be prepared and its difficulties evaluated, in another year another party could make the final climb. Secretly, however, each one of us hoped that ours would be the group to reach the summit.

Chapter IV

Into Kashmir

Robert H. Bates

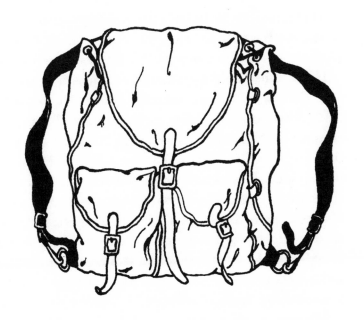

Chapter IV   Into Kashmir

WHEN the dusty Frontier Mail from Bombay slid into Rawalpindi station on May 8, four travel-stained Americans might have been seen peering from a second-class carriage window in search of Captain Norman R. Streatfeild of the Bengal Mountain Artillery. This blue-eyed, black-haired, vivacious Scot, whom we had never seen before, was already awaiting us, and soon we were chatting like old friends. He had brought with him the six Sherpas selected for us in Darjeeling by William Tilman, leader of the 1938 attack on Everest, so with the exception of Charles Houston our entire party was for the first time united.

Houston had been forced to leave America two weeks after the rest of us, had taken the *Queen Mary* to England, flown from London to Karachi, and was now crossing the famous Sind Desert by rail—the temperature at 121°—in order to join us early on May 9 in Rawalpindi. Twelve hours later, when the Lahore train arrived, the expedition was complete. At the hotel Houston spent much time scraping off layers of dust acquired in his torrid journey, then joined us at the breakfast table, where we let loose a flood of questions about details cables had not settled and made heavy inroads on an Indian breakfast.

All were eager to get on to Srinagar, where there was much to do, so we stowed the Sherpas in two lorries crammed with crates and bundles, arranged ourselves more expansively in two cars, and began the 180-mile drive to the Vale of Kashmir.

For an hour the road crossed dry, sun-baked plains north of Rawalpindi. Then we began to climb toward the evergreen-covered hills around Murree, where the air became cooler. As switchback after switchback carried us up into soothing forests of blue and Himalayan pine, our excitement mounted rapidly. Soon we had crossed the pass at Murree and were dropping down through terraced fields, green with young rice shoots, to the narrow canyon of the Jhelum River. Here the road skirts a mighty gorge where precipitous walls rise high above the trail and drop sharply away to the roaring river below. Rock and mud slides frequently close the road and maintenance work is practically continuous.

At Kohala we were speedily passed by customs officials and at last found ourselves in Kashmir. For hours we drove along great cliffs that seemed nearly vertical, with only a low rock wall on the outside. Occasionally, where the terrain was milder, we passed groups of bullock carts. Until a few years ago they carried most of the freight between Kashmir and Rawalpindi, but now the irrepressible motor car is rapidly replacing them. The slow-moving, ponderous wains, piled high with produce, are not allowed to use the road during the daytime because it is so narrow. They rest in the shade while there is daylight and when night falls creep along until dawn forces them to the roadside.

Such carts are one of the last reminders of days when jeweled bullock and elephant trains transported the courts of the Mogul Emperors from Delhi and Agra to the summer palace at Srinagar. What had taken them six weeks of tiresome travel, we were doing luxuriously in two days.

Gradually the gorge opened out, the sheer rock walls

became easy slopes, and we suddenly entered the peaceful, steamy beauty of the Vale of Kashmir. On every side stretched so many carefully irrigated fields of deep green that from the stratosphere the Vale must have resembled a giant emerald—90 miles long and 25 wide—in a setting of brown rock. As we sped along the firm poplar-lined highway that runs straight to Srinagar, we could see the rampart of the Pir Panjal range completely circling this verdant, misty valley; and once we had a fleeting view of the white summit of Nanga Parbat, monarch of the Northwestern Himalaya.

At Srinagar we found great confusion as our honking cars wound through streets seething with people. Most of the traffic is on foot, although the cheery bell of the tonga, a two-wheeled cart drawn by a single horse, is continually heard. The main thoroughfare, however, is not on land but on water. As we crossed the murky Jhelum River we could see banks lined with moored boats which had been poled into the city. Some of these, we learned later, were luxurious affairs where Europeans live all the year round, for no European may own land in Kashmir. Other boats also were numerous, especially the lithe, graceful *shikaras* which glided swiftly by, propelled by men with heartshaped paddles. In a few more minutes we had left the Jhelum, driven past the Maharajah's splendid polo grounds, and turned in at Nedou's Hotel, where days of concentrated work awaited us.

Streatfeild had made careful arrangements for stor-
ing the tea chests shipped from New York, so next
morning we could at once start making up coolie loads
for the long trip to the mountain. But first there was
unpacking to do. We went to work en masse, ripping
off the lids we had so painstakingly sealed six weeks before, and checking to see how each item had come
through the rough journey. Nearly everything had survived, though a tin of red pepper had become blended
with some cocoa, a 5-pound can of jam had been pierced
with a nail, so that its contents decorated every single
object in a 120-pound case, and a large tin of honey had
soaked its contents into Houston's fur-trimmed, windproof suit. Otherwise all was well.

The next problem was to weigh out loads of 55
pounds each and pack them in boxes that could be carried by either ponies or coolies. For this purpose we
had brought from America knocked-down plywood
boxes which would be far lighter and less expensive
than the local leather *yakdans*. The plywood needed to
be assembled, so while some of us were sorting equipment and food, building a weighing platform and making up loads, Petzoldt became foreman of a box factory
operated by the Sherpas. They enjoyed the work immensely, and the hotel rang with the sound of their
saws and hammers as they followed American methods
of mass production. When they discovered a neat little
screwdriver which operated by pressing down the han-

dle, they were so delighted that we had to restrain them from screwing on the lids before the boxes were packed.

As soon as we started filling the containers, it unfortunately became obvious that they would hold far more than 50 pounds, and as their contents had to fit snugly to survive the rough handling that was coming, we were at a loss what to do. The box factory responded nobly, however, and sawed in half most of the boxes they had so painstakingly assembled. Each case was numbered and its contents listed both on it and on a separate tally. We tried to scatter essential food and equipment throughout the loads, so that the loss of one or more would not cripple the expedition, but in the rush we did keep all seven of our primus stoves in their original box. This fact we bitterly regretted later when we saw the dangerous trails over which our loads must be carried.

The greatest event of preparation as far as the Sherpas were concerned was the distribution of equipment. They were particularly proud of their boots and spent the evening stamping around among the barefoot Kashmiri with conscious dignity and pride. We were careful, however, not to give them all their equipment, for the wiles of the crafty Kashmiri would probably have prevented some of their kit from seeing the mountain.

A pleasant interlude in this furious activity was an invitation from the British Resident and his wife, who entertained us beneath the huge chenar (plane) trees on their lawn, with true British hospitality.

On the last morning the work of packing proceeded even more rapidly. The box factory turned out better boxes, while the packers weighed out loads, packed them tightly, and delivered them to the factory for closing.

The Captain and Burdsall spent most of the morning in the bank trying to arrange for the transfer of some of our funds to the Government Treasury at Skardu so we could avoid carrying many pounds of rupees, an Indian coin the size of a half dollar and worth about forty cents. This was only one of the thousand and one instances where Streatfeild saved us trouble and facilitated our departure from Srinagar.

On the evening of May 12 we were at last ready. Then for the first time we had leisure to see the city, so we engaged a *shikara* and were paddled through the beautiful canals. In these sheltered waterways swarm hundreds of boats, while others are anchored along the bank. Thousands of Kashmiri live and die on the water, but they are usually married on shore. We saw the preliminaries of a wedding. Alongside us were mosques, Hindu temples, and the palace of the Maharajah. We floated down the Jhelum in the moonlight past the doorsteps of Srinagar, while hundreds of natives swam and splashed in the water beside us. An hour before, the sunset had been glorious as it gleamed from shining temple roofs and tinted the water; now everything was silver. We regretted every swish of the five paddles that brought us nearer to the hotel. In the distance we could hear shoutings and wildly throbbing drums of a native wedding procession. The romance of the East seemed epitomized by that sound. Only with difficulty did we restrain ourselves from running off in the moonlight to follow the torches, but there were lists to check and last minute letters to send. We turned regretfully back to the hotel. When we crawled into bed at 1:30, the furious booming of the wedding drums still sounded in the distance.

Chapter V

Over the Zoji La

Robert H. Bates

Chapter V   Over the Zoji La

"GOOD morning, sahib, *chotah hasri.*" The words
broke strangely into my dreams of a sunny Alpine pasture and I sat up quickly in bed. For a moment
nothing looked real; then I remembered. This was the
morning we had been looking forward to for six months.
Today the American Karakoram Expedition was starting on its 330-mile march from Srinagar, Kashmir, to

the base of K2, and, impossible as it seemed, I was a member.

For another moment I stared vaguely out through the bamboo window shade to where a faint pink light was showing behind the hills on the other side of the Vale of Kashmir. Five o'clock. It was indeed time to be getting dressed. The aristocratic looking Mohammedan servant bowed and went silently out, leaving only the tray, with its apple, cup, and steaming teapot, and the curtain, with its gently swaying strings of beads, to show that anyone had been within the room.

Five minutes later I had drunk my tea, and, dressed in shorts and marching shoes, was standing on the porch of Nedou's Hotel sniffing the early morning air. Dew sparkled on the beds of scarlet geraniums and the air was heavy with the smell of moist earth. In a great plane tree across the garden some unseen bird was trilling, while almost at my doorway an ungainly myna fledgling, hopping awkwardly along and croaking hoarsely, was discussing with himself the long pile of duffel bags, food boxes and oddities of expedition equipment. He seemed especially impressed by the Captain's collapsible rubber bathtub, but I left him to admire it alone and headed toward the dining room.

Breakfast was unusually quiet. However, Streatfeild, his normal chipper self, glibly remarked that we were casting off, for at least 100 days, both our razors and the yoke of fashion. Naturally, expressions brightened at this comfortable idea, but slowly the talk lagged again as we thought of our near departure and the immensity of the job ahead. Many days would pass before we should see Srinagar again, and each of us was probably secretly thinking the same thing! "There are only six of us. I hope I won't let the others down."

None of us was especially hungry (and Petzoldt had only two helpings of scrambled eggs), so before we knew it we had finished eating and were starting to load the two lorries that were to drive us to Woyil Bridge, 18 miles from town. Houston and I began to check the numbered boxes while grinning Sherpas hoisted them carefully aboard. Each of these six boys, perspiring cheerfully, was dressed in his very finest to impress the Kashmiri. High-altitude windproof jackets, which next made their appearance six weeks later at Camp II, were surmounted by a bizarre variety of pearl gray or black felt fedoras, worn derby style (without a crease); and treasured ice axes—the badge of office —were carried continuously unless both hands were absolutely required for carrying purposes.

Major Hadow, the charming British officer who had done much for the expedition before Captain Streatfeild was appointed to it, had risen early to see off his close friend the Captain and "the rough looking crowd" he was transporting. The Major in a couple of weeks would also be pulling on his climbing boots, as he was to be transport officer for the 1938 German Expedition to Nanga Parbat. The two men, strikingly different in appearance, each in his way presented as fine a liaison officer and companion as any expedition could desire. Last handshakes were given; the Sherpas climbed into one lorry, where they entirely disappeared save for the new hats and the grins; we boarded the second truck, and the expedition with its food and equipment for 100 days rolled joyfully out past the splendid chenar trees of the hotel compound.

It was still early morning. The mist was curling lazily above the calm surface of Dal Lake as the Great Shah Hammadan mosque slipped behind us. Already at 7 o'clock the light was bright. Soon it would be blinding, for the sky was dry and bare of clouds. As the sun rose, fruit and vegetable sellers became more numerous and jostled along the road to the city in their squeaky bullock carts with ungreased wheels. These were crude affairs drawn by great, mud-caked, sleepy looking brutes who took no more notice of the dust, the flies, the insistent blowings of the lorries' horns than they did of the thumps and curses of their masters. Horses and asses with top-heavy loads helped swell the traffic, and poorer Kashmiri vendors, carrying wide wicker trays of potatoes, ducks or strawberries, swung from their shoulders or balanced deftly on their heads, perspired past on their way to the great bazaar. Those with heavy loads progressed at the inevitable coolie trot, resting frequently, and shouting unintelligible

words at us in the second or two before the lorry overtook them and the opaque wake of dust following the
truck swallowed them from view.

The road was rough. As we jolted and bumped along,
the driver swerving round corners an inch from the
ditch, grazing cows and bullocks with placid equanimity, and continuously blowing his raucous horn
(which sounded like the grunt of a catfish magnified
100 times), we were cheered only by the knowledge
that if we survived for another hour we should be
there. Meanwhile, below us, feathery green spikes of
young rice plants colored the landscape, as field upon
field of flooded paddies, staggered in artistic irregular-
ity, dropped away to the lake. Sometimes the road bent
down toward the water. There along the shore bobbed
flocks of tame ducks, yellow bills flashing and pink feet
kicking in the sunlight as they up-ended greedily to
pull at the water lily and lotus roots below the surface.
And always in the background, beyond the ancient
lake bed famed through history as the Vale of Kashmir,
we could see rising above the hills ringing the valley
the snowy summits of the Himalaya.

Soon the lorries turned away from the lake and we
began passing through small villages where occasional
fields of gorgeous scarlet opium poppies bordered the
road; it was hard to imagine that such fragile flowers
could cause greater suffering than all the flies and the
smells in the narrow little bazaars we were going

through. Far less beautiful but more amusing were the naked little brats who screamed *"Baksheesh!"* (money) at us as we slowed down for obstructions in the road. Wherever there are tourists in the East, children learn this word first.

Soon the lorries jerked to a final stop in a cloud of dust, and our uneven ride was over. Before us, Woyil Bridge, a steel link suspension structure too frail to support lorries, spanned the rushing Sind River. Here our first pony transport awaited with far more ponies than we could use. The baggage was at once unloaded by the roadside, the lorry drivers were paid, and amidst tremendous confusion the Captain began hiring men for the five-day journey to Dras.

As we piled our kit into loads of some 150 pounds each, eager pony men dragged their horses right into the baggage to show us the animals' virtues, while others waved their arms and swore we were making the loads too heavy. Salesmen, beggars and wretched hangers-on added to the turmoil as they stood fawning in the middle of the duffel bags, displaying their cheap trinkets, or sneaked cautiously about looking for unconsidered trifles. Soon, however, the Captain's cries of "Chase that man, Ghaffar Sheikh. *Nikel jao!* Go away, you silly old man!" took effect. The vultures were chased to a safe distance, from which they watched as a numbered metal disc, to be exchanged for money when the expedition reached Dras, was handed to the owner of each load.

Within two hours the Captain and Ghaffar Sheikh, the major domo (shikari), had adroitly brought order from confusion, and our awkward caravan was ready for the trail. Two of the more restless members of the party had even spent the last fifteen minutes endeavoring to find a "route" to the top of the nearest bridge pylon, so it was clearly time to be moving. As we swung out across the creaky bridge, Petzoldt and the Captain filmed our jaunty gait. Everyone was bubbling over with enthusiasm, for at last the months of preparation lay behind us. Even Srinagar was behind us. Ahead lay the joys of the open road.

The immediate march was a long one for the first day. Dust from the caravan of 25 ponies rose about our heads as the six Sherpas, the shikari, the cook, and the cook's cook escorted us along the dry path skirting the west bank of the Sind. (In India every servant has his own servant.) The dust from the horses was choking, so despite the sun's force we stepped out sturdily and were soon a considerable way ahead.

The trail fringed the tumbling stream descending the Sind Valley, and from this path we could frequently glimpse ahead snowy peaks rising from green forests of deodars or silver firs. Everything looked cool, but the heat dampened our spirits as well as our shirts and made us linger under trees that occasionally bordered the path. Frequent pauses to bathe hands and feet in the river encouraged us, and lunch time found us on a green bank of turf bordering the Sind some ten miles above the bridge. Here our convoy passed us as we ate dry sandwiches, dunked ourselves briefly in the frigid water, and speculated whether our shoes and feet would last for the 300 miles still ahead.

When we started on again, the sun bored into us until we were "spitting cotton." Finally most of us gave in, as the Captain did, and drank from the roaring torrent. Paul was especially thirsty; the more he drank the more he perspired, till water streamed from his glowing face. Still, his sense of humor remained with him, even when he remarked that the sweat dripping from his nose was averaging three drops to the step.

All afternoon we put one foot in front of the other *tenderly*, as if walking on thin ice, but visions of tea drew us on, and finally at 5 o'clock the party rounded a curve at cautious speed and sighed gratefully to see tents being pitched in a grassy field along the river. Houston, as befitted the head of the expedition, came first; he was plastered with sweat and dust, but had drunk no doubtful water and had reached camp at the front of the column. At the clearing he found the Sherpas still grinning happily, looking as fresh as if they had covered the 17 miles in a special train, while Ahdoo, the cook, crouched over a snapping fire of knobby juniper and promised Kashmir curry for supper.

As we sat in stocking feet, Ahdoo and his helper brought steaming pint mugs of tea, which we drank while I was ransacking pony loads for the sugar. Two pints apiece of tea made such a fine appetizer that when the hot curry appeared we swallowed it ravenously. So vicious was our attack that fifteen minutes later Ahdoo nearly scraped a hole in a new cookpot in showing Paul that unfortunately the curry was *bus* (finished). [*Bus* is a whole vocabulary in itself. It is the word one uses when there is no more butter, the camel is ill, a wheel comes off the car, a coolie has a sore toe, or one is leaving the country.]

One thing more remained to be done that night—a division of Sherpas so that each of us would have an orderly. Every climber wrote down his first and second preference, the names were examined, and to our surprise and joy there were practically no conflicting choices, so uniformly good were the six men Tilman had sent us. The sirdar (head man), Pasang Kikuli, went to Houston, whose orderly he had been on Nanda Devi. Tse Tendrup had been with the Captain on the French Expedition to Hidden Peak, so he was quickly accounted for. Kitar, the smallest of the wee laddies, went to Petzoldt, whom he had faithfully followed everywhere since the day that he had shown him how to drive nails and make boxes. Pempa, the handsomest Sherpa, went to House. Phinsoo, a Nepalese who turned out to be the humorist of the crowd, came to me; and hard working Sonam fell to Burdsall, whom he served with the greatest zeal.

Each of us got into his Meade tent and sleeping bag that night almost too sleepy to undress. My next memory is of a torrential downpour, of reaching out to tie the tent door and falling asleep again before I could get my arm back in the sleeping bag. The eiderdown felt unusually cosy next morning when we waked at 5 to hear the rain hammering on the tent. The storm, the first we had experienced since leaving New York, was so violent that we stayed abed till 7, when we rose and ate a soggy breakfast. Unfortunately we could not then appreciate the humor of our appearance. Dressed in long green raincapes, and porous helmets or droopy felt hats, we stood solemnly in a circle on the unsheltered river bank and consumed our oatmeal, while the water streamed off our noses into uplifted spoons and gradually made the milk on the cereal become almost transparent.

Away at last, we were glad to warm ourselves by walking. The dust of yesterday had become mud, but the air was clearer and eventually it stopped raining. About lunch time we halted by a little stream, boiled some drinking water in a film tin, and dozed briefly. The canyon walls closed in as we started on again, trudging over old avalanche remains in a gorge where the roar of the river grew harsher. On both banks lay melting piles of packed snow, littered with fine spruce branches, traces of winter snowslides of unusual severity. It was here, the Captain told us, that in late April, 1936, one of the Sherpas of the French Expedition had been carried down 50 feet in a small avalanche. The ponies managed to cross these slopes extremely well, though we shuddered as some of our more precious belongings wavered on the narrow path. Still the valley steepened and the cliffs above our heads grew more abrupt, while the trail wound unevenly through a maze of boulders.

Camp that night was very jolly, though a cool wind speeded our open air supper and we had far too little time to examine several magnificent 17,000-foot peaks that lay across from us. Eventually we were forced to agree that the only routes to their summits must lie "up the other side," but we were so intrigued by these splendid bastions that had we not known of K2 we should have traveled no farther, being content to remain near Sonamarg, only 31 miles beyond Woyil Bridge!

The third day was the sweetest one so far. After climbing a few hundred feet above camp, we found ourselves in what might well have been an entirely different valley. As we marched along pastures high above the river, cuckoos called from the Himalayan pines above and the whole valley was full of life and cheer and sunshine. Everything was bright and gay. Here the sparkling water, the dew on the snowdrops and anemones, the birds' cheerful tunes as they bobbed across our path, and above all the jagged summits etched against a clear mountain sky made a scene we can never forget.

A black Himalayan thrush was singing in the woods above Sonamarg as we passed through the little village and continued on toward Baltal at the foot of the Zoji La. Yellow crocuses were everywhere, and even edelweiss appeared on exposed slopes. Meanwhile, Burdsall, the ornithologist of the party, was eagerly swinging his glass on eagles, kites, redstarts, wagtails, skylarks and other birds, most of which we could not recognize. Crows and choughs were most numerous, and I once saw a large flock of red and yellow billed raiders swoop down on a rookery of doves in some shale cliffs.

Between Sonamarg and Baltal avalanche tracks became more frequent along the valley, showing that the route must be distinctly dangerous in late winter or early spring; and at Baltal we even found that part of the dak bungalow in which we expected to pass the night had been crushed by a winter snowslide. Here the chill of melting snow was in the air and all was desolate. Across from us rose an avalanche-torn slope where rotting tree trunks were strewn like a box of spilled matches.

After making camp on a flat terrace in a field of crocuses, we bathed in the Sind, and then worked over food lists till suppertime. An air of anticipation had settled over the whole convoy. Tonight we were to go over the Zoji La, the 11,230-foot pass that crosses the great Himalayan chain. For ages, through this break in the range, the wealth of the East has come over the Baltistan watershed to Kashmir, brought by countless caravans from Turkestan, Western Tibet and Ladakh.

In the afternoon we gazed with awe as exhausted troops of heavily laden ponies passed our camp. Their drivers were wild looking, splendid specimens. They had slant eyes and black beards and wore big boots and heavy cloaks. When they said "Salaam," they looked us in the eye and never cringed. On their sleeves were sewn prayers in little patches of colored cloth—charms which made us wonder what winter blizzards and wind-swept marches they had seen. But what interested us most about these husky traders was the sign of toil and strain in their faces; more than ever we began to realize that to cross this pass two weeks before it was officially open would be a test for us all.

That night we turned in early with everything ready for a midnight start, for we must be on the trail by 12:30 A. M. if we were to be sure of passing the steepest part of the La before the morning sun could cause avalanches. Just at midnight the cook awakened us, and, while we were gulping our breakfast of tea, our Sherpas rolled up our sleeping bags and tents and put them on the ponies.

About us spread a wild sight, which in our sleepy condition seemed unreal. As Pasang's resinous torch flared and sputtered, the light rose and fell. It gleamed on the high cheekbones of his eager face, flickered over our tousled hair and well wrapped bodies as we bent over our cups, and made even the tea at the bottom of Ahdoo's cookpot gleam dully. Meanwhile other hissing torches were bobbing unevenly as the drivers sought with shouts and whistles to locate the last of their hobbled, 500-pound ponies, who did not at all like the idea of carrying 150 pounds apiece over the backbone of the Himalaya.

While we were waiting around the juniper fire, loath to depart, a pony man with skin boots came to me and said, *"Huzzur, taklif"* (I am in trouble, sir). He then pointed to his forehead where a cord tied tightly around his head was supposed to cure a headache. At least that was the Captain's interpretation. We told the lad to loosen the band, and then gave him a fruit drop to suck, for the medical kit had long since been packed. He felt immensely better at once, judging from his expression, and went back to his ponies; for, where medicine is hard to get, the power of suggestion will work wonders. A native doctor would have cured his headache in a different way—by branding his foot with a red-hot wire. The ponyman would have completely forgotten he had a head after that.

Meanwhile camp had been broken and a slightly

luminous patch of sky over one of the great rock walls across the valley showed that somewhere the moon had risen. Down in our black canyon all was darkness. Slowly we stumbled away, feeling rather than seeing the narrow trail at our feet. In the eerie light about us existed no such thing as distance—just gray things and black things whose shape one could not tell. Over a rough snow surface (the remains of amazing winter snowslides), our new boots crunched pleasantly until, without warning, the Captain swung us sharply from the regular trail, where it lay buried under avalanche debris, and turned abruptly into a black chasm.

Here was a pass that a handful of men could defend. Black walls towered above on either side, and our path lay up the snow chute between. The snow became far steeper now and we had to kick with the toes of our boots in order to keep our footing. It seemed impossible for any ponies to go where we were climbing, but our condition was bad, and we had worry enough to get our own reluctant bodies to the top.

Something about the gulf made us redouble our efforts to reach the heights. The stars directly above appeared very bright; the air was clear and cold and the world seemed devoid of space. We might have been sinners condemned always to climb from the black pit toward the stars, for it seemed as if we could jump off and fall a thousand miles into nothingness, or climb until we reached the bright specks far above. Never have I known such an eerie light or such a strange feeling. The mystery of the ages seemed locked in that magic land.

Nobody spoke, and the only sound was the crunch, crunch of boot nails on the crust. Then suddenly as we pressed over a little rise, the friendly moon appeared over a ridge. It was like meeting an old friend in the middle of the Gobi Desert, and our feelings changed. We could appreciate the steep walls now and the silver shoulders of snow and ice gleaming so mysteriously high above.

The valley had widened perceptibly and a raw wind told us we were near the top. As we rested here and passed the thermos round, Burdsall, chilled though he was by the icy blasts, took a barometer reading to check the instrument. The pass appeared to be its stated height, a fact recommending both the barometer and Burdsall, so we went on more cheerfully. Everywhere about us old avalanche tracks crossed the valley. As we climbed among ice blocks that had fallen months before, weird black shadows extending across the snow seemed waiting to swallow our tiny figures toiling along the corridor. And high above us the great snow summits shone cold and unearthly.

Ahead lay the bleak country of Baltistan, with mile after mile of snowy peaks stretching toward Ladakh. Chilly introduction it was too, as the morning wind flicked our faces, and a cloudy dawn broke slowly over the arctic landscape, dark and cheerless, contrasting grimly with the pleasant scenes of the day before.

Under the snow beneath our feet we could hear a stream flowing; we were at the source of the Dras River, which we were to follow to its confluence with the dusky Indus. Before we knew it, the stream was running in the open and we were hard put to cross. In one place we thrashed about in semi-darkness for half an hour before a crude bridge, its planks slick with ice, presented itself. Here we suddenly found House missing and feared that he had slipped into the tumbling river. He soon appeared, however, having only gone back up the trail to warn Burdsall, who was behind, of a short cut.

Six o'clock found us dragging our weary legs up to the resthouse at Machoi. We were sleepy, tired, and much in need of a belated breakfast. At our shouts, a surprised choukidar (resthouse keeper) ran up, gaped at us, then dashed off for wood, so that in a short time we had tea water brewing in a pan on the stove. A tin of ham, some crackers, butter, and malted milk tablets improved the morale of the party, and we soon moved to the porch, where sunlight was showing through the early morning screen of gray. From a few miles away a stunning 18,000-foot peak stared calmly down on our motley group and on the caravans that were toiling westward toward the Zoji La. As we sat and smoked, we could see our *bandobast* spread out over the snow fields before climbing through the muck of filthy little Machoi and passing on toward the next village of Matayan.

By now caravans were everywhere. A few, loaded with such prosaic goods as salt and sugar and kitchen pots, were going our way, but most were coming from the East, laden with numdahs (rugs), woolens, Tibetan tea, and bales whose treasure-trove we could only imagine. Many of these caravans used *dzos*, great shaggy animals with huge heads and rings in their noses. The *dzo*, a cross between a yak and a cow, is much valued, for it is said to combine endurance with docility. These shaggy brutes with hair over their eyes reminded us of their wild looking drivers, and like their masters they could absorb great physical punishment. Unlike the Indians we had seen in the plains, most of these men treated their animals kindly, though there was tremendous shouting and cursing when softening snow began to bog down the heavily burdened animals. Luckily our train had pushed right on, for soon the trail was choked for a mile or more with floundering horses and grunting *dzos*. One caravan in trouble would stall the rest, and sometimes loads and even animals slipped down the snow slopes into the river. In the space of an hour we passed the carcasses of several dead ponies.

Some five miles from Matayan we stopped for another bite, and here I found tracks of a bear—a Himalayan red bear, the Captain said. Snow leopards we also looked for, as they were supposed to be numerous, but we saw none.

Matayan had appeared to be a fine place when we viewed it from up the valley, but it was a disappointment when we finally panted into it. The village was still snowbound, and its square mud houses, which looked like forts, were dismally mucky. The main occupation of the inhabitants seemed to be carrying baskets of manure (of which there was great abundance) from one pile to another; village and people alike had a strong smell which foreign tourists would probably label picturesque. We were in no mood for seeing or smelling the sights, however, and after Houston had treated Burdsall's severe blisters, we stretched out on the bungalow floor.

Chapter VI

The Indus Trail

Robert H. Bates

Chapter VI   The Indus Trail

AT six the following morning we arose scratching, for a starving battalion of local fleas had attacked during the night; and the victory was all theirs, for where is the contortionist who can catch a flea in a sleeping bag? The sun was already shining brightly on the bold ridges to our west as we emerged stiffly from the squalid cowshed euphoniously termed "the resthouse." A typical Himalayan morning confronted us. Half the world was in blinding sunshine; the other half, Matayan included, in frigid shadow.

After crossing the Dras River, several of us saw three Baltis taking a short cut across some cliffs instead of continuing along the trail. Naturally we followed them, and our scant respect for Baltis immediately increased when we observed what rock climbing assets they had in their toes. While we were pursuing these Balti guides somewhat uncertainly, one of the Sherpas was nearly struck by a stone from above. He looked startled for a moment, then grinned broadly. Why worry about trouble after it is all over?

One other incident impressed me on the trail to Dras. As we were following the trace high above the river, I noticed that the stream was running into a small canyon. The water roared against the sheer sides, tumbling and tossing below the track, which was only a nick in the valley walls. The trail was narrow—a *dzo's* breadth wide in most places—and some of the corners were awkward. One of these was caused by a huge fragment of coarse marble (polished by the river years before Alexander the Great was a boy); it now projected into the path, where it lay gleaming in the subdued light of the river gorge. Ragged scratches on the shiny surface caught my eye. "H. H. G.–A. 1861–2–3," it read.

Here was the mark of the famous explorer Godwin-

Austen, for whom K2 was named. What infinitely greater problems had been his when he first scratched his initials on this rock while making his original explorations in Northern Kashmir! For him each corner had led into unknown country, each village had threatened possible ambuscade; and how carefully he must have plotted and planned his moves for each following day!

Dras was only 13 miles from Matayan, child's play after the march across the Zoji La, and even the bungalow was pleasanter. As we approached it, curious natives stared at us openly. Men forgot their yokes of *dzos,* women put down their baskets of manure, and some of the younger generation even cheered briefly before running off to a safer distance. The women here seemed very numerous. Bright-red trousers peeped from under their black, sacklike dresses, and clumsy anklets and silver bracelets dangled heavily. Baltistan jewelry is inherited, and the size never changes.

At the bungalow we found much to do. First came the job of paying off the pony men, and as bright rupees (16 annas) and half-rupee pieces were clinked cheerfully into the hands of each man, he began a monologue that went something like this: "Sahib, I am extra good man. My sons they are extra good too. I always work extra hard. Someday my sons will do much work for you. Therefore do you give me please, sahib, just twelve times as much *baksheesh* as you give me

now. Eight times, sahib; four times. Oh, sahib, give me
two annas more!" The men did not seem grieved when
their shares were not increased. They accepted their lot
philosophically and went back to the horses.

Our next duty was to check over the loads, to find if
anything had been lost or broken in transit, before we
hired another group of drivers to escort us to Karghil.
This scene, if anything, was more confused than the
last. At least a hundred bearded rogues were seeking a
dozen jobs, and from the start a small riot seemed inevitable. The Captain, however, was very efficient, and
his commands were voluntarily enforced by the Sherpas, who despised the local coolies. Sonam, himself a
coolie when at home in Darjeeling, took special delight
in swaggering among the natives, ice ax gripped bravely
or hand on *kukri,* while the Baltis respectfully made
way for him. Only once did the pushing, yelling crowd
make the Captain angry, and then he drove the whole
lot from the compound with shouts of *"Nikel jao,* you
silly fools, *juldi."* Momentarily his face was so stern
that the choukidar ran off with the others and hid behind a mud wall, from where he watched open mouthed
to see if Streatfeild would tear down the bungalow
with his bare hands.

Half an hour later, arrangements were amicably con-
cluded with the drivers of 23 horses, and we bought a
sheep to celebrate our successful arrival at the first
stage of our journey. Intensive bargaining was neces-

sary before the headman of the village, an engaging, white-bearded rascal, would sell us the sheep, for his price was four times too high. He repeatedly weighed the 60-pound animal, poking and punching it as he expatiated on its virtues and the plumpness of all its ancestors. Finally House could stand it no longer and started to weigh old Gray Beard himself on the scales. Then, when we began to poke *him* in the ribs appraisingly, he immediately gave in and sold us the sheep for only 10 rupees—still double the normal price.

From Dras the trail descends the Dras River to Kharal, and by 6 next morning we were striding along the river bank with pleasant expressions caused by a generous breakfast of scrambled eggs and sheep's kidney. The day was soft and springlike and again we marveled at the color contrasts of high peaks in glaring sunlight and deep valleys cold in shadow. Birds hopped about at the water's edge, though the vegetation steadily became sparser. Lizards were there too—little orange-stomached fellows eight inches long who rattled swiftly across the trail like tiny armored cars.

For hours we followed a V-shaped gorge of bare rock and broken stone, passing only a few goatherds on the way. Tasgam Bagh was our destination, 17 miles from Dras, and our idea of what it looked like was vague. When a small village shaded by apricot trees appeared ahead, we put our broken Hindustani to use and asked a withered old crone how far it was to Tasgam. The old witch drew a corner of her black smock over the lower half of her face; then, pointing with her arm, on which hung handsome silver spangles with rough turquoise settings, she indicated that we had only a short way to go. After this her courage collapsed and she fled squeaking into the nearest mud hut.

A mile down the road we did find the *Bagh* (garden), a shady terrace with poplar trees overlooking the river. It was nice to be camping in tents again, and the commissary produced a large tin of cheddar cheese to go with tea, while the Sherpas put on an unrehearsed floor show. It started with Phinsoo and Pempa seeking wood to cook their dinner and ended with great rivalry to see who was the more acrobatic tree climber and wood chopper. They swung like monkeys from limb to limb, tearing off dead branches and hacking away with their curved *kukris* at living boughs.

Fortunately some of the trees were left, for our porters' next move was to come up very humbly to borrow the oldest climbing rope. Permission was quickly granted. Then, amid squeals of laughter, these husbands and fathers forgot their dignity and, after fixing the rope to a tree, began to swing like five-year-olds. They swung one another till the branches groaned, then swatted each swinger as he went sailing by. Next they swung four or five at a time, all the while laughing so hard that somebody was always losing hold and falling to the ground. At last someone began turning the swingers round and round, then suddenly letting the twisted rope spin. Of course they became dizzy and fell off, then walked in circles and fell down, giggling continuously, and finally ran back to the swing to do it over again.

What joy it would be if everyone could get such sheer pleasure from such simple play! But the performance was not over. Tse Tendrup, whose turn it was to cook for the Sherpas, went back to start his fire, and reluctantly Phinsoo and Sonam began to take down the rope. Just as Phinsoo was slowly coiling it, however, he noticed a very mangy village dog sneaking toward the Sherpa food. Immediately a light came into Phinsoo's eyes and he began slowly to stalk the brute, who was in turn cautiously stalking the food. We watched breathlessly as the Nepalese made a slip noose and crept quietly toward the prey which he pretended was a ferocious and dangerous enemy. His showmanship was superb, even till the last minute when he flung his lasso over the mongrel's head and then held tight as the dog bounded and yelped about the garden. After much gloating by the other Sherpas, with Phinsoo showing modest pride, the quarry was turned loose and camp became more normal. That night we sent the Sherpas a present of sheep meat and the whole camp went to bed happy.

The march from Tasgam to Kharal turned out to be a rough one. About a mile and a half from camp we

found 10 feet of track washed away by a swollen river.
Most of us promptly jumped the gap and started on,
but the irrepressible Sherpas, lovers of engineering
problems, improvised a bridge over which the loads
could be backpacked. Beyond this *mauvais pas,* miles
of dull going brought us to Shimsa Kharbu with its
neat bungalow among green fields, an oasis in the barren country. Steadily the wretched trace grew worse,
many times being washed away as it skirted the stream
bed. It led over several snow patches, and in crossing
one a pony slipped off into the raging river.

This news was brought us by a pony driver as we sat
lunching under some beetling crags two miles downstream. The pony had been rescued with difficulty, the
wallah said, but the load appeared irretrievable. For a
moment we felt a sinking sensation, each hoping it
wasn't the load containing all the primus stoves—without which the expedition could not exist in the mountains! Gloomy scowls took the place of contented smiles
as we stared aghast at one another. How could we have
been so careless as to leave all our stoves in one box?
Each one of us felt personally to blame. Another pony
driver appeared before long, calling in Hindustani before he reached us: "Horse go in water. Much work.
We get him out. Saddle gone. Load gone. Cook sahib
very angry."

"Good old Ahdoo!" we thought, "always so anxious
about his master's belongings. If anyone can get the

load he can." But a few more words from the pony wallah changed our ideas and made us yell with relief. No wonder Ahdoo was anxious. The lost load contained only his own bedding!

The rest of the march to Kharal lay along rocky hillsides marked infrequently across the river with terraced villages shaded by cool groves of apricot and mulberry trees. Brilliant green fields of barley soothed our eyes, even as in our imagination the shade of the trees cooled our bodies. Our side of the valley, however, felt like an oven. The parched rocks were hot to the touch and they reflected light dazzlingly into our streaming faces. Toward the middle of the afternoon we reached the modern suspension bridge at Kharal where the Dras-Shingo River meets the Karghil River. There we found a motley crowd of black-bearded pony men squatting round a hookah. With them was an under-Tehsildar in khaki with a red fez, and a chuprassi (local policeman) in splendid purple robe and white turban. They had brought from the Tehsildar (local governor) of the district a note which said he had arranged horses to take us to the next town. To our rage and disgust we found this was all he had done, for he had not arranged through transport to Skardu as Streatfeild had thrice requested and as the Revenue Minister had ordered him to do. Instead of having through transport to Skardu, we now should have to pay off a set of coolies each night and hire a new batch of them each morning.

The blow was more irritating than severe, and we sent the chuprassi off with a blistering note to the Tehsildar.

For supper we had a red-hot curry (filling up House and Petzoldt for the first time since Srinagar), and shortly afterward, as we sat smoking and watching the purpling shadows in the river gorge, the chuprassi rode in on a foaming horse with another note from the Tehsildar. It said that through transport was impossible but arrangements had been made for us day by day. The Tehsildar was patently lying, prompted no doubt by local graft; however, we could do nothing more and went to bed angry and dusty, for at Kharal the only camping place is a barren gravel flat perched well above the murky river.

Considerable confusion marked our start next morning, for the pony men had evidently sat up late the night before smoking *bhang* or some other drug mixed with their tobacco. At least this was the Captain's interpretation of their being so bleary-eyed, nervous and quarrelsome. Our sullen escort finally got under way and we crossed the suspension bridge to the other side of the river. During the first half hour of the march a vexing problem was settled to the great delight of Bill House. The night before, we had observed an irrigation ditch cutting across the cliff on the opposite side of the river. So level was it that none could tell whether it had flowed from left to right or vice versa, and sundry bottles of ice-cold beer were wagered on this momentous problem. The fact that no beer was to be had in this parched land and we should see none for at least three months to come made little difference.

The irrigation ditches never failed to fascinate us. They cut across great expanses of bare cliffs where only generations of human labor could ever have built up such clever waterways, traversing as they do shining walls where it seems the intense reflection of the sun must make the water boil away into steam. Mile after mile such ditches run. We could trace each threadlike course across the river as it gradually descended from snow fields high in the mountains to some tiny village close to the river's edge. There the patches of emerald barley looked greener than fields ever looked before, set off as they were by miles of rocky desert. It was as if we had been camping for months in winter snow fields and had suddenly come down into a meadow of spring life and greenery.

Our path itself was a mountain engineering problem to make any Swiss or Austrian expert proud. Sometimes it followed tiny ledges 200 feet above the river, with a balustrade a foot high to keep one from falling off the edge. Again it would drop down to river level, descending precipitous walls by an ingenious system of braces and switchbacks. Timbers bore the weight of the trail in gullies which would not support stonework, and frequently 10–15 feet of rock, built without benefit of mortar, would hold up the outer edge of the trail as it hung over the river hundreds of feet below. Like the irrigation ditches, this trail was the result of centuries of work. In the year that Porus and Alexander were fighting for India this route was being used by hardy merchants who brought the wealth of interior China to beautiful Kashmir. And then, even as now, winter avalanches must have damaged sections of trail. No wonder the Baltis are clever stonemasons, for they have a long heritage behind them.

The march from Kharal was a short one of 13 miles, topped off by a steep climb of 800 feet to the top of the village of Olthingthang. This is the largest village in the valley of the Shingo. Every inch of its 800-foot slope is taken up by little terraced fields as wide as the angle of the slope permits. Through the middle of the town the steep trail threads its way; and up the middle in the noonday heat we sighed and grunted and perspired till we felt the path must be turning to mud behind us. At the top we pitched our tents among the boulders of a rocky orchard.

In the afternoon Houston and I set out to see the town and walked for miles along rows of terraces and irrigation ditches shaded by rustling poplars. The squalid mud and stone huts look out on magnificent gorges to the south and west, with rock peaks towering beyond them in the distance. With modern houses and a little plumbing, a Shangri La could spring up in the midst of this waste of splintered rock, for the situation is truly remarkable.

A self-appointed young Balti guided us about town. He took great pride in his position, grinning with delight whenever we spoke to him. The local Rotary Club was shown us also, and the members left off sharing a very stained and ancient hookah to smirk and stare. Our guide was prouder of his linguistic achievements than of his fellow citizens, for somehow in the course of his eventful youth he had picked up a smattering of Hindustani and four or five words of English. He was very proud of the latter accomplishment and kept saying, "Right, left, right, left. Good morning."

Less learned or less daring Baltis followed us at a respectful distance as we walked over the roofs of houses that were built into the terraces. From them we could see the women working in the fields. They looked like so many crows when we saw them in the distance, for their smocks are a funereal black. When we came on them suddenly in the yards of the houses, however, we saw that most of these unlovely creatures had invested their love of color in heavy silver and turquoise jewelry or strings of bright beads. The women seemed very curious, but always watched from a discreet distance and hid their faces if we looked at them. It was enough to give any man an inferiority or superiority complex, depending on how ferocious he thought his beard looked.

The houses were overpopulated with Baltis, from nursing babies to aged grandsires; and naked, potbellied little urchins were everywhere. To one of these houses—a square, mud and earth, one-room dwelling—our guide brought us, depositing us at last before a very elderly gentleman who was clearly dying. His greenish white face, dull eyes, and spasmodic breathing told us he would build no more barley terraces. What was there we could do for him now? "Medicine," said the guide, "medicine." The old man was beyond help, but we gave him a fruit drop (all we had with us) for psychological effect, and started for camp, explaining to our guide on the way that the old man was very ill. "Grandfather," we called the old man, and the boy picked up the word quickly. When we left him with a present of cigarettes in his hand, he was grinning broadly and salaaming over and over again as he shouted after us: "Grandfather! Grandfather!"

In camp we found our companions surrounded by would-be coolies who watched their every action as if they were men from Mars. Gradually they would come closer and closer until the Sherpas rushed at them with upraised axes shouting, "*Jao, jao!*" in an effort to obtain breathing space for their harassed sahibs. At last all was quiet and we had a pleasant supper under the apricot trees, though we knew that in the background many pairs of eyes were peering from behind rocks and bushes in frank wonderment at the strange scene.

Each day we were becoming more familiar with the routine of camp life, which generally went something like this. At 5 A. M. (about dawn) Ghaffar Sheikh would wake us by blowing a police whistle and shouting "Breakfast, sahibs." Then he would go from tent to tent, shaking each gently in turn and calling, "Good morning, sahib." After this there would be a few moments of silence, marked by a hearty yawn or two, before singing would be heard in the Captain's tent. How he sang so cheerily almost the moment he got his eyes open was one of the wonders of the expedition, for whether at Base Camp or along the steaming Indus Valley the Captain's morning song was always there, and usually the same: "Widdicombe Fair." By the time that "Uncle Tom Cobbleigh and all" had been referred to for the last time, the Captain was usually outside his tent and sousing his face with water in his wash basin. At about the same moment Houston and I would be staggering sleepily out of our tents, with Petzoldt and House close behind. Last would come Burdsall, always cheerful, and far too good-natured to mind if the oatmeal was already cold.

Breakfast would consist of cooked dried fruit with hot cereal, tea, and some kind of eggs, served on a box circled by duffel bags. House and Petzoldt always groaned loudly at the small portions of "egges" (as Ahdoo called them) and promised each other an 18-egg omelet apiece when they got back to Srinagar. Breakfast often included a floor show provided by House and the Captain. House always had something witty to say to the Captain about his disgraceful habit of singing in the middle of the night; and the Captain, lighting up his Barney's Mixture, would make adequate reply, not forgetting to call Bill, Dick—a name he thoroughly dislikes.

While we were eating, the Sherpas would pack our tents, so that by 5:45 camp would be broken once more; and when we rose from the duffel bags, these seats would be snatched by waiting coolies and the last of the caravan would be on its way. Each man selected his own pace, so sometimes we went singly and sometimes all together, as chance offered.

The Captain and I were usually the fastest walkers and kept ahead, perhaps because we so much enjoyed sitting in the shade and resting while the others came up. We never got far ahead, however, for I carried the lunch and was always carefully followed. Petzoldt's red cowboy shirt impressed the natives immensely and it made a good landmark, as did House's brown felt hat or Houston's black one. The Captain's green shirt was his distinguishing feature. Petzoldt and Houston (especially the former) loved to run downhill, and when the track dipped down they gained perceptibly on the rest of the company—even on House, who had the most uniform pace of all. Burdsall formed the bulwark of the cavalry, having had the ill luck to blister a heel on the day we crossed the Zoji La, and from Dras to Yuno he rode horseback. Houston joined him for a few days with a bruised instep, and later a pulled tendon forced me to ride, but House never rode and the others rarely joined the cavalry.

All of us carried small loads on the march in to the mountain, to improve our condition, and it really seemed to help us when we reached the higher altitudes later on. My load always included the lunch, which consisted generally of *chupattis* (native bread of wheat flour and water made like Mexican tortillas), hard boiled eggs or cheese, and chocolate. After lunch we would plug along till 2 or 3 in the afternoon, when our camping place was reached. There each of us would plant his ice ax where he wanted his tent to be and then retire to whatever shade was handy, to await the arrival of the coolies and the tents.

It was really Millionaires' Row in expeditioning. I hate to imagine what our sourdough friends in Alaska would have said had they seen the daily performance when our coolies came into camp. Often the natives would give each of us bouquets of flowers and then beg for the honor of being allowed to help our Sherpas smooth the ground and put up our tents. Then came the real struggle. Several coolies would plead for the privilege of being allowed to blow up the sahib's air mattress, and if his Sherpa permitted it, the victorious coolie was overjoyed. He would puff and strain away, often blowing for a good five minutes with the valve shut if the Sherpa in charge didn't watch him closely.

Next each Sherpa himself would lay out his sahib's sleeping bag, diary and toilet kit, and then come up with a change of shoes and personally take off his master's marching boots, if he would let him. Such luxury doesn't exist in civilized countries.

The day we left Olthingthang was bright and cloudless. Similar mornings had taught us to walk rapidly in the cool of the day, for the afternoon sun gave off blistering heat. As we struck out smartly along the narrow track, we could not but marvel at the great walls above and beneath us that the path traversed. Three hundred feet below raced the Shingo as we rounded a corner and found it merging with the mighty Indus in a smother of tossing brown. And now the route from Srinagar followed a fourth stream. Up the Sind we had come until the Zoji La was reached, then down the Dras to where it reached the Shingo, and down the surging Shingo to the murky Indus. Now at last we were following the father of waters, one of the great rivers of the world, the mighty Indus.

The 15-mile march to Bagicha was an easy one, but I pulled a tendon in my left leg while jumping a stream, and only with difficulty hobbled on to a waterfall where we had decided to lunch. Here we sat comfortably in the grass and watched the water in its 150-foot plunge from the rocks above. The water sparkled in the bright sunlight while rainbows played through the mist about us. High above the glistening spray we could see small

BURDSALL

ALONG THE INDUS

THE EXPEDITION AT SKARDU

Standing: Ghaffar Sheikh, House, Houston, Streatfeild, Bates, Burdsall, Petzoldt, Ata-Ullah. Seated: Pemba, Phinsoo, Pasang, Kitar, Tse Tendrup, Sonam

stalactites hanging from the opposite walls, and among these rock pigeons were nesting. As we sprawled on the grass just out of reach of the wet, we wondered how many other travelers had come unexpectedly into this garden in the wilderness.

Five miles farther on, in the grassy garden at Bagicha, Burdsall and the Captain paid off the noisy crowd of local coolies as soon as the last load was in. Meanwhile Houston and I sat soaking our legs in the Indus and kneading our tired muscles. We did not like the idea of being "cavalry" and hoped soon to be in good walking condition again. Horses, we knew, could go only two days' march beyond Skardu, the capital of Baltistan, which we were fast approaching. As we sat glumly, each on an individual rock with his feet in the river, something close beside us attracted our attention. It was a little cave near the water's edge lined with pretty pebbles and a fence of twigs and stones. The dirt floor was packed and smoothed and so neat we could hardly credit it to one of our crude coolies. A man could enter only on hands and knees, for the whole estate was scaled in miniature; probably it was owned by some Baltistan leprechaun who bitterly resented our sudden intrusion and had just departed. Whoever the owner, I hope his wrath was softened by a shiny 8-anna piece Houston left just inside the hearthstone.

Perhaps the little elf put an idea into Ahdoo's shaven head, for he suddenly manufactured a magnificent rice *pilau* for supper. Rice and raisins and pieces of cinnamon bark were blended skillfully with delicious bits of fried onions, fruit seeds and dozens of other amazing and indistinguishable items. Petzoldt was so delighted by this kingly dish that he yodeled every time his plate was being refilled, and after dinner started a rope tying contest among the Sherpas. Lesson I he informed us was to be on bowline tying. It was as good as a circus to see him explaining in English to our grinning, eager little boys, how the rabbit (end of the rope) came out of his hole, went around the tree and then back into his hole again. He tied the knot on Kitar and then pulled the rope tight to show that the knot would not slip. He also showed how easy it was to untie, and the boys chattered with delight. Then they practiced on themselves and on each other as if it were a matter of immediate life and death. The boys learned so quickly that they ruined our plans of holding a contest and giving a package of cigarettes to the best student. In fact they humiliated us by tying knots faster than we could, so we gave cigarettes to all.

Next morning we were still in the best of spirits as we trod the rocky ledges of the trail. Below us the coffee-and-cream-colored Indus now lazily slid along, now viciously roared on her journey westward. Across from us we could sometimes see tiny houses clinging like swallows' nests to the rocky walls. To their occupants we must have seemed like ants crawling along the face of the great cliffs, for rarely did the trail descend to the level of the river. When it did, the cause was a tiny village perched precariously at the water's edge. As we passed through, wide-eyed urchins and staring grown-ups followed our every move, hardly more curious than the long-tailed magpies and golden orioles in the tree-tops.

In these remote villages we were often amazed at seeing tire tracks in the dust of the trail. No auto road existed within hundreds of miles, but we soon realized that many upper class Baltis were wearing *chuplis* (sandals) made from the rubber of old automobile tires. Where the tires came from in the first place I don't know (possibly Srinagar), but it was astonishing to us to see familiar treads showing clearly in the dust of this narrow, far-off caravan trail. Probably the natives would gladly make practical use of old razor blades too!

In the early afternoon we reached Tolti, where we were greeted by men with flowers for us. Most of the Baltis here wear flowers in their hair and the effect is very favorable. Even the Rajah—for a minor one exists here—wears rosebuds in his turban. This dignitary, whom we had to term Rajah Sahib, sent his prime minister around with special rosebuds, then called and invited us to play polo. We declined, but he put on a game for us anyway.

Eight players, one of whom was the Rajah dressed in

spotless white, rode wildly up and down a field fairly free of stones but blessed with a large mud puddle and a small stream bed. The game started when one rider dashed madly down the field, ball in hand. Halfway down he threw up the ball, and still at a gallop smacked it in midair so that it bounded ahead with eight men in hot pursuit. Play was continued till a goal was scored, when the scorer would fling himself from his horse and touch the ball down. Sometimes something like a fight around the goal posts ensued. It was all very mystifying, for we never knew who was ahead or what the score was or who won. We didn't dare cheer for anyone but the Rajah, so whenever he had the ball there were loud yells of "Come on, Rajah, Sahib!" The Rajah, however, would have been unpopular with an American football crowd, for more than once he had a clear field ahead and was going on for an easy goal when the ball hopped into the mud puddle. Each time the spotless Rajah would ride off to one side and shout at one of his men to hurry up and knock the ball out, so he, the Rajah, could go on and score a goal. The explosions of muddy water were lovely and the crowd yelled. Sometimes the players would lash inaccurately at the chipped wooden ball and a sheet of muddy water would soak everyone but the aloof Rajah.

At half time, hookah smoking was indulged in. The Rajah's pipe was a carved silver one with a curved stem at least three feet long. The great man puffed on it till he was tired, then handed it to his prime minister (Tolti's chief "yes-man" and referee of polo games) who took a few whiffs before passing it on to lesser dignitaries. While the men were resting, the juvenile stars of the village performed on the same horses, to the great delight of the spectators, who offered them free advice. This gallery was colorful. Nearly every man wore roses or a sort of phlox over his ears, and there were countless half naked little urchins who turned somersaults and fought and ran and shouted just as American boys like to do between the innings of a baseball game.

Since the horses were tired, the second half was shorter. Later we had tea with the Rajah and presented him with some chocolate and tins of cigarettes. He was not well bred, despite his rank, for he asked for more presents and later sent his polo players round to ask for a tip.

The scenery beyond Tolti specialized in goats, which ate flowers, weeds, lower branches of trees and anything reminiscent of green. The goats were all stunted, probably from lack of food in the winter, and were often no bigger than large terriers. One of these dwarfs with a melancholy eye so struck Houston's fancy that it took the combined efforts of the crew to keep him from carrying the little fellow into the resthouse. Willie Goat, however, had his revenge. At least I think he was responsible for the virility of the fleas in the Parkutta resthouse that night, though Houston received credit for an assist.

Parkutta was a fine village from the Balti standpoint. Splendid old chenar trees, 15 feet in circumference, shaded the village compound where the old men sat and watched the handsome magpies quarreling with the roosters over bits of food. These grandfathers could look out over the waving wheat fields to the distant mountains beyond; and perhaps, like us, they marveled at the way water had been carried down from these mountains to permit crops to thrive at Parkutta. The irrigation streams could be turned off or on at will, as we had seen at Tolti when just before game time natives had turned off the stream flowing through the polo field.

Parkutta was an interesting town, but none of us desired to spend another night with the particular brand of fleas engendered there, so we were glad to leave early next morning for Gol. En route we passed the place where the River Shyock pours its silted water into the Indus. Then for several miles we plowed across arid sand flats where a hot wind and blowing grit gave us the illusion that we were crossing the Sahara in a sandstorm. Beyond the sand beds we found great loess deposits which continued to Gol, where we camped in the lambardar's (headman's) garden in the shade of his mulberry trees. He brought us two large plates of dried apricots, then left us to enjoy them and the soft tinkle of his brook.

Only one more march now separated us from Skardu, the Balti capital we had so long been approaching. The march turned out to be a severe one. For the first part of the 20-mile stage we followed the canyon walls of the Indus till we emerged gradually into the Valley of Skardu. Here for the first time in 20 days we were not shut in by mountains rising from our very feet. The 5000-foot high valley is ringed with 15,000-foot peaks, to be sure, but its breadth, like the Vale of Kashmir, gives one a pleasant feeling of freedom.

A real sandstorm struck us a few miles from the city. With heads bent low to save our eyes, we plowed forward over the yielding surface where a sparse cactus growth formed the only vegetation. The storm so increased that two of the cavalry were slightly damaged when they rode with closed eyes into low-hanging poplar branches that border Skardu Boulevard. Our second error followed quickly on the first. Two hundred yards farther on we met the Rajah of Skardu, dressed in purple and riding a fine horse. He dismounted till we passed. Not knowing who he was, we acknowledged this courtesy with only a salaam!

Later in the afternoon the Rajah called on us at the resthouse. He turned out to be a fat, dissipated, self-important person who wished us to take many pictures of him. Not wishing to offend, yet not wishing to waste our precious movie film, we took movies of him from countless angles—most of them with no film in the cam-

era. Quite different was the Rajah of Shigar, a boy of
twelve, who visited us with his Munshi (teacher), a
big, black-bearded, handsome man who was his guard-
ian. We all solemnly smoked cigarettes while Streatfeild and the Munshi conversed.

Later the Wazir (Governor) of Baltistan, the Tehsildar of Skardu and the Assistant Tehsildar came to call.
These high caste Hindu officials wore European dress.
They turned out to be grand people and old friends of
the Captain. The Wazir was a keen, vivacious man of
real intellect, and, like the Tehsildar, he spoke excellent English. They seemed to enjoy having visitors in
Skardu, even though we bombarded them with questions. The Tehsildar told us of his ideas for foresting
Baltistan and of what he had done in Skardu and Shigar, while the Wazir told stories of his journeys to Leh
and other outlying parts of his territory.

Among other things we heard how 150 Tungans had
come down to Leh last spring armed to the teeth but
not wishing to fight. They said they had fled from Chinese Turkestan where a war was going on. "Do what
you want with us," they had said, "but don't send us
back." The Wazir immediately confiscated their arms
and the four maunds of gold (320 pounds) they had
brought with them, and directed them to be fed. Then,
on orders from the Kashmir Government, he sent them
with an escort to Srinagar, where they were interned.
The Wazir also told of a single Tungan who had

recently been caught entering Srinagar with eight *maunds* of hidden gold. It was all the Tungan could get of his store of 100 *maunds* before bitter fighting caused him to flee. Who was fighting and why the Wazir did not know. Evidently the world hears little of what is going on in Chinese Turkestan.

We were now over halfway from Srinagar to the Base Camp and it was unanimously agreed that we should spend a day at Skardu making a general shakedown. Accordingly next morning we were all busy. The Captain went to the Skardu Treasury where he obtained the 75 pounds of money we should need to pay off our coolies, then made arrangements with the postmaster for handling mail or telegrams we would send out. In the bazaar he also bought some *tsamba* (barley flour), rice and *dhali* (curry powder) for the Sherpas, some odds and ends for Ahdoo, and sugar and tea for us. I, as commissary, was becoming concerned over our tea and sugar consumption, for in the heat of the Indus Valley we had each been averaging some two quarts of tea a day. The extra supply would help. Meanwhile Houston was hard at work with numerous letters, I was composing an article for the London *Times,* and House and Petzoldt were doing yeoman service in stringing aluminum snowshoe frames and weighing food.

In the afternoon the situation was under control and we compared notes. Our supplies had all arrived at

Skardu in good shape, though some of Petzoldt's splendid boxes had received harsh treatment and he had to repair them. Confident now that we were ready for the next 150 miles, we went for a stroll en masse through the streets of the capital. The city was rather disappointing. A medieval looking stone and mud fort did lord it over the town from a rocky eminence, it is true, but the rest of the settlement was less glamorous. It was like any of the Balti villages we had gone through, though considerably larger and with a bigger bazaar. Each tiny shop was filled with knickknacks and gaudy ribbons, while charms galore dangled everywhere. They were covered by bits of brilliant cloth or beads and came in all colors. We saw 20 kinds of cigarettes, and matches, and turban cloth, and looking glasses, and cheap flashlights—in fact almost anything one would not want to buy in a low grade 5 and 10 cent store at home. We saw no *bhang* or *chang* (Ladakh beer) for sale, though we were told that young Mohammedans no longer strictly follow the laws of the Prophet. One enterprising salesman even offered to sell us movie film. The cartridges looked good, but when the Captain told us they had been discarded by the French in 1936 as worthless, we declined the offer.

In the evening began a frantic search for suitable clothes to wear to the Wazir's, where we had been invited for dinner. Each had his first hot bath in weeks (for this resthouse boasted a tin tub), before searching duffel bags for odds and ends of clothing less malodorous than marching togs. Our wardrobe was neither extensive nor uniform, and we appeared on the scene in everything from windproof trousers (meant for high altitudes) to shorts and climbing boots.

In the Governor's garden we were graciously received by the Wazir's boy, who escorted us through the fragrant beds of flowers to a shady spot where our host, with the Tehsildar and the lieutenant commanding the fort, awaited us. Many polite words were spoken there amid the fragrance of the flowers before we were led into the house. At the entrance we all took off our shoes —to the consternation of two members of the party who had holes in their socks—and then the Wazir poured water from a silver pitcher over our hands before we sat down cross-legged on rich silk rugs. On the tablecloth before each of us was spread a tray containing a large silver dish heaped with two kinds of rice and surrounded by several small bowls with spiced meats and sauces. This huge portion was only the beginning, however, for a servant kept coming in with bowls of vegetables, thick *chupattis* and even more poignant sauces.

Knives, forks and spoons were lacking. The Wazir started the meal by taking rice in his fingers, dipping it into the various sauces and transferring it to his mouth with gracious skill. For us, eating with the hands was a difficult matter. Both rice and sauces dripped from our clumsy fingers—into beards that I fear in some cases changed color with the foods. It was also a problem in our cramped position to lean so far forward that the food would drop back onto the plate and not onto the rug. Meanwhile, as our legs went to sleep, our abnormal sitting position rapidly became unbearable.

Even worse was the effect of the sauces. At first we had swallowed them in large amounts, for they did not affect us till the middle of the dinner. Then a thirst that would have choked Tantalus seized us. Vast gulps of water seemed only to fan the flames that were raging in our stomachs, tears came into the corners of our eyes, and our breath felt like a blast from the Sahara. Someone had drunk from the silver goblet on his right, and as we each followed suit we were horrified to find that this left one of us with two goblets and the Wazir with none.

As the banquet continued, most of us were quickly filled, for we already felt as if what we had eaten was cooking away in our stomachs. Red-bearded Paul, however, was made of sterner stuff, for he not only ate all of his own trayful but had three extra helpings besides. At last we staggered to our feet, adjourned to the hallway, where water was again poured on our hands, and put on our shoes. From here we went to the reception room where a delicious dessert of almond custard was brought. The cool custard made us all feel better, and as we sat smoking afterward we felt this had been the pleasantest evening of the trip.

The Wazir told stories of political difficulties and cases that he had judged in court. Violent crimes are very rare among the Baltis, it seems, and most disputes concern boundaries and water rights. Among other things he said that Baltis may marry for a month or a day or for any length of time they wish, so that infidelity is absolutely unknown. The Tehsildar meanwhile was telling of shooting wily ibex, sharpu and markhor, and of killing a far rarer quarry, the beautiful snow leopard. Both Tehsildar and Wazir were Brahmins of the noble warrior caste and each greatly venerated the military. Over and over again the Tehsildar told us of how his father and his brother were army officers, and that he would have been also had his eyes been good.

Despite slight astigmatism the Tehsildar was an athlete, and, among other things, an enthusiastic tennis player. We were then unable to play on his tennis court, but on our return to Skardu some months later I played with him. On that grand occasion the backstops were made of purple turban cloth, the net topped by red cloth and hung with gorgeous red tassels, and the ball boys—who competed to get each ball—numbered in the dozens.

The evening was too soon over. When we departed, we were escorted to the resthouse by the Wazir and others, preceded by several torch bearers. It was with real regret that we said good-by that evening to these hospitable, genuine Hindu gentlemen. Next morning we were to leave at dawn for Shigar.

Chapter VII
To the Last Village
Robert H. Bates

"ALEXANDER'S" BARGE

A GOAT-SKIN ZOK

FOUR BALTIS. NOTE THE GOITER ON THE MAN AT THE LOWER RIGHT

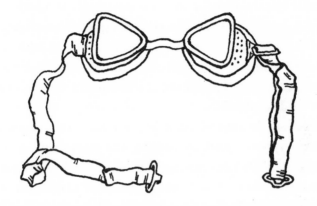

Chapter VII   To the Last Village

D AWN had scarcely broken on the morning of May
27 when we tipped the bungalow keeper and said
good-by to the little tin bathtub in the resthouse. Not
till our return to Skardu would we see this or any other
tub, and before that eventful day many rivers had to be
crossed. The first river, literally speaking, lay almost
at our feet—the rushing Indus.

At Skardu in the springtime the stream is broad and the water swift. Across it an ancient ferry curves a diagonal course to the other side, then is pulled laboriously upstream again to reverse the process. This barge, locally rumored to be the handiwork of Alexander the Great, is of the sturdiest construction. The planks of the flat bottom and square sides are fastened with hand worked iron clamps and the timbers themselves are massive enough to withstand the bolting and shying of the wildest ponies.

Before we shoved off with our load of 3 horses, 5 sheep, 7 goats, and 17 people, the steersman, a huge goitrous Balti who manned an enormous sweep oar in the stern, paused to spread wide his arms and pray loudly to Allah that we should not be drowned. Then the Balti equivalent of "Eastward Ho" was shouted and we were pushed out into the fierce grip of the current. Everybody worked. Paddles and sticks lay handy on the planks of the ferry, and young and old alike, without stroke or rhythm, hacked furiously at the water as if the devil were chasing them. The river bank shot by alarmingly fast but only imperceptibly did we edge out toward the middle of the stream, though all the while the giant Balti steersman leaned on his sweep oar and shouted encouragement. Suddenly we were out of the current and into the slower water of the northeast side of the river; in a few more minutes we were headed into shore and came grinding against the sandy north bank, where we disembarked nearly half a mile below the place we had started.

A 12-mile march across broad stretches of soft sand took us to Shigar, a large town on the river of the same name. Here we were again the center of interest. The high bank which surrounds the polo field where we camped soon filled with Baltis, who struggled for front row positions so that not a single movement of ours would escape them. The playing field at Shigar is the largest in Baltistan and its grandstand is shaded by a fine walnut and an immense plane tree. Beyond the polo grounds, paths lined by stone walls stretch away. Baltistan, like New England, has countless stone walls, firmly built and well cared for.

We had little time to observe this prosperous metropolis or its inhabitants, however, before a tall youth with a faded red fez appeared and invited us to the Munshi's for tea. The Munshi and the little Rajah of Shigar were still in Skardu but they had sent word that we were to be entertained despite their absence. And princely hospitality it was. First we were taken to the balcony of the Munshi's house, where we sat looking down on a garden of almond, pear, and apple trees. Birds were whistling in the fragrant garden below as we sat watching the Baltis plowing in the green barley fields along the river and, in the distance, rugged peaks rising grandly well above the snowline.

Nor was the entertainment itself less satisfying. We

were ushered into a heavily carpeted room where we took our places around a table, trying as we did so to stop casting inquisitive glances at a pile of near-by delicacies. First came tea. Not the kind we know at home, but delicious cinnamon tea made of milk, tea, sugar and cinnamon (with no water). During the repast that followed, never were the delicate cups allowed to become empty. Either our tall host or a large servant with an amazing turban would refill them from an immense dragon-ornamented teapot, which like the magic pitcher of antiquity seemed never to get empty. Cakes of all sizes and textures streamed past. Great platter-sized dainties of eggshell thinness alternated with others thicker than doughnuts and many times more solid. Still others were brittle and full of bubbles, but one and all were good, so that we had cookies and *chupattis*, ghi cakes and honey cakes heaped in a great pile before us, although we were eating as fast as we decently could.

Finally, when we could eat no more, extra cups were brought and we were treated to Lhassa tea. To us it seemed completely unlike tea, for it was chocolate-colored and made largely of salt and butter. I thought it most like clam broth; someone else said it tasted like Epsom salts, and none of us could agree. The bitter tea, however, made an agreeable contrast to the sweets we had had, and after it our host produced cigarettes. As we leaned back contentedly in our chairs, smoking, and chatting with the tall Balti through the medium of the Captain, we had leisure to observe the splendid rugs from Turkestan, the carving of the woodwork and the incongruously cheap photographs of mosques that hung on the walls.

When it was time to depart, we thanked our generous host and started slowly back to our encampment at the polo grounds. From Shigar on no banquets would be ours, for we would be climbing steadily through thinly populated country till we reached the Base Camp; but now for the first time we would be going in the direction of our mountain and not zigzagging all over Baltistan.

Ahead of us next morning stretched the 18-mile stage to Yuno, the last march where we could use horses, so the three cavalry members each rode part of the way. For miles we followed poplar shaded lanes and skirted mud and rock villages till we reached barren valley slopes soaked by the hot sun. Glad we were to reach the tiny village of Yuno near the confluence of the Shigar and the Braldu. Now only 25 miles separated us from Askole, the last village we would see before reaching the mountain.

After paying off our horsemen, the next step was to hire coolies for the following day, but on arrival they demanded 4½ rupees apiece for the 25-mile carry to Askole and insisted on taking 4½ days to do it. This seemed excessive, since we had been paying in most places only one anna (¹⁄₁₆ of a rupee) a mile and the Captain thought that for the sake of future expeditions we ought to pay only the official rate. The men seemed happy enough with the 2 rupees 8 annas we offered them—a month's wages in Baltistan—but they were led by two trouble makers who rudely insisted on their rights.

Finally we stepped into the Logan tent to have supper and discuss what to do. When we came out, the crowd of coolies refused to go, the ringleaders having induced them to stage a sit-down strike, making them swear on the Koran not to go for the wages we offered. Bitter words followed. Before we knew it, someone had shoved one of the ringleaders; and the wretch, stepping backward, lost his footing and sat down. At this, the mob of 60 men yelled and surged forward. Both sides were really angry and spoiling for trouble, and for a moment it looked like war. The hindmost men shoved the foremost ones into us, while one fellow struck Ahdoo on the head with his rope. Meanwhile the Sherpas had taken out their ice axes and *kukris* and had started forward to carve the enemy to bits. This was serious, for our little Nepalese boys hated to see their sahibs thwarted. They kept saying: "Let us at them, sahibs. We do not like these men." While we were stopping our angry boys, the Munshi's son, who had followed us to camp, restrained the coolies.

The 60 Yuno men began to disappear into the darkness and we and the few coolies who had stayed passive but loyal remained. The Munshi's son immediately went after the fugitives, while we huddled in a council of war. We didn't think these natives would actually attack us, but we were afraid of damage to equipment which would ruin our chances on the mountain. All of us were deeply ashamed of our anger at the coolies, but things had happened so suddenly we had been taken by surprise. Even though we felt that only a handful of men were to blame, we foresaw a delay that might prove most unfortunate. The Sherpas, meanwhile, had placed each man's ice ax before his tent and were standing guard over the camp. The spare axes were placed neatly in the center of the ring of tents, showing that the Sherpas were sure we were in for a night attack.

Finally the Munshi's son returned and said we would have to go back to the Tehsildar for help. He said the men had been smoking *bhang* and talking wildly while we were at supper and had been led by their two leaders to swear on the Koran not to go with us except at their own price. This settled it. We should be delayed at least two or three days while somebody went to Skardu. Luckily, however, we found that a goatskin raft (a *zok*) was handy in the village, so it was decided that next morning the Captain and I should float down to Skardu and make as speedy arrangements as possible with our friend the Tehsildar. Meanwhile the others would either split the party and go on with a few supplies to

Askole, or stay at Yuno to wait for us.

Early next morning we awoke to find that no savage attack had been launched, but a high wind, which our boatmen refused to face, was creaming the waves of the Shigar, and another delay appeared inevitable. About eight o'clock it died abruptly and to our joy the four wild looking boatmen carried the raft down to the water. The contraption consisted of 28 goatskins covered with a framework of slender poplar poles on which we were to sit; the whole raft weighed less than 100 pounds, so the "zokmen" could easily take it apart at Skardu and carry it upstream. The Captain and I took our places gingerly. Wild cheers from the rest of the expedition greeted this maneuver, and almost before we could sit down the *zok* began bobbing off downstream.

For the rest of the morning we were completely in the hands of our boatmen, who spent the time alternately grounding us on sandbars, spinning us round and round in the swift water, and examining our shoes. When we approached rapids in the river they put down their poles and prayed loudly, while we spun and tossed and held on grimly; but the raft seemed unsinkable and we soon agreed that as long as it didn't turn over we were safe. We urged the boys into swifter water, but they were conservative and stayed in traditional channels. Most of the time one or two of them would be blowing up leaky bladders or splashing water on the raft to keep the sun from cracking the skins. The lung power of these fellows was amazing, for with perfect equanimity they would blow up the very ones we were sitting on, even while the *zok* was being tossed violently by the waves.

The Captain and I were generally dry, sitting as we were on our sleeping bags wrapped in slickers, but the boatmen had only short coats to keep out the wet. Cold water was continually sloshing up between the skins to soak our gondoliers, who fortunately didn't seem to mind anything as long as they could stare at their passengers. Our slickers and especially my crêpe-soled shoes amazed them, even as their peculiar haircuts astonished us. One of the boatmen—a 6-toed fellow—had a half-inch part shaved down the center of his head, while the rest of his hair hung lugubriously over his ears. On the whole it seemed like a clever idea. By this method one could part his hair neatly in the morning without needing to look in a mirror or even open his eyes.

These boatmen prayed repeatedly that we would not drown, but as the swift Shigar was not wide, their prayers soon ceased to alarm us. I began to watch for ibex on the slopes above till my eyes closed and I slept soundly. When I awoke, the sun had gone and a stiff breeze from the north was blowing clouds of dust upstream. The high wind worried us, as we knew the boatmen might refuse to cross the Indus while it was blowing, but cigarettes encouraged them, and by 2:30 we were creeping along the sandbars at the mouth of the Shigar, ready for the wild race across the Indus. A moment later and we were again booming downstream in the clutch of the great river, while our "zokmen" encouraged one another with shouts and guttural grunts. Headway was hard to make. For a time it looked as if we were in for a long sail downstream, but a rest on a sandbar so helped the men that, with the "cabin class" cheering loudly, the zok finally scraped against the gravel of the south bank only two and a half miles down river from Skardu.

We paid the happy boatmen and went immediately to the Tehsildar's house, where several score shoes about the door informed us that he must be holding court. Past this maze of pointed brogans we were ushered to the inner sanctum where the Wazir and the Tehsildar sat in two thronelike chairs. They immediately adjourned the meeting and invited us to the Wazir's garden, where we soon found ourselves sipping tea, eating an onion omelet and relating our sad story. No officials of any country could have been more kind. The Tehsildar offered to go with us himself to put things right, and when we wouldn't hear of that he arranged for a chuprassi (a sort of captain of police) to go with us.

Once our business was settled, we began discussing pleasanter things, and the Wazir told us how he had been holding an oral examination for the position of tax collector when we came in. His system was to ask a riddle or tell a story requiring a solution. Then, like Haroun-al-Raschid, he would immediately appoint the man who gave the cleverest solution to the catch problems. At least in one part of the world it seems that political appointments are unknown!

One story of the Wazir fascinated me. He told how the Baltis of this area actually manufacture *artificial glaciers*. Artificial teeth and flowers and wood and ice, we have all seen, but as far as I know even Hollywood has never made artificial glaciers. The Wazir went on to explain that ice streams are the life blood of Baltistan. Without water in this barren country there can be no life, and as glaciers feed streams throughout the dry season a new glacier must be built before a new village can be started. The last artificial glacier, according to our host, was made about 35 years ago by the grandfather of the present Rajah and is still flourishing some 30 miles from Skardu.

Glacier building follows an ancient formula. Ice is first carefully taken from male and female glaciers. (The sex is determined by the character of the melt water, but how, the Baltis would not tell us. When we asked about it they only laughed.) It is carried by coolies who may not speak a word throughout the whole operation. It is then deposited in a high valley where a glacier could easily exist were it once started. Many invocations are made while a vast number of ice blocks are assembled and covered with charcoal and thorn bushes, which in turn are hidden by numerous goat-skins of water. The water keeps things cool before the thorns prick the skins and let the water drip slowly through the charcoal to the ice.

This water, freezing in the cool fall nights, helps the glacier to survive, while in the winter snow packing in around the ice helps it to expand. Baltis carry snow to the glacier for the next 20 years to help it along, till finally the ice river is firmly established. At the end of this time the Baltis have another stream for irrigating purposes and another village can be begun. Whether this is the true process or not I don't know, but the two Hindus certainly believed it and they pointed out to us men who had helped build "the last artificial glacier."

As we sat in the garden with punkah men fanning us, the Wazir apologized that the high tea was not more elaborate. The Mohammedan Rajah of Skardu had asked the Hindu Wazir to dinner on this evening, and the Wazir had already sent his best cook to the Rajah's to prepare Hindu food. Of course a Hindu cannot eat Mohammedan food, and vice versa. We were asked to join the party but declined the honor. I was glad we did, for the Captain informed me secretly that the Rajah's cook was famous for food so hot that it would make the Wazir's sauces of a few evenings before seem like ice water.

Next morning the chuprassi, a stocky chap originally from Hunza in Turkestan, woke us and showed us a note from the Tehsildar ordering the Yuno men to go with us. He said that ringleaders of the strike were to be sent to court at Shigar for trial and punishment.

Then for a second time we left the resthouse and once more crossed the Indus in "Alexander's barge." This time ponies carried us over the hot, sandy miles to Shigar, which we reached five hours later. There the Munshi's son again met us, seated us at the handsome tablecloth in the richly carpeted room, and feasted us with ten cups apiece of cinnamon tea and delicious sticky cakes.

Refreshed and with greatly stimulated morale, we changed horses and pushed on toward Yuno 18 miles away. It was sizzling hot. We watched the magpies along the trail, stripped occasional half ripe mulberries off the trees, and damned all Balti ponies and wooden saddles a good many times before we saw Houston in the distance.

Soon cups of dark tea were soothing away the hot miles behind us, and afterward we celebrated House's birthday with a *pilau* of the very finest. Then, over a small bottle of rum (donated in Pittsburgh and carefully smuggled in from Srinagar), we toasted the ex-president of the Yale Mountaineering Club and our mountain, before starting to compare notes for the past two days.

While the Captain and I had been down river, the

others had discussed sending a two-man or three-man party on toward K2, but in the end it had been decided that the two or three days gained would not compensate for splitting the party at such an uncertain period. The time was spent, therefore, in putting drawstrings in the Meade tents, sewing, checking over the supplies and, most important of all, giving the Sherpas a course in the proper use of the rope. Later on, this two days spent with the Sherpas paid high dividends, for their belaying and general rope handling on the mountain were steady and reliable.

Again there was difficulty about the coolies when we sought to leave Yuno. Though the chuprassi was very efficient, he could locate only 44, and we finally decided to leave him, Ghaffar Sheikh, and 24 loads behind. The chuprassi said he had sent a *zok* across the river to the village there and would have men soon, but "soon" is an indefinite adverb in Baltistan so we decided not to wait.

The coolies went slowly at first, for they stopped to smoke and chat every few hundred yards, but when we came to stiff going they went well. Most of the men were the same rogues who had blackmailed us three days before, but they had no hard feelings about the matter. Like most Asiatics caught lying, they took the attitude: "I didn't get away with it today, but maybe I'll have better luck next time. The sahib will please to forget."

The trail cut along ledges high above the Braldu River, and about 4 o'clock we finished what the Captain claimed was a 500-foot climb. To us it seemed more like a 2000-foot ascent before we finally crossed a wind-swept shoulder and descended to a shepherd's hut near some ancient terraces. Here, 500 feet above the roaring Braldu, we found a spring, wood, and ground level enough to camp on. Though Ghaffar Sheikh and the chuprassi had failed to overtake us, we pitched our tents confident that they would catch us soon.

The march to Foljo, the next village, took most of us by surprise, for we climbed about 6000 feet, all told. The trail continually led up and down round cliffs falling sheer to the river. Some of the footing was precarious and in one place the barefoot coolies negotiated a slab that we dared not attempt in nailed boots, only friction keeping them on the cliff. As the trail continued, we found ourselves at times picking our way along the river bank, at others scrambling up slabs of granite or resting gratefully on a sunny shoulder 2000 feet above the water. From one such place we could look ahead into a great hollow where the river had chiseled out of the rock a pocket three miles long and 5000 feet deep.

It was pleasant to sit in the shade of a boulder and gaze ahead. A sweet smell of flowers was in the air and incredibly pointed peaks rose in the distance around us. Astonishing monoliths edged the track, putting to shame the famous Chamonix aiguilles. On one of these, according to the local legend reported by Godwin-Austen, a pure white bird guards a lump of gold placed on a velvet cushion. Any object not to be found in the morning is supposed to have been stolen by this *Pir* and kept on the rock. Fortunately no bird visited us here, nor was anything "eaten," as the Sherpas say when something mysteriously disappears.

A long afternoon march took us to Foljo where the few huts and green fields high above the river made us think of Kipling's Shamlegh. We saw no lady of Shamlegh, unfortunately, but a kindly lambardar did present us with a sack full of delicious apricot seeds, tasting very like tiny almonds. The lambardar was delighted to see us, as we were only the second group of white men to visit his village in 25 years. He immediately brought several villagers in need of medical treatment, one of whom, suffering from an advanced stage of trachoma, was his own brother.

The sufferer was nearly blind and begged Houston to cut his eyelids off. Little daylight was left, so our doctor could not operate, but he did trim off the old man's eyelashes and give him something to relieve the pain. The man's friends crowded around, offering us bags of apricot seeds (a sort of local currency) to cure him, but we could only shake our heads.

Houston's clinic was increased after supper when he found that Petzoldt had a temperature of 101°. Our expeditionary John Ridd had been carrying a heavy load and the exertion might have combined with a touch of sun to give him a fever. It didn't seem serious, however, and he, like the rest of us, was greatly cheered by the arrival of Ghaffar Sheikh, the chuprassi, and 24 men. They had done well to catch us so soon. The old shikari was glad to join us and was further delighted that he had seen five ibex. Again and again he told us each individually, "Ibockus, sahib. Many ibockus." Like most Kashmiri Ghaffar Sheikh could not pronounce the letter x.

On this part of the journey we felt much cheered by the loyalty of certain natives who had come with us as porters for many days. Two of them had come from Askole to Tolti to enlist. They were brothers called Sulim and Mussa. Sulim was a good-natured giant of a fellow with a perpetual grin, always happy and nearly always with flowers in his hat or over his ears. His amazing chest and breadth of shoulders, plus a short black beard and single gold earring—a great rarity in Baltistan—made him look the perfect pirate; yet he was soft-hearted as a child. If he were allowed to, he would each evening do half the work of pitching the tents, and he would always go back from camp to carry in the loads of slow or tired coolies. Sulim was a fine chap, and though we could not understand his Balti jokes, at which he himself laughed uproariously, we did appreciate his humor and his kindness to everyone. Had it been anyway possible we would have added Sulim to our permanent camp entourage.

Mussa was also a good man, though lacking his brother's nobler qualities; shrewder in money matters, he made all business arrangements for the pair while Sulim did most of the work. These two men and eleven other carriers from Satpura, who had joined us at Gol, were the backbone of our transport. We worried less about our Yuno coolies when we knew that the cheerful Satpura men were with them. In fact one of these chaps, named Hussein Ali, seemed so well bred that Houston insisted he must be a C.I.D. man in disguise.

Before leaving Foljo we presented cigarettes to the kindly lambardar and dark glasses to the trachoma sufferer. Then, with the whole village watching us, we paraded out of town in the direction of Hoto. At first a level stretch of going gave us hopes of an easy day, but soon a series of discouraging heights showed that the path would hardly be a level one. The climb became steeper and steeper, and as the sun bored into us a great thirst settled over the party. We found streams, but so much mica was suspended in them all that we dared not drink for fear of serious internal troubles. At the high point, Burdsall's barometer registered 11,400 feet, about the height of the Zoji La.

More difficult was the 2000-foot descent on the other side down a path of ladderlike steepness. We were threatened here by falling stones, for much of the slope was made up of rocks lying near the angle of repose, but the only ones that fell close to us were started by two foolish *dzos* who were grazing on the edge of a perpendicular grass patch above. In several places landslips had occurred which left smooth slabs of a most unpromising sort. Only friction holds could be used on these rock plates, which provided us with many interesting moments; but the footing did not bother the coolies, who pranced gaily down with their 55-pound loads, quite putting to shame those of us who modestly imagined ourselves rock-climbers.

After 10 hours of fairly constant going we reached Hoto, 12 miles from Foljo. Not far from this town Sulim had stationed himself at a small stream and insisted on carrying us over on his back one by one. Our weight was nothing to this brawny fellow and we should have lost face among the coolies had we refused. Hoto is a small village only six easy miles from Askole, but as we had already had a rough day we decided not to push on till the morrow. One reason for this decision was Petzoldt's illness. He had felt better in the morning when we left Foljo, but the cruel trail had taken much of his strength and only grim determination carried him on. When he finally reached camp on sagging legs, with faithful Kitar close behind, we found his temperature was 103°.

Here was the most serious obstacle to the expedition so far. What had caused the fever we could not guess.

It did not seem to be sunstroke or trouble caused by bad food. Weakness, a high fever that varied, and a severe pain in the back were the main symptoms. That evening we anxiously watched Houston treating the patient, seeking to learn if Petzoldt could possibly have pneumonia. I am ashamed to say I slept fairly well that night, while our doctor slept hardly at all. At repeated intervals he got up to see how Petzoldt was faring, for he had dosed him heavily with aspirin to break up the fever. Paul sweated all night and in the morning said he felt much better. Although his temperature was still fairly high, he insisted on pushing on to Askole where he could be more comfortable, and Houston somewhat reluctantly let him go.

About a mile from Hoto hung the only rope bridge we should pass on the trip to the mountain. We had seen others, but were thankful that we had not needed to cross them, for the Captain told us how one such bridge had overturned when two expedition members leaned on the same handrail at the same time. They had been rescued only after hanging for several minutes to a single cable high above the stream. Perhaps this explains why a member of another expedition is said to have refused to cross any rope bridge unless blindfolded and carried over by coolies! We were not yet in this condition, but we approached respectfully the three sagging cables, made of twisted willow twigs, which spanned the 200-foot gorge. No wonder the rope creaked like an abused wicker chair, for it had been made on the spot from local pollarded willows, twisted into thin strands before being braided (in groups of 15 to 30) into the cables themselves. These three main supports—one for the feet and one for each hand—were joined at intervals by lighter lines, and in places sticks were jammed between the two handrails so that pressure would not force them together and eliminate room to walk between. These sticks seemed to bother the coolies not at all, for many natives practically raced across the bridge, but with us it was a slightly different story.

As we one by one stepped gingerly onto the central cable, which appeared brittle and cracking with age, we thought of the Balti maxim, "No rope bridge should be repaired until it is broken," and groaned inwardly. Slowly we paced along the six-inch width of the middle rope, holding to the sharp surfaces of the twin handrails. Below our feet, which we watched intently, we were well aware that a turbulent mountain torrent was swirling. At every step the rope contraption squeaked a protest and tremors bounded along the foot cable. The sticks between the handrails were perhaps the jolliest part of all. Just as one of us would get his left foot higher than his hands in order to clear the obstruction, the foot support would start bouncing up and down and swaying from side to side while the water spun dizzily below.

Once in the center of the bridge, one felt uncommonly close to the water, for the cold air rising from the racing stream was chilling. From the middle onward a steady climb took one to the ring of grinning, encouraging native faces at the other end, where one could step off the straight and narrow trail with all the enthusiasm of a football player breaking training. Paul crossed easily despite his illness, and our only casualty came when the wind blew off the ancient hat of a coolie. We paid for a new hat on the spot, happy that we would not need to pass a rope bridge again for many weeks.

Sulim and the chuprassi had by now herded the last weak-kneed Yuno man across the strands, and the road to Askole lay clear before us. House and I forged ahead past some old sulphur spring deposits that reminded us of Yellowstone Park. Two live sulphur springs were near by, though out of sight. We missed these, and while we were basking on a sunny rock overlooking the outskirts of Askole, the others found the springs and spent a delightful hour soaking in them. Before entering the water, they had been forced to eject Ghaffar Sheikh from one pool and 15 coolies from the other, but this in no way detracted from their enjoyment. Their first shouts when they reached us were, "Unclean! Unclean!" as they pointed at us with scornful fingers. They, on the other hand, we were informed, were now pure as driven snow and entirely free of lice and fleas.

Pure and impure, we entered Askole together. It is a small village of mud huts, with tiny goats, green terraces high above the river, and beautiful surrounding peaks. The lambardar of the village and the local zaildar (a government tax collector) came forth to meet us and welcomed us to a compound where we were set off from the rest of society by a circle of low stone walls topped by thorn bushes. Our fame, however, had spread before us, for, long before the tents could be set up, a circle of staring faces appraised our every move. It was exactly as if a circus had suddenly come to town and everyone had turned out to see the fun. The show started when the Sherpas began setting up our tents and getting tea. By the time Petzoldt had entered his sleeping bag, the circle was three deep or more, and the Captain began to put on a real performance.

Streatfeild I fear would never be happy as ruler of a native state, for in all his trips to Baltistan—and I believe he knows the country better than any other white man—he has never grown accustomed to audiences of 50–200 whenever he sits down for a bite to eat. Long before he is half through his first cup of tea, a savage gleam comes into his eye and he springs from his duffel bag shouting: "Go away, you silly fools. Why do you need to watch all the while? Hit that man, Ghaffar Sheikh. No, throw water on him. Frightful manners, these people. *Nikel jao, nikel jao!*"

This was the part of the show the people liked best.

Squeals of joy would come as we pretended to throw stones at the natives, and loud yells of delight when an unfortunate one of their number was splashed with water—something that every good Balti abhors to take externally. Time and again the circle would come closer, and at odd intervals throughout the afternoon the Captain would loudly raise his voice in additional attempts to teach the Baltis manners.

A few of the waiting people were in need of medical attention and they were placed aside to be looked at by Houston later in the afternoon, but first there was much to do. Petzoldt's temperature was up again, so, after making him comfortable, Houston had a conference with Ahdoo about soups and eggs and simple things for the sick man's table. Meanwhile the rest of us, with Streatfeild and treasurer Burdsall at the helm, were paying off the Yuno coolies. This part of the show thrilled Askole, and only the valiant efforts of our Sherpa boys with their ropes and ice axes and pails of water kept the crowd from stampeding in on us. The next job was even worse, for we now needed to secure men to go with us from Askole to the mountain.

The moment the Captain told the lambardar we were ready to hire the men, 300 yelling natives burst enthusiastically into the compound. Some came over the thorn-topped walls and others knocked down stones so that in no time at all a maelstrom of humanity was seething through the camp. The Sherpas and our Sat-

HOUSE

BATES CROSSING ROPE BRIDGE AT ASKOLE

An Unpleasant Corner on the Trail near Paiju

Ice Pinnacle on the Baltoro Glacier 150 feet High
(Note figure on right slope of cone)

pura boys behaved manfully, and with sticks, ice axes and ropes we chased the job hunters into some semblance of order.

Finally 50 loads were given out and the rest of the crowd was driven away, for the tents, kitchen and other loads could not be issued till morning. The good-humored but jostling crowd outside the walls kept returning and returning, while the Sherpas, armed with sticks and pails of water, protected the camp. Eventually, quiet came; Houston looked over the sick Baltis and cared for Petzoldt; we had a late supper and turned in.

Next morning Paul's temperature was 104.4°, so we spent the day in Askole arranging to break our group into two parts. Houston and Petzoldt were to stay behind while the other four went on to the mountain. It was all very hard on both men, but especially on Houston, who had lived this expedition for six months past. We had no idea what Petzoldt's strange malady could be, or when he would recover. It might be a severe chill, or the strange tropical fever that Tilman had on the Shaksgam Expedition a year before.

With these thoughts oppressing our spirits, the day rolled slowly on. Burdsall carefully checked over the accounts and money on hand, while House and I separated the food going with us from that staying with Houston. Later we slipped away from the compound and bathed luxuriously in a mountain stream, returning to find the Captain still talking with the lambardar, the zaildar and Ghaffar Sheikh about the amount of atta for the coolies and other details of the transport. Eggs cost 8 cents a dozen, and Streatfeild had found a man with a huge wicker basket packed with straw who would carry 20 dozen to the Base Camp for us.

Houston meanwhile was tremendously busy. As soon as he would finish temporarily with Petzoldt, he would go out to his clinic where Ghaffar Sheikh would have the lame, the halt and the blind neatly arrayed on the grass. The people were of all shapes and ages, and many of them were tearfully thankful for Houston's treatment. Cases of goiter were fairly common, as they had been since Skardu. Numbers of our coolies since we left the Indus had had huge bunches at the neck, though their physical strength seemed unimpaired by the deformity; little boys and old men alike were marred by this lack of iodine, and we saw several cretins.

The sufferers in Houston's clinic had a vast assortment of ills, but luckily he found no cholera, the dread disease that had so hampered Guillarmod's expedition at Askole. The ward procedure went something like this: Charlie would say to Ghaffar Sheikh, "What's wrong with this man?"

The shikari would say, "He has pain in stomach, sahib."

"How long has he had it?"

"He says fifteen years."

"Give him this."

Charlie would give aspirin or bicarbonate of soda or some other simple remedy, which would at least have a psychological effect, and then go on to the next patient. Some said they had had a bad cough for many years or headaches for a quarter century, and all asked cheerfully for a magic pill to make them instantaneously well.

Charlie didn't brand his patients with a red-hot wire as the village doctor did or make them swallow charms or pay heavy fees, so he was easily the most popular man in town. Trachoma and blindness, swollen hands, bruised feet and backs—almost every sort of ailment was there, but his most remarkable cure was made on a woman whom he never saw. To look at a group of patients in Baltistan one would suppose Balti women never are ill. Of course this is because of Mohammedan prejudice about showing a woman to any man, even a doctor. Men would come up and say: "My wife has pains here and trouble here. What shall I do?" And on these vague symptoms the doctor was supposed to base his cure.

In this particular case a man told about his daughter's trouble. From the description it sounded as if she were suffering from lack of calcium and might be helped if she could get some. Just then Houston's eye fell on an enormous can of tooth powder, which one of

Petzoldt's cowboy friends had presented to him before he left Wyoming. It was full of calcium and perhaps just the thing. Hurriedly Houston poured out half the contents into an envelope and gave the man the bulging packet with specific details as to its use. Then he promptly forgot about it. Many weeks later, however, when a battered corps of expeditionaries were returning to Askole, this same man was there to meet us. Fortunately his daughter had not died—the thought which immediately entered our heads. Instead she had somehow been cured and was now well and happy. Her father was profoundly grateful, and as a result some day a surprised salesman will probably sell out his whole supply of tooth powder to the happy villagers of Askole.

Last-minute preparations were made in the evening, and heads were shaken when Houston reported the bad news that Petzoldt's temperature had "spiked right up to 104.6° again." Next morning the big fellow was slightly better and could even joke with us when we came in to say good-by. Then, after giving him a cheery word apiece, we marched out through the streets of the last village we should see in many days. Ghaffar Sheikh, who spoke Balti, was to stay behind with the others, but, like the chuprassi and Houston, he escorted us to the edge of town. There, near the two crude stone forts which the Askole people built 100 years ago to protect themselves from raids of the Hunza bandits, we left Houston and began the last 60 miles of our long journey from New York to the slopes of K2. We had no way of knowing whether Houston and Petzoldt would ever traverse those last miles to the mountain.

Chapter VIII

K2 at Last

Robert H. Bates

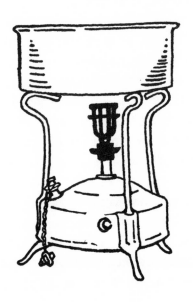

Chapter VIII   K2 at Last

THE two ruined forts we had just passed reminded us that we were now going into even less civilized country. Less than a century ago raiders from Chinese Turkestan had swept over the icy Muztagh Pass to pillage Askole and carry back loot and prisoners to the other side of the Karakoram. As a matter of fact these formidable raids were only ended by an English military expedition which conquered Hunza and Nagar and annexed them to Kashmir.

To reach Askole these amazing marauders traversed the Hispar Glacier, crossed the pass, and descended the Biafo, covering 65 miles of ice on the way. The last raid, according to Godwin-Austen, came in the autumn of 1840, when 700–800 robbers seized rich booty and returned with it toward Hunza. On the way, unseasonable storms swept down on the pirates as they labored over the ice fields, and all but the leader perished.

Now no longer do Askole mothers tremble at the thought of robbers from the northeast, for ice has closed the pass. Today the trail eastward from Askole is only a trace worn by sheep and goats that are brought in the summer time to fatten on the slopes at Paiju or Urdukas.

Before us, through the walls of a natural gateway of crude, polished marble, soon appeared the Biafo Glacier, where our only American predecessors, Dr. and Mrs. Bullock-Workman, had carried out their splendid survey work and glacier studies. Legend has it that the Biafo at one time pushed across the Braldu River and formed a great lake; when the dam broke, the resulting floods swept away a whole village and carried its mosque all the way down to the Shigar Valley. Here the mosque was rescued, taken apart and rebuilt. It was still standing for Godwin-Austen to see in 1861.

The Biafo in 1938 was far from the banks of the Braldu. Between it and the river lay a delta of sand and boulders on which grew wizened patches of dwarf juniper and wormwood. We did not choose the best route, however, and tried to cross the two-mile stretch of detritus-covered ice rather than follow the longer route along the delta. Ahead of us lay the great Paiju Peaks, looking for all the world like the sharp, unearthly mountains in some Maxfield Parrish illustration. High summits were in view all around as we paused in the shade of a huge boulder the shepherds call Korophon, to eat lunch and marvel at the summit cap of Mango Gusor (20,600 feet) across the valley.

In the afternoon we made a sensational traverse along a steep wall whose base was washed by the brawling stream. The Captain, House and I all took different routes across the cliff, and all sweated great drops before we arrived safely at the other side; but what was our intense disgust shortly afterward to watch the coolies wade around the foot of the cliff in murky water only two feet deep! Beyond this point we forded many minor streams and then the two main parts of the Dumordo River. Though the water was very swift, we saved a three-mile detour upstream to a rope bridge by forcing a way across. Here, on a terrace called Gurrah, we camped with our backs to the Punmah Valley, which leads in turn to the New Muztagh Pass—one that no white man has yet been able to cross.

We had difficulties nearer than the Punmah Valley to worry about, for the whole troop of coolies demanded 1 rupee 4 annas a day, claiming that such was the amount they had been promised by the zaildar. The rogues had also brought an additional seven men to carry their atta (which we had paid for), and it soon became evident that the zaildar had dispensed patronage only where it was profitable to him. We insisted that the men stand by the agreement we had made with the official. They refused, and the afternoon was filled with wrangling and shouting till suppertime. We had two alternatives: to pay the very excessive charge or dismiss all the natives but seventeen loyal men and relay loads on to the mountain. As our treasury, like our temper, was almost exhausted, we discussed far into the night our immediate problem and the gloomy days that had befallen the expedition. Meanwhile the brushwood fires flared brightly in the darkness around us, illuminating the circles of Baltis in violent conversation.

We were up early to drink our tea made from river water, which was so full of sediment that the beverage tasted gritty and looked like pea soup. Almost at once we were met by a delegation of natives who told us they would have their pay and their ropes and go home. The Captain said they would get neither their ropes nor their pay and could go to a far hotter place. At this they rushed angrily away out of sight, pretending to go home; but they didn't. An hour later, while House and I sat gloomily over a chessboard, the men returned and agreed to a compromise. Much time, however, had been lost by the wrangling, so we made only five miles before it was necessary for us to camp.

A few pug marks of snow leopards and a bear were etched in the mud of the trail as we continued on across a level tableland toward Paiju and the Baltoro Glacier. Along parts of the route the path disappeared under hardened clay, traces of the mammoth mud avalanches which in wet weather slide down on startled natives in several parts of Baltistan. Now the surface fortunately was firm and we could raise our eyes to admire the amazing spires and pinnacles that soared like old-time Alpine prints about us; so pointed were some of these Paiju summits that even an artist would have hesitated to grace their pinnacles with the traditional chamois. Once, as we rounded a bend in the river, we were greatly thrilled to see a few miles before us the gray back of the Baltoro Glacier, looking like a huge reptile, and, many miles beyond, the bulk of a giant peak outlined against the horizon. Perhaps it was K2!

Paiju is the last little island of vegetation to cling to the bare valley walls before the traveler crosses the final spur and feels the cold breath from the Baltoro. Here Baltis are said formerly to have washed for gold brought down in the granites of Masherbrum, but no trace of workings exists now. Beyond this tiny coppice lay the dismal, boulder-strewn surface of the Baltoro, which strangely enough has no terminal moraine. A lateral moraine on the north side of the ice provides a convenient stairway to the glacier proper, and up this we were soon toiling over mounds and ridges of loose debris. For us the uncertain footing was little more than irritating, but for our coolies, with straw or goat-skin moccasins, the passage was severe. Their pace was slow as they wound single file behind Rose Ali, a Balti specialist in glacier travel. Each native carried a coolie crutch, a sort of crude wooden ice ax, good for rudimentary step-cutting and for resting loads.

Leaving the north side of the ice to avoid *seracs* caused by the influx of the Uli Biafo Glacier, we zig-zagged diagonally across to the glacial trough at the southern edge of the ice where our boot nails grated on solid footing for the first time in many hours. Here we passed the curved horns of three dead ibexes that had been killed by snow leopards or winter avalanches. An air of death and decay hung over this part of the glacier. No birds or flowers brightened the dismal gulch at the edge of the ice, even when we came to a dried up lake bed between steep ribs of moraine and cliffs of glacial drift where we were to camp. Boulders as big as automobiles hung threateningly from the crumbly till, while continuously from some part of the glacier came the rattle of small pebbles or the slither, slither, plunk of a large stone sliding off into a glacial pool.

The Baltoro must have seemed to the Baltis a malevolent monster awaiting the precise moment to strike, for it was clear they had no love for it. They crouched as far from the ice as possible and shifted uneasily when solitary rocks slid suddenly off a ridge as if pushed by an unseen hand.

While the coolies were huddling in tiny groups over fires of wormwood to cook their *chupattis* (made by wrapping unleavened dough around heated stones and baking them in the fire), we were admiring the vertical walls of the Trango Towers across from us. Certainly nowhere in North America or Europe can one see such thousands of feet of smooth, sheer walls capped by pinnacles of rock. Some of these great rock fortresses are so well defended by bastions at every angle that even the most ardent rock-climber trembles before them. Beyond these castellated ramparts project still other fangs of stone, while farther off rear snow-splashed summits of even higher peaks.

We had come up vertically about 1000 feet since leaving the foot of the glacier, so we reckoned our elevation at about 12,000. Still the altitude did not bother us. Nor were we troubled when we moved on to a second camp at Urdukas (13,200) where we camped on grass for the last time. This is a delightful camping place. In the midst of some of the mightiest peaks in the world rises a grass slope sprinkled with flowers where the Baltis sometimes drive their flocks in times of drought. Here we heard the call of the *ram chikor* (the giant partridge) and saw the blue stars of the primula and the blossoms of saxifrage and potentilla. An ancient avalanche has spattered this slope with giant boulders 30 feet high, which lend it the atmosphere of another Stonehenge. Near the base of the largest stone, a clear spring breaks from the grass within a rope's length of the flattened ground where the Duke of Spoleto pitched his tents for three months while carrying on his elaborate survey in 1929.

While we were lazing in the grass of this delightful oasis, and looking for ibex (whose sign was everywhere) the greatest surprise of the expedition took place before our eyes. Pasang suddenly shouted from the slopes above camp, "Sahibs, sahibs, look see!"

Our gaze followed the line of his outstretched finger to the great hills of moraine that litter the central portion of the Baltoro, and there among the boulders we saw something red moving. Black dots were visible too against the sky and in a second Burdsall had his fine binoculars fixed on the spot.

"Why, it's Paul!" he shouted. "Paul and Charlie! How in the world did they do it?"

That was the question we asked ourselves as we hurried excitedly across the glacier to meet them. Petzoldt's flaming plaid shirt was a fine beacon to aim for and in a few minutes we were standing beside them. Petzoldt, though his shirt hung a trifle loosely and his face was

HOUSTON

THE TRANGO TOWERS FORM A PRECIPICE A MILE HIGH

BURDSALL

CROSSING A GLACIAL STREAM

HOUSE

HOUSE

A Length of Rope and a Karabiner get Kitar across with Dry Feet
Coolies using "Crutches" on the lower Godwin-Austen Glacier

MITRE PEAK (18,930 FEET)
GASHERBRUM I (26,470 FEET)

somewhat wan, looked surprisingly strong for a man who four days before had been seriously ill at Askole —35 miles away.

"Charlie fixed me up," he said simply. "How is the food holding out?"

A few minutes later, sprawled on food boxes, we had immediate evidence that Petzoldt was himself again, for after three pint mugs of tea and untold quantities of crackers and cheese, the big fellow said he hoped we were going to have a really large *pilau* for supper. And then, as Charlie winked at us, he went on to describe how his sickness had probably been caused by not eating enough. At least that was the only reason he could think of, so he vowed to eat really hearty meals in the future and never become ill again.

Though we had been separated for only a few days, it had seemed far longer, and we had many plans to discuss that evening as the shadows crept up the steep walls of the Trango Towers across the glacier. Again we could plot a six-man reconnaissance and plan which ridge should be investigated first. At every mention of K2 our excitement increased, as we longed for a first sight of our mountain. Meanwhile the Baltis were likewise chattering eagerly while they passed a primitive *narghile* (water pipe) around the circle. Others, less fortunate, had to make their pipe, which they skillfully did by burying a bent twig in soft earth. A small hole, roughly shaped like a pipe bowl, was dug, and then the twig was tunneled through the adjacent six inches of soil till it emerged in the bowl. After this the stick was carefully removed, rank native tobacco was placed in the hole and lighted, and the coolies took turns at inhaling smoke through the tunnel.

Long after we had gone to our sleeping bags the coolies were still talking, but lack of sleep did not prevent them from starting off cheerfully up the glacier as soon as it was light. We left almost at their heels, for we were eager both to get well up the Baltoro this day and to see the great bulk of Masherbrum (25,650 feet) before the threatening clouds could draw a curtain over it. Unfortunately only the lower half of Masherbrum was visible when we paused four miles from its base to wonder how James Waller and his partners were faring in their attempt to climb it from the south. They were the only other expedition in the Karakoram this year, and we regretted we knew so little about their plans. The fact that they had probably established their base camp three weeks before, while we had not yet even *sighted* our mountain, made us chafe again at our annoyingly slow progress.

Beyond this point we began to glimpse the magnificent solitary ice pinnacles for which the Baltoro is famous. These amazing glacial freaks are duplicated on no other glacier, as far as I know, and even their origin is disputed. The ice blocks, 50–150 feet high, are so pointed it is impossible to climb them; they seem to grow right out of the glacial ice and their sides shine in the sunlight. How they are formed we couldn't tell. They do not seem to be melted *seracs*, fallen from above, but appear to have been thrust up by pressures and strains on the surface, later weathering into their present shapes. In any case, to the traveler advancing up the glacier they look like the sails of a vast armada as it drifts slowly along a channel.

We were still within view of these ghostlike figures when, for the Baltis' sake, we decided to camp. Fine rain, driven by a raw wind, bit into the faces of the poor wretches, some of whom had worn out their sandals and were walking barefoot in the snow. Accordingly we put up the tents on a wet patch of shale across from the obscured Muztagh Tower and gave the Baltis our extra tarpaulins and raincapes. The poor carriers were blue with cold, but they soon had their pipes going and seemed happy.

In the morning we found they had pulled off all their clothes, put some above and some below them, and slept in a big pile between. Bodily heat must have kept them warm, and as a Balti cannot have a sensitive nose, I suppose they were fairly comfortable. At least they started off so quickly in the gray dawn that they soon had a good lead on us. All day we zigzagged through crevasses and clattered along poised piles of debris where a footstep would send stone after stone rattling downward. Again the weather was cloudy, and though we were being robbed of some of the world's finest mountain scenery, we enjoyed the coolness the clouds gave. In the afternoon the famous Mitre Peak beckoned us on, and despite the slowing effects of altitude we managed to get nearly to the Godwin-Austen Glacier before dark.

Now we were camped in the very heart of the Karakoram, only a long march from the towering south wall of K2. Behind us, Masherbrum and the Muztagh Tower stood swathed in cloud, while almost alongside jutted the upthrust wedge of The Mitre (18,930). At the end of the Baltoro rose the vast bulk of the four Gasherbrums—all of them over 26,000 feet! One of these, better known as Hidden Peak, was in 1936 the object of the first French Expedition to the Himalayas. Farther to the left we could see part of the bold southern ramparts of Broad Peak, another 26,400-foot giant. The rumble of falling stones came from this direction, as it did from Marble Peak, a lower, fantastically blended mass of black schist and white marble which forms the corner between the Godwin-Austen and Baltoro Glaciers.

We were now at Concordia Amphitheatre, 15,000 feet above sea level, so it was no wonder that many coolies complained of headaches. Most of them were not seriously ill, however, for we found that when Charlie gave a man aspirin to cure his headache, the

Balti promptly turned his back, spat out the tablet, and put it carefully away for use when he would be really ill. We had previously provided cheap glasses for the carriers, and this prevented an epidemic of snow blindness or sore eyes, such as had hampered earlier expeditions.

On the 12th of June—one month to the day after leaving Srinagar—we swung slowly away from the Baltoro Glacier and onto the surface of the Godwin-Austen. Before us the valley was dark with sullen clouds, but directly ahead of us a rift in the vapor suddenly disclosed, not ten miles away, though high in the air, the glittering apex of a ghostly summit. It was like something from another world, something ethereal seen in a dream. For a few stunned moments we stared at the peak we had come so far to see; then it was gone. The glacier stretched ahead for miles into a void of blank, swirling mist.

Part way up the glacier Houston and I reduced our loads, left the others to encourage the porters, and swung ahead to find a suitable place for our Base Camp. We were now higher than the highest mountain in Europe, and as we pushed ahead to get a lead on the natives, I for the first time began to have a mild headache and a slightly uncomfortable feeling. Houston seemed less affected. He plowed through soggy patches of winter snow like a Bactrian camel and was soon 100 yards ahead of me.

We joined at the height of land where a desolate waste of glacier, like a shell-torn no man's land, stretched mistily before us. Houston went one way, I the other, as we searched for a suitable campsite. Minutes later, as panting Sulim led the host of coolies over the last rise, we selected a hollow in the moraine and shouted to the carriers to pile the loads there. This debris-strewn depression was close to the south wall of K2, it was somewhat sheltered from the wind, and it was safe from avalanches. For the time being we could ask no more.

The coolies refused to go another step and demanded their pay at once, for they wanted to get well down the glacier before nightfall. Then came frenzied counting out of 1 and 2-anna pieces and the usual pleas for more baksheesh. We gave no tips to the labor agitators, and told them why, but presented money, cigarettes and matches to Sulim and Mussa and the Satpura boys who had worked so well. The faithful ones thanked us respectfully, asked once more if they could stay to work for us, and then after many salaams struck out toward the lower glacier.

Base Camp had been reached! No rivers or labor troubles could stop us now, for under Captain Streatfeild's guidance we had reached our mountain without mishap or serious delay. That night as the chill of the glacier worked up through the Logan tent where we were eating, our enthusiasm rose. We could not tell what lay ahead. But at last we had come to grips with the mountain we had traveled halfway round the world to find.

Chapter IX

Preliminary Reconnaissance

William P. House

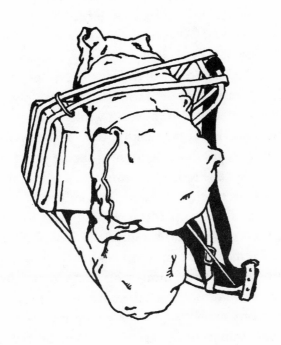

Chapter IX   Preliminary Reconnaissance

BASE CAMP as it slowly took shape June 12 and 13, stood for more than a position from which to make sorties on K2. It marked the completion of the month's march from Srinagar as a job well done. All the planning of the early days of the expedition in America had proved sound, every load had come through safely, our party of six climbers and six Sherpa porters were

in good health, and the realization of obstacles successfully surmounted gave us confidence in ourselves as a
group. With that behind, the far more serious obstacles
that faced us on the reconnaissance were not discouraging. We looked forward to it as a challenge against
which we could pit our whole strength and feel that it
was being expended in a worth-while manner.

The circumstances attending our first day in camp
made an exciting introduction to the beginning of the
reconnaissance. From the cluster of tents in the little
hollow between the ridges of the Godwin-Austen Glacier we could look up at the cloud-dimmed lower wall
of K2 rising only a few hundred yards away. The summit still remained completely hidden as did the upper
slopes of all the great mountains that encircled us. We
were well aware of what lay above, having memorized
photographs taken by earlier expeditions, and knew
what form the mountains took above the clouds. To
lend reality, rumblings at intervals reminded us that
avalanches were falling from the upper slopes to the
glacier. Some of these seemed to come from immediately above camp although they did not spread far
out on the ice. Nevertheless it was some time before
their thunder came to be accepted as a part of camp
life and we ceased to feel alarm.

We had little time that first day to think of what
lay about us hidden in clouds, for camp had to be put
in order so that exploratory work could begin imme-

diately. The ever busy Sherpas cunningly relaid the rock floors beneath the six Meade tents, joining them with smooth paths of rock to prepare against the ravages of hot days later on. Others constructed a dining shelter of rock, roofed with tarpaulins, where we could assemble in comfort. Bates, with his usual solicitude for our food supplies, drafted several of the Sherpas and built a snug storehouse for our provisions. Made of boxes piled on their sides, forming an enclosure roofed with canvas, it was a mysterious den into which he and Houston were wont to disappear with notebooks and pencils, to reappear solemnly hours later with fresh decrees affecting the commissary.

We were glad to assemble in our new camp to go over plans; not that these had not been discussed repeatedly before, but now the finishing touches had to be applied and our first moves planned to accomplish the most possible. We had decided to place this camp near the juncture of the Savoia with the Godwin-Austen Glacier, because this position made the west, south and east sides of K2 readily accessible.

To the west the Savoia Glacier curved out of sight around the western buttresses of the mountain to its source in the cirque below Savoia Pass. From this glacier two of the main ridges of the mountain could be reached—the northwest and the west. The first of these, rising from Savoia Pass, seemed to offer one of the best prospects of a route to the summit. Previous study of

Sella's excellent photographs, taken on the Duke of the Abruzzi's expedition 30 years before, showed the strata to be sloping upward. This was most important, for although the angle of the ridge was uniformly steep it meant that holds for climbing would be good and there would be abundant ledges for campsites.

Most encouraging of all, the rock ridge rose from the top of a pass at 22,000 feet. Between this pass and the Savoia Glacier were only 3000 feet of snow slopes. The guides of the Duke had gained the pass without great effort, and if a well-stocked camp could be placed on it, only a little over 6000 feet of steep rock would need be climbed to the summit. Reaching such a high point with little difficult climbing would be a tremendous asset, as on most great Himalayan peaks troubles begin far below 22,000 feet.

One thing tempered our perhaps premature optimism—the report of the Duke's guides. It was vague and indefinite and said nothing about the northwest ridge itself. It did conclude that there was "no hope" on this side of the mountain. Perhaps bad weather or the lateness of the hour when they reached the pass had been partly responsible. We could only hope so. At present it looked good to us. Of the other ridge rising from the Savoia Glacier we could tell little from photographs, but closer examination of it could be had at the same time we studied the northwest ridge.

From the juncture of the Savoia and Godwin-Austen

Glaciers immediately above Base Camp rose a third ridge, beginning with The Angelus, a 22,330-foot minor peak, and continuing northeast toward the summit. Of this also we could tell little except that the rocks above the glacier were very steep, and as with the southwest ridge the Duke had not considered it worthy of description.

Broken by the above three ridges was the west face of the mountain—photographs of which revealed great precipices almost devoid of snow and ice but subject to ice avalanches from the summit cone.

To the east, up the Godwin-Austen Glacier, were two more ridges, photographs of which had long fascinated us. The southeast ridge, a huge rounded rocky shoulder ending on a hanging glacier 3000 feet below the summit, had actually been attempted by the Duke. On it he had placed one camp. From this base his guides had reached about 20,000 feet, where they had turned back because of the increasing steepness and smoothness of the rock. This was not surprising, for the strata —in contrast with the northwest ridge—sloped down. Although the angle was not as steep as some of the other ridges, it was continuous without any let-up.

Still farther east a spur of the northeast ridge joined the glacier. We considered this a possibility, although the Duke had not attempted it. Unlike the other ridges it was of ice and snow and apparently not very steep until it touched the summit cone. One thing made it a fearsome chance for a route—a mile-long knife edge at 22,000 feet. If this could be traversed safely it might offer a route to the summit, although a long and exposed one. The south and east faces, like the west, appeared to be too exposed to avalanches, but it looked as though their upper parts might if necessary be traversed safely.

Of the one remaining side of the mountain we could only conjecture. The north face, cut off as it was from the Baltoro Glacier system by high passes, could not be reached by a party concentrating on the south side. Reconnaissance of the north would have required another group going in by a different route. However, reports and photographs taken on this side by the successful 1937 Shaksgam Expedition were not encouraging. They showed the north face to be much higher above the base than any of the others and to consist of rock and ice precipices offering little in the way of safe, practicable routes.

We had before us, therefore, five main ridges to reconnoiter and several intervening faces to study for possible variations. Since all these rose 10,000–12,000 feet above the glaciers, it was to be a Herculean task.

To speed reconnaissance and utilize our resources as efficiently as possible, we planned to split up into two parties. One of these would go up the Savoia Glacier to the western side of the mountain to study the northwest and west ridges and report on their feasibility. If

HOUSE

LUNCH—THE BEST HOUR OF THE DAY

BURDSALL

Petzoldt   Streatfeild   Houston   Burdsall   Bates

BASE CAMP

HOUSE WORKING THROUGH ICE BLOCKS OF THE SAVOIA GLACIER

necessary, they were to try to reach Savoia Pass and actually climb on the lower part of the northwest ridge to discover what climbing conditions there were like. At the same time a smaller party would retrace their steps down the Godwin-Austen Glacier and gain the view of the south side of the mountain not vouchsafed us as we had approached several days before. Since the Savoia Glacier reconnaissance would take longer, we decided to use the entire carrying power of the expedition to establish a camp on the lower part. From this, four climbers without Sherpas would move higher under their own power.

Accordingly, on the morning of June 14, we started toward Savoia Pass, carrying very light packs in order not to rush acclimatization too fast. On the day before, Petzoldt and I had prospected a route up the crevassed middle section of the glacier, believing it safer if more difficult than the avalanche-threatened edge underneath The Angelus. Roped in threes and fours, we attempted to continue this route. It was not a happy choice, for many of the crevasses were covered with deep layers of soft snow, indistinguishable from the solid areas between them. One by one we took turns leading, each firm in the belief that he was a better route finder than the man he had succeeded. One by one we broke through the treacherous coverings and were stopped a few feet down by the rope and the watchfulness of the man at the other end.

By noon we were thoroughly disgusted with such progress—the more so as we had covered only three-quarters of a mile since leaving Base Camp. It was not an auspicious beginning for the reconnaissance of one of the greatest mountains in the world. To make matters worse the sun shone hotly, softening the snow and burning through the layers of glacier cream on our faces. When we finally saw a spot that looked safe enough for a camp, it took the twelve of us almost an hour to reach it, despite the fact that it was only 100 yards away. An intricate maze of crevasses surrounded it, so once there we felt as safe as any feudal baron protected by his moat.

After lunch Bates and Streatfeild left with the six Sherpas for Base Camp in order to get their part of the reconnaissance started the next day. Houston, Burdsall, Petzoldt and I remained with two tents and food and fuel for a week. The great heat of the forenoon had brought an attack of fever, so Paul rested in camp while the three of us set out unloaded to try to find a way out of our predicament.

Almost as soon as we had left the tents, clouds started to form and within a half hour it was snowing heavily. We were glad we had brought Bates' black-painted wood dowels to mark the trail home, for to get lost on that part of the glacier would have meant a night out or worse. Abandoning our prejudices against the edge of the glacier below The Angelus, we proceeded directly toward it and after two hours of careful route picking reached the trough between the ice and the rock wall of K2. There were no traces of rock or ice fall from above and as the corridor continued in the direction we wanted to go, we decided that this should be our route the next day.

The return to the two Meade tents was exciting, for by now it was snowing hard and the visibility was reduced to 50 feet. One by one we passed the black wands, looming through the storm like telephone poles, until we made out the dark splotches of our tents, already partly covered with snow.

We found Petzoldt suffering from alternate chills and fever, unable to keep warm in spite of his sleeping bag and all his clothing. There was nothing to be done at the moment except to give him hot things to drink and take turns rubbing his back. We were worried, for it looked like a recurrence of the illness he had had at Askole. If he were no better in the morning we must take him back to Base Camp. While we discussed this sudden setback, the storm rose, the wind hammering at the tent walls and blowing fine snow through the ventilators. With the two small tents set end to end we cooked a supper of pemmican over the primus stove and crawled into our sleeping bags, wondering how long it would be before we could get the sick man to Base Camp. Home seemed very far away that night.

Morning brought two good things. One, the wind

and snow had ceased and the clouds gave evidence of parting. Two, Petzoldt's smiling, bearded face informed us that he was feeling fine—a trifle weak perhaps, but very hungry. Anxiously we plied him with oatmeal and Klim until he began to talk of carrying a double pack. Hastily vetoing this, we prevailed on him to rest while we carried one set of loads over to the trough. On our return we would break camp and leave forever this slough of despond.

Two hours saw us back, and we were not sorry to shoulder heavy loads and make a second relay. Soon we were laughing over the discouragements of the day before and hurrying up the channel toward a corner that hid from view the upper Savoia Glacier. When we rounded it, what cheer! There, rising ahead of us, we could see the white gleaming slopes that led from the glacier to the crest of Savoia Pass. They did not look too difficult and there were no cornices to threaten them from above. Even better, we had a good profile view of the northwest ridge. There was no denying it looked steep, but the upturned strata were very evident.

It was impossible not to be encouraged. I recall even feeling a little regretful that the reconnaissance was to be so short, for it seemed as though there would be no question of gaining the pass and making fast progress on the ridge itself. Only 6000 feet above the pass towered the rock-faced summit cone, deceptively close in the rarefied air. Stimulated by the sight, we made two fast relays from our cache in the trough, and by late afternoon had pitched our tents halfway up the glacier, only a day's march from the cirque at the end.

As the sun fell behind the sharp rim to the west, plunging the glacier into a rapidly deepening twilight, a great cold descended on us. By 6 o'clock, with the peak of The Angelus blazing in the last sunlight above, we were in the grip of the Arctic. The thermometer registered 15° above zero and was still dropping, but inside our little tents the primus stoves purred brightly and we talked cheerfully of what we might find on the pass. That night the maximum and minimum thermometer recorded +2° F.—the lowest temperature measured on the trip.

The morning dawned clear, but so bitterly cold that it was not until nearly 9 that we started out. With the great bulk of The Angelus ridge between us and the rising sun, we were in frigid shadow. Not far ahead, sunlight streamed through a jagged gap in the ridge to warm a pattern on the frozen snow. Long before we reached this oasis we had to take off frozen boots and try to thaw chilled feet. No sun-worshiper had more love and respect for his god than we when at last we left the shadows and stepped into the blazing light.

Mountains are characterized by extremes. Less than an hour afterward the once blessed sun had become so oppressive that we might for all the world have been in the Sahara. Not a breath of wind stirred the dead air or intercepted the blaze of heat reflected from the snow surface. As the morning advanced, the snow softened until we were sinking to our knees, and breaking trail became exhausting.

Our goal, a snow hump below the pass, seemed to grow no closer as we trudged hour after hour toward it. About us ice-and-snow-hung walls towered above both sides of the glacier. They sent thundering down avalanche after avalanche, shaking the snow beneath our feet but not coming near us. Safe on the middle of the glacier, we were even grateful for the cool wind thrown at us by the larger falls. Such forces of destruction can sometimes be a boon to man, but woe betide the mountaineer who treats them too lightly, for behind those cold winds are thousands of tons of falling ice and snow whose power dwarfs any that man has yet been able to harness.

Wet, tired and groggy, we at last collapsed on a little snow platform in the mouth of the cirque. Here, at 19,000 feet, Houston and I were to remain to attempt the pass the next day. Burdsall and Petzoldt, after leaving their loads, would return to the glacier camp and spend the next day climbing high on the slopes across from the west face of K2. From those points of vantage they could study both ridges and the face itself through binoculars and get a better idea of their character than was possible from the glacier.

It was all that Burdsall and I could do to set up the tent and crawl exhausted into its welcome shade, but Petzoldt and Houston indefatigably continued on to prospect farther for the morrow. When they returned an hour or so later, they reported that the upper part of the cirque did not look bad and that the line of attack plotted from lower down on the glacier seemed free from serious obstacles.

All too soon the departing pair had to leave, for they had a long way to go and the snow was soft. It was with good spirits that we said good-by, for it seemed almost certain that we could gain the pass next day. Perhaps from what we should see there we could send the welcome word down to Base Camp to start moving supplies preparatory to attacking the ridge. Although committed to a thorough reconnaissance, it was not impossible that we should find the northwest ridge so obvious a route that there would be no question of searching farther.

Long before dark we were in a twilight all our own. It was a strange contrast preparing camp in the steely chill of the approaching Himalayan night and at the same time looking down at the glacier below still flooded with light and warmth. Far in the distance we could see the two tiny figures of our friends, infinitesimal in a mountain universe.

My feelings that night were mixed. Over and above the optimism inspired by the appearance of the slopes leading to the pass was an indefinable dread of something. Perhaps it was the darkening cirque that rose behind our tent to the unknown above the pass. Perhaps it was that we were actually in the shadow of K2 for the first time—not where it could be viewed from a distance, from the strength-giving companionship of our party, but with a single companion, temporarily cut off from all support, dependent on ourselves and ourselves alone. We were no longer the proud American Karakoram Expedition, but two men slightly appalled at what they had challenged.

This was our first night as high as 19,000 feet. Houston was little affected, but I slept poorly, waking often to gaze drowsily at the pale moonlight seeping through the thin tent fabric.

Early next morning we started out, following the steps kicked in the now hard-frozen snow the day before. Above them we continued on a line of our own toward a narrow point in the *bergschrund* that separated the upper from the lower snow slopes. Before reaching this we had to cross several great cracks on flimsy snow bridges. These were negotiated carefully on all fours, for one glance into the delicately tinted blue depths made one look anxiously back at the second man to make sure he was belaying the rope well.

At last we reached the *bergschrund,* having stopped several hundred feet below it to don crampons. Above, the angle steepened to 55–60°, or somewhat more than

SAVOIA PASS WHERE THE EXPEDITION THREE TIMES TRIED TO REACH THE NORTHWEST RIDGE

BURDSALL

Petzoldt on the upper Godwin-Austen Glacier

that of the average house roof. In several places ice seemed to come close to the surface, but we were confident that we would find little trouble. The rock-studded pass 800 feet above us appeared to be a goal already won. Our hearts quickened as we realized that in perhaps a half hour we would be on the pass. The anticipation of what we might see from there was almost too great to bear.

With Houston securing my rope around his ice ax, I leaned across the *bergschrund* to carve out steps on the other side. The wide blade of my ax bounded back and I called down that there was ice a few inches beneath the snow. This was not too alarming, so I hewed out several good steps and a few minutes later stood on the upper edge. There was no mistaking here that the character of the surface had changed. Everywhere I could reach with my ax was tough green ice camouflaged by an inch or so of frozen snow.

We looked upward. The nearest rocks were less than 800 feet away, but it did not seem possible to cut steps for that distance in such steep ice. In the Alps it would not have been an insurmountable obstacle, but at 21,-000 feet it was more than we considered wise to attempt. Quite aside from the difficulty we ourselves would have was the more important consideration that as a route for porters it was out of the question. Possibly by spending the whole day we could have cut those steps and the next day climbed to the pass, but it

seemed obvious that such a slope could not be safe-
guarded for porters. We realized that another way
would have to be found if the northwest ridge was to
be considered a route at all.

As we stood at the bottom of that appalling slope,
the sun flooded it with light, revealing the same consistency right up to the pass. From the lower glacier
the day before we had not been able to distinguish
this, so completely was the ice masked by the innocent
looking layer of snow. Regretfully we started the descent, experiencing that devastating uncertainty that
all climbers must feel when they turn back without
achieving their object. How much due to the mountain; how much to the climber himself? *

The Duke's guides had reached the pass from a lower
camp than ours without great difficulty, so we could
only surmise that conditions must have been different 30 years ago and earlier in the season. Perhaps
there had been more snow on the ice then, requiring
little step-cutting. How we would have liked to talk
with those guides!

We reached our tent before noon and almost immediately Houston left for Base Camp to send a party
to the east side of the mountain. Far down below us we

* Later we had some doubts of our decision that the pass could not be
attained from the floor of the cirque. There was a possibility that incomplete
acclimatization as well as the fact that neither of us had stood on steep ice
for two years had influenced us unduly. These doubts, however, disappeared
later when, well acclimated and trained to heights, we revisited the cirque
and reached the same conclusion.

could see the figures of Burdsall and Petzoldt on the edge of the glacier still searching for a route on the upper part of the northwest ridge. How disappointed they would be when they learned what we had found.

After they had been told the sad news, Burdsall accompanied Houston to Base Camp, while Petzoldt came up to help me move down our high camp. He was still optimistic about the northwest ridge, although he agreed that we would have to find another way to it. He and Burdsall had seen several difficult-looking pinnacles which might cause trouble lower down, but he thought if the ridge could be reached it might be possible to gain the summit by it. An indefatigable route finder and our strongest rock-climber, he announced that he had spotted what might be an alternate way up a rocky spur just to the right of the pass. His confidence was like a good drink after the disappointment earlier, and I readily agreed to remain with him at our lower camp and essay it the next day.

Alas, the weather broke during the night and a heavy storm in the morning prevented any climbing. Leaving the camp intact, we started the descent to Base Camp, but had only gone a third of the way when through the blowing snow we saw three figures approaching. They were Burdsall with two Sherpas to help us down with our loads. He told us that he and Houston had found a very good route down the glacier, eliminating the crevassed section and making the journey much easier. We were cheered at this good news, but disturbed when he told us that Houston had twisted his ankle and would be laid up for several days.

The new route to Base Camp proved as easy as Burdsall had said and by noon we were home enjoying one of Ahdoo's excellent meals. We had found our culinary technique rather rusty after the luxuries of the trip in and were quite willing to have someone else do the cooking and dishwashing.

Refreshed by a good night's sleep and the comforts of Base Camp, Petzoldt and I returned the next day to the Savoia Glacier. It was still snowing, but with three Sherpas helping us we planned to carry up more food and move our lower glacier camp to the eastern corner of the cirque. From there, if the weather let us, we would try to reach the northwest ridge. That night we were well established at about 18,500 feet at the foot of the spur which Petzoldt had thought might yield a route. It started to snow again early in the evening and the wind quickly rose, battering the little tent and making sleep difficult. To make matters worse, Petzoldt had another attack of fever and chills. He was feeling much better in the morning, but the storm continued and already there was a foot of new snow around us. Avalanches were crashing down the great walls above with almost monotonous regularity.

Thinking it unwise to exhaust our strength and morale by being stormbound for several days, we returned once again to Base Camp. There we found Bates and Streatfeild, who had returned shortly after we had left the day before. They had descended the Godwin-Austen Glacier almost to Concordia and in brief spells of clear weather had gained good views of the whole south face. The face itself, they said, was out of the question, due to avalanche danger; nor had the Abruzzi ridge impressed them favorably, being continuously steep to a snow and ice plateau at 25,000 feet. After making valuable sketches from this point, they had advanced east up the Godwin-Austen Glacier and established a camp a little above the base of the Abruzzi ridge. Bad weather forced them to retreat without getting a complete view of the northeast ridge, the third main possibility.

Reunited for the first time in almost a week, the expedition held a long conference. The true character of the mountain was shaping up in our minds. Although we had not yet set foot on its rock, we had found its ice uncompromising. It was evident, now that we had begun to grasp the scale of things, that earlier ideas of what might be accomplished had been very optimistic. We had expected difficulties, but not the immediate and apparently complete setbacks of unnegotiable ice and continued stormy weather.

Since the east side of the mountain, with its two ridges as yet little known, now offered the most promise, we decided to concentrate on it. Later, if we were still blocked, we could complete the reconnaissance of the west side. Less confident by now in our own individual judgments, we decided that everyone except the Captain should go up the Godwin-Austen Glacier and together study the possibilities there. He would take Tse Tendrup, his Sherpa, for survey work farther south toward the Baltoro.

In the evening, as if to give us new hope, the weather cleared. The darkening peaks stood out sharply in the twilight, the sky cloudless save for little flurries of dry snow blown from their summits.

Chapter X

Up the Godwin-Austen Glacier

William P. House

Chapter X   Up the Godwin-Austen Glacier

O N the morning of June 21 the second stage of the reconnaissance was begun. Five sahibs and five Sherpas set out toward the camp established by Bates and Streatfeild several days earlier. For several miles the surface of the Godwin-Austen was smooth hard ice. Up this we walked unroped at a safe distance from the ice-encrusted south face of K2. On either side rose great walls of ice and rock culminating on our left in the summit cone peeping over a snow shoulder 10,000 feet above our heads. To the right rose the three summits of Broad Peak, the highest towering to 26,400 feet. The glacier formed a broad highway between the two mountains, its narrowness and the masses of ice poised thousands of feet above it making us apprehensive of avalanches which might sweep entirely across. There was no evidence, however, of any falls which reached across the glacier, so by staying far out from dangerous looking places we were reasonably safe.

All too soon the good walking came to an end in a maze of crevasses, some covered, others open chasms. It was a labyrinth of troughs and pinnacles through which we swarmed single file. Higher up we emerged from the chaos to find the surface broken by huge lateral cracks, some 30 feet wide and hundreds of yards long. Most of these were bridged over with masses of snow and it required careful work on the part of the lead man to avoid falling through into them. We took this opportunity to train our Sherpas in glacier travel, letting them lead the way, though a sahib was always next to stop them with the rope should they fall in. They enjoyed leading immensely and it soon became a matter of disgrace among them for the leader to go through the snow or arrive at an impasse.

Crevasses on a glacier are much like the cracks in a drying log or beam. Their ends never meet, but overlap, leaving ridges of solid ice between. The cracks constantly change, due to melting and movement of the ice, and the ridges tend to melt away, causing the crevasses to coalesce into longer ones. By zigzagging back and forth a way can generally be found via these ridges through the worst system of crevasses.

Early in the afternoon we reached the cache, where we found the pyramid tent completely snowed under, but everything in it intact. Our route had been well marked and all the bridges tested, so we had no anxiety in sending the Sherpas back unescorted. Under Pasang they were in good hands. With food for more than a week we were now in a good position to explore all possibilities on the south and east of the mountain. For the remainder of the afternoon we busied ourselves variously fixing camp, Petzoldt and Houston, as usual immune to the intense midday heat, climbing a short way up a rocky slope to look at the Abruzzi ridge. When they returned with a more favorable opinion we were all encouraged, for the long horizontal knife edge of the northeast ridge had almost decided us against it as a possibility.

Supper was a hilarious affair that night. A brief battle raged over the commissaries' alleged stinginess with the pemmican. This was settled amicably by Petzoldt and me eating an extra half pound, partly to disprove the contention that a pound of this substance was *more* than enough for six strong men. Later Bates regaled us with some stirring Alaskan ballads and I read aloud from "Pickwick Papers." Mr. Pickwick's breach of promise suit made all our difficulties pale into insignificance and we retired to our sleeping bags in remarkably high spirits.

The next morning we split into two parties in order to cover the vantage points more thoroughly. Burdsall, Bates and Houston walked over the now almost level glacier toward a snow-crested spur which dropped from the northeast ridge. They climbed up the lower part of this until the snow gave way to ice. Here they could have gone higher, but more was to be gained by penetrating a little valley on the other side of the ridge. The appearance of the ice towers on the crest indicated that perhaps there was an extensive ice or snow field on the other side just beneath them. If this were so the ridge might still be climbed, though a traverse of the ice pinnacles for such a long distance was out of the question.

The north side of the ridge, however, proved as uncompromising as the south, consisting as it did of long steep ice slopes exposed to avalanches from above. There appeared to be no campsites high up on either side. Continuing on to the foot of Skyang Kangri—a 24,750-foot peak 6 miles northeast of K2—they studied the upper part of the ridge. Here they reached the conclusion that a great mass of hanging ice just beneath the summit would render unsafe the juncture of the

BURDSALL

BURDSALL

BRIDE PEAK (25,110 FEET)
THE LONG KNIFE-EDGE OF THE NORTHEAST RIDGE OF K2

K2 FROM THE EAST

ridge with the summit cone.

Petzoldt and I had an easy day compared with theirs, trudging as they did for eight hours in the merciless glare of the hot sun. We climbed up a rocky spur across the glacier from the Abruzzi ridge and attempted to get an idea of the climbing difficulties above the first few thousand feet. The Abruzzi ridge is really more of a shoulder than a true ridge, being composed of a number of small rock ribs interspersed with ice *couloirs* converging on a snow and ice plateau at 25,-000 feet. From the upper edge of this rises the summit cone—a pyramid of rock 2200 feet high. Halfway up this cone is a great hanging glacier which sweeps the upper part of the northeast ridge as well as one corner of the Abruzzi ridge. Care would be needed in crossing the plateau from this last ridge, but it looked as though it could be done safely. From our vantage point 1000 feet above the glacier the ridge looked difficult, particularly just below the plateau. Of the summit cone we could tell little because it was in clouds most of the day.

Another serious conference was held that night. The outcome was that two men were to climb up the lower part of the Abruzzi ridge next day to get a firsthand idea of climbing conditions. The others would journey again to Savoia Pass to complete that study. It was hardly a decision at all, but we agreed that if the climbing on the Abruzzi ridge was not too difficult we would attack it and call in the Savoia Pass party.

Petzoldt and Houston originally planned to investigate the Abruzzi ridge together, but that night brought
another attack of fever to the former. In the morning
he had not recovered as usual, but thought he could
make Base Camp all right. Houston and I formed the
team to investigate the ridge. The others, taking on
part of our loads, started toward Base Camp. Seeking
a short cut, they followed a trough between the ridge
and the glacier, hoping to find a better route through
the maze of crevasses lower down.

An hour's steady climbing brought Houston and
me to the top of a scree slope from which smooth polished cliffs rose as far as we could see. Parting company
in order to cover the ground more thoroughly, we followed different gullies around this obstacle until we
met on a little col about 1000 feet above the glacier.
Except for the rocky slope below, this was the only
place we had seen where tents could have been erected.
Nowhere else on the ridge did there seem to be anything better.

It was here that Houston discovered a few small
sticks of wood—evidently from one of the Duke of the
Abruzzi's boxes. These identified the col as the highest
point where supplies had been carried in 1909. From
this point his guides had climbed for 500 feet up a
couloir before coming to the conclusion that farther
progress was unjustifiable. It was thrilling to find these

traces of the earlier expedition, even if we knew that on the basis of what they found here they had turned back.

After a rest we roped up to ascend the snow *couloir* attempted by the Duke's guides. Higher up it looked as though there might be some ledges which did not slope too steeply for tents. The higher we climbed the more disillusioned we became. What looked from below like good honest ledges turned out to slope so steeply that they held only the rock frozen into them. The remarkably clear air and brilliant lighting must have some effect on the climber's estimation of angles. Or perhaps it is an effect of the altitude on the mind of the climber, making his judgment less dependable. We were fooled again and again until, the slabs on each side of the *couloir* becoming steeper, we left it 500 feet above the col.

This maneuver was a hair-raising one, Houston leading over treacherous snow-covered ice to the west crest. I did not realize what he had done until, trying to hurry—for it was getting late—I slipped off and found that, even with pulls from him, it was no easy matter to reach the crest. Once there we crawled along a narrow ledge to the head of another gully. The rocks here were well broken and although steep and uneven might have yielded a campsite. It would require much work in building up tent platforms and would be used only as a last resort.

This last impression was strengthened when we came to descend into the bed of the gully. On several overhanging stretches we had to slide on our rope. From there we had to pick our way cautiously down one at a time, racing the shadows which were fast lengthening. A slip on the part of either would have been serious, for neither of us had much purchase on the ice, and we were glad when we reached solid snow where we could travel more securely.

Returning to the base of the ridge we were surprised to find deposited there beside our light packs the loads of which we had been lightened that morning by the party returning to Base Camp. With them was an apologetic note from Bates saying that they had run into terrific difficulties trying to get through the icefall and had had to retrace their steps after several hours' futile search. Worse still, Petzoldt had very nearly collapsed and, as they were already carrying his load, they did not dare add more, since they might have to help him into camp.

Thoroughly discouraged and deadly tired, we shouldered our full loads and started the long trip down to Base Camp. The only bright spot in that trip was meeting our gallant Sherpas. Hearing Bates' story they had immediately volunteered to go up and carry in our loads for us. Such thoughtfulness endeared our helpers to us many times.

Supper that night was a gloomy affair. Rarely even

on high mountains is there such a dearth of campsites as we had found that day. The continued steepness of the slabs gave us little hope that anything better would be found higher. It is absolutely necessary in Himalayan climbing to have camps between which a round trip can be made easily in a day. If they are too far apart the strain of carrying loads may be too great, and, more serious, the margin of safety in case of a storm en route is greatly diminished. If too close, much time is lost establishing camps. To have found such a long stretch on the ridge devoid of any places where tent platforms could be built and reached by loaded men was serious. It seemed to close up the last avenue of hope we had had for finding a route on K2. On top of this setback, one of our strongest climbers was ill. Without him our strength was greatly reduced. Although able to reach camp without help, Petzoldt was very weak and it looked as though his recurring illnesses would make it impossible for him to continue.

Little by little the story of the descent of the larger party came out. It was a nightmare whose description could be fully appreciated only by those who have been frustrated for hours in a bad icefall. At one point they had had to rope down 40 feet of sheer ice. A little farther they came to an impasse and had to climb back up the rope hand over hand. It was here that Petzoldt collapsed. Had he not after a long rest regained some of his strength, they might have been in serious trouble.

Only part of the bottle of excellent Demerara rum donated by Houston's father gave some measure of cheer that evening. It seemed hopeless to lay new plans after having found such apparently insurmountable obstacles on all three of the proposed routes.

However, as a last resort, we decided to look at the Savoia Pass and northeast ridges again. Houston, Streatfeild and Burdsall would retrace their steps up the Godwin-Austen, search farther on the Abruzzi ridge and then see if the lower part of the northeast ridge could be climbed. Bates and I would return to the Savoia Glacier to try to force a route up the east side of the cirque. Petzoldt would remain in camp resting and trying to regain his strength. Even the Sherpas were gloomy that night—a rare mood for them. It was hard for them to see their sahibs apparently beaten.

Chapter XI
The Abruzzi Ridge
William P. House

Chapter XI   The Abruzzi Ridge

WE parted company on the morning of June 24 with the unspoken thought that if we had not found a route when we next met, we would probably spend the rest of our time without getting higher than we had already been.

By the middle of that afternoon Bates and I, with three Sherpas, had moved a camp again to the head of the Savoia Glacier. We spent the rest of the day studying the east side of the cirque, trying to get some encouragement for our attempt on the morrow. The rocks looked steep and fairly smooth, but there were breaks and it seemed as though we might be able to get around the steepest sections by skirting the ice high up. A discussion developed at one point as to the safest and most feasible way of getting onto the lower part of the rocky rib. I was in favor of a little chute of ice and snow which led to a good ledge 400 feet above camp. It was partially overhung by masses of ice, but it looked to me as though these would fall farther off to the side. Bates favored a harder and longer route far to the left. He did not, he said, like the looks of that hanging ice. And with good reason, for a few minutes later several large chunks came tumbling down with (to him) a very satisfying clatter.

We always carried along a small folding chessboard and that night continued a series of games which had begun in Srinagar and had involved most of us in close intra-party competition ever since. Aside from this, cooking supper as usual was in itself an interesting game.

First a large pile of snow is scraped together outside one end of the tent. From this an aluminum pot is filled. After guy ropes have been tested and everything outside made shipshape, the two men climb inside, carefully knocking all snow off their boots. With the tent door partially closed, a small piece of meta—solidified alcohol—is placed beneath the burner of the primus stove and lighted. After a few minutes it is hot enough to vaporize the liquid fuel, and some of this is pumped up by a pump built into the stove itself. The flame sputters for a few minutes, but after that generally settles down to an even purr—a sound even more suggestive of content in a primus stove than in a cat.

While the meta has been burning, the pot with the snow has been placed over the burner and as the heat increases the chunks of snow slowly melt, sometimes not disappearing until the water is quite hot. As the water approaches the boiling point, enough is drawn off to make tea. Into the remainder, part of a can of pemmican is scraped. Five or ten minutes of boiling, depending on the altitude, plus the addition of some dried vegetables, makes a thick stew, which is eaten as soon as the mugs are emptied of their tea. With the addition of crackers, butter, jam and chocolate, quite a satisfying meal results.

Pemmican, though very high in nutritive value, is naturally low on bulk. Therefore the addition of bulk foods like crackers, vegetables and fruit is necessary, not only to give feeling of fullness, but to enable the stomach and bowels to function properly. To this fact were due many of the complaints which our commissary, Bates, accepted so patiently, for the calory content of most of our meals was very high.

While this dish is being consumed, the remaining heat in the pot and stove is used to melt more snow—either for the pretense that goes for dishwashing or for oatmeal. In the latter case the oatmeal is cooked up—usually in water not previously used for dishwashing—and poured into a thermos. Carefully wrapped in extra clothing, it is saved for the morning. No desert traveler ever hoards his store of water more carefully for, except when the sun is hot, all moisture is tightly locked up and can be released only by burning precious fuel.

After supper the stove is placed at the foot of the tent where it will not be knocked over, and the two occupants, if they have not already done so, retire to their sleeping bags. There they may play chess, read, or write in their diaries until about 8 o'clock when it is too dark to see. Then the tent doors are tightly tied, the small ventilators above them propped open and the soft air mattresses generally bring sleep quickly.

At 8 o'clock on the morning of the 25th we were stamping the spikes of our crampons into the hard snow slopes behind camp. The frozen surface was ideal for walking and we mounted rapidly toward a notch behind one of the ribs. We thought if we could reach this we could cross behind it and stay on rock the rest of the way to the pass. Equipped as we were with pitons and extra rope, and well acclimatized by now, we were determined to push on just as hard as was justifiable. After having climbed 500 feet or so we advanced directly toward the rocks, encountering steepening slopes with the ice underneath close to the surface. It was very delicate work, but the rocks were only 100 feet higher and we could afford to take time to reach them. We needed more than time, however. As we came close to the rocks we found the ice only a few inches thick, adhering to smooth rock and covered in places by fluffy masses of snow.

The rope was little protection here, but Bates made what use he could of his ice ax jammed into a shallow crack, looping the rope around its head. About 20 feet below the notch I encountered the hardest problem. The ice had given way to rock slabs lying at between 65° and 70° and with only tiny irregularities for holds. There was no opportunity to take off my crampons, so I had to continue on, the two-inch spikes grating and slipping on the sloping surface. At last, only a few feet below a good ledge, I realized that I was at a point where farther progress would be unjustifiable in view of the precarious position of Bates, who could not have stopped me had I slipped. After some intricate acrobatics I managed to drive a long ice piton into an ice-filled crack a little above me. With the rope passed through this I felt more confident and with a little moral support from Bates climbed up onto the ledge. It was happily placed, for I was at the end of the 100-foot rope and he had already moved up as far as he could and still give me any protection. The entire pitch of 150 feet had taken two hours.

Once on the crest of the rib our hopes were dashed. We could not follow it, for the rock was too smooth and on the other side was the same kind of ice. A route for porters might have been made the way we came by stringing lots of rope along it, but beyond it seemed impossible even for us, unloaded as we were. We found some compensation for our hard climb by sitting in the warm sun and eating our lunch of crackers, cheese, chocolate and dates. We were now close to 20,500 feet, but still 1300 feet from the top of the pass. All too soon we had to return, for we knew the hot midday sun would soften the snow slopes and perhaps make them liable to avalanche.

The descent over the ice-coated slabs proved more difficult than we expected, for, as the only route was a diagonal one, we could not slide down a fixed rope. It was 400 feet straight down to the nearest resting place and, since we did not have enough rope for that, we had to inch our way cautiously back the way we had come.

A few hundred feet above camp with all clear below, Bates' crampons became balled up with snow. He lost his footing and shot down the 40° slope. I was caught off guard, and before I could jam my ax in was whisked off my feet to follow him. Once he managed to brake himself with the shaft of his ax, but before he could make himself firm I had catapulted past and jerked *him* off his feet. We both stopped on easier slopes below, laughing, our clothes filled with snow. No harm was done, but it was a timely reminder that at these altitudes the climber must consciously combat the tendency to carelessness.

A little before dusk light clouds blew in over the pass and soon the entire west face was streaked with them. Snowflakes were falling gently, and by the time we were ready for bed a full-fledged storm had developed. Again the wind battered at the tent, but the pegs were well frozen into the snow and we were safe.

Plans had to be changed in the morning, for the storm had continued all night. About 10 inches of snow had fallen and the great cirque invisible above us resounded with the thunder of avalanches. Clearly it was no place to be on that day, so we gave up the plan of penetrating it and attempting a slope at its far end that did not look as icy as the rest. Instead we tied the tent flaps securely and started out toward where a minor glacier tumbled into the main one underneath the west face of the mountain. From a dome part way up this we hoped to be able to look at the south side of the northwest ridge, in the hope that it might yield a route.

Bates' keen glacier sense led us unerringly through a maze of giant crevasses right up the side of the hump. The crevasses were the largest we had yet seen; some of them were 50 feet wide and hundreds of yards long. In the obscurity caused by the falling snow their ordinarily dark depths were almost indistinguishable from the slopes that rose above them. Our way led through these on hair-raising, tilted snow bridges over which we crept on hands and knees one at a time. In this sort of going a single rope would be little use if one man fell, for he would fall far, and, with the rope cutting into the edge, the second man would probably be unable to pull him out unaided. A doubled rope is much safer, for with it the man in the crevasse can help pull himself out while the other man merely takes in the slack and holds him while he reaches for a new grip on his rope.

The doubled rope never came into play, however, and after several hours' work we reached what would have been a vantage point had it not been in the clouds. We dared go no closer to the wall, for we could hear small avalanches ahead and knew that to advance much farther would expose us to them. There was some hope that the clouds might break, so we coiled the rope on the snow and sat down on it to wait.

It was a long vigil, but at last the driven clouds thinned momentarily and we could get fragmentary glimpses of the south side of the ridge. Each succeeding glimpse showed what we had feared. The rocks there were glazed with ice and were of the same general character as those we had climbed the day before. It was a wild sight; the icy precipice rose 3000 feet, framed in a jagged hole in the clouds. Puffs of light snow cascading down were evidence that avalanches were at work here as well as on both sides.

We were forced at last to the conclusion that no route existed to the east of the rib we had attempted the day before. This left only the chance that the far corner of the cirque would prove to be snow rather than ice. Perhaps the storm would abate enough to enable the cirque to shed its excess snow so we could venture in the next day. As if to blast even this faint hope the wind increased in fury, blowing the rope stretched between us into a great arc to the leeward. Fine snow particles beat into our faces and completely obliterated the footsteps we had made coming up. Bates' skill was equal to the task, however, and he found our previous route down through the crevasses without misstep.

Back at our snug camp we spent the afternoon writing letters on pages torn from diaries. We did not know when they would be mailed, if ever, but somehow in that lonely spot, with failures behind us and perhaps others to come, it was comforting to be in some sort of touch with family and friends back home. The next morning the storm still raged. There were 18 inches of new snow and it was obvious that entry into the cirque would not be possible for several days. It had been a slim chance anyway and we felt we were not abandoning much when we agreed that this year no safe route existed to the northwest ridge—a discouragingly negative finding. Perhaps when we reached Base Camp the others would have better news.

Carrying all we could from the dismantled camp, we pushed down through the storm, arriving in camp to find Streatfeild and Houston just returned from the upper Godwin-Austen. They had carried out fully as important a reconnaissance as ours, but had had a much rougher time of it.

On June 24 they had left camp intending to search farther on the Abruzzi ridge, but believing the several days of fine weather had made snow conditions good, they continued on to make use of these on the northeast ridge. With three Sherpas they moved most of the glacier camp up to the base of it and on the 25th had climbed up the first 800 feet. This required much step-cutting and they realized after several hours of hard work that the crest could not be gained without the expenditure of much labor. Their decision to return was a timely one for, as if to punish them for neglecting the Abruzzi ridge, the weather broke swiftly, driving them to the tents. That night they had to build a wall of snow blocks around their tent, so fierce were the gusts.

As on the Savoia, the weather was bad the next morning, but in spite of this Houston took two of the Sherpas down to the lower cache to bring up more supplies. It was a nerve-racking trip for both. Broad Peak to the south of the glacier and K2 to the north were sending down huge avalanches, some of which might have swept across the width of the glacier. It was on this trip that the Sherpas said they heard voices high up on K2. They were vastly pleased when, passing the same spot on a new route chosen by Houston, an avalanche fell partially covering their former tracks. This was conclusive proof to them that their gods were watching out for them, and it strengthened their morale considerably.

The existence of these spirits in the Himalaya has been a matter of considerable interest to explorers. To the Sherpas, with their Bhuddist superstition, they are genuine and undoubtedly play a very real part in their lives, particularly when they are in high mountains with foreign expeditions. It is not surprising that these people should connect unusual noises or even suggestive imaginings with the spirit-filled world in which they live. There have been many instances of this on the Everest expeditions as well as on others.

It is somewhat more surprising, but understandable, that these same noises should be noticed by white men and in some cases ascribed to the forces that dominate the religion of these superstitious people. This has stimulated talk of the "snow men" which have come to figure prominently in British Himalayan expeditions.

That there should be controversy among white men as to whether these spirits exist or not is surprising. Illusions and fantasies are common enough in the altitudes of the Alps. It is not unreasonable to assume that susceptibility to them should be increased at higher altitudes when the workings of the mind follow less easily the grooves channeled by centuries of conventionalized western thought. Perhaps with the mind freed somewhat from restraints it reverts naturally though superficially to the strength-giving superstition of primitive religions. In the midst of natural forces which emphasize man's insignificance it is not unnatural that he should unconsciously accept part of a faith better adapted to maintaining his mental equilibrium than are his intellectualized western beliefs. This is only one explanation; no better method of stirring up an argument among climbers exists than to support firmly or to deny the existence of these spirits.

It goes without saying that these rationalizations are not formed while dodging avalanches, nor is much thought provoked at the time as to whether they are started or merely anticipated by the mountain spirits.

By the 27th it was as obvious to the northeast party as it had been to Bates and myself on the Savoia that no more climbing could be done for several days. Moreover, what they had seen two days before had nearly convinced them of the unfeasibility of the northeast ridge.

Although it was still storming very hard, they started out with the Sherpas for Base Camp. There was much new snow on the glacier and the blowing particles made the journey through the crevasses hazardous. Weak spots in the crust were covered over and, in spite of the willow wands, which had been left to mark the trail for just such an emergency, they had a hard time following it. At one point it looked to them as though they would have to bivouac in a crevasse, so violent had become the storm. Fortunately before they had to resort to this a lull came and they were able to reach the smooth going below the bad icefall. Once here they were able to fight their way back, arriving in Base Camp exhausted, but with no frostbite.

The expedition spirits were now at very low ebb. From one side of the mountain to the other we had been unable to find a route. Two weeks had been spent apparently to no other purpose than to convince us that no way we had seen was possible. We remembered rash statements we had made back in the United States to the effect that we were prepared to spend the whole summer reconnoitering and would do so until we found a way up the mountain. Two weeks of continual discouragement made the prospect of a whole summer of the same depressing to say the least. Every one of us would have liked to be clear of the whole business right then.

Had we been able to spend an afternoon relaxing at the seashore or getting very drunk, we might have realized that two weeks of reconnaissance on a mountain as big as K2 could not possibly be conclusive. By gaining a little perspective we would have realized that perhaps some of our earlier judgments might have been incorrect—or at least would stand checking. As nearly all the reconnaissance had been done in bad weather, we might have overlooked something. At that time, however, it seemed as though each succeeding judgment had been upheld by later checking and that there was no hope at all. Unfortunately the seashore was a thousand miles away and our supply of rum far too slender to indulge in as an escape.

A conference on the evening of the 28 found a division of opinion. Houston and Burdsall still favored the northeast route and thought we should concentrate on it. Familiar with it as they were, they thought that eventually some sort of a route could be made up to the mile-long knife arête.

Petzoldt and I thought that the Abruzzi ridge was the only remaining chance. Although previous search had failed to yield campsites, this route looked safer than the northeast ridge and we knew climbing on it was possible for some distance. We still had over a month's food supply, were strong and fit, and should be able to find some foothold on the ridge. With so much time on our hands we would be justified in spending a day or more constructing tent platforms on sloping ledges. There the Sherpas' skill in building with rock would be a great asset and somehow we ought to be able to make tents stay, even if we had to anchor them with ropes and pitons. Bates and Streatfeild held less positive views, with the result that after several hours' discussion we arrived at a plan which was acceptable to all.

We would move all supplies up the Godwin-Austen Glacier and establish a well-stocked camp near the foot of the Abruzzi ridge. From that we would first make a thorough investigation of the ridge and then, if it still proved hopeless, concentrate on the northeast. If no route was found on either, we would devote the remainder of the time to further reconnaissance and give up all idea of trying to climb the mountain this year.

As before, when we had been driven to Base Camp by continued stormy weather, the next day dawned clear and we were treated to several days of incomparably clear skies. Relaying loads up the glacier to a cache near the Abruzzi ridge became a chore, indeed, for the heat of the sun in the middle of the day was almost unbearable. However, we could always count on a cool wind blowing down the glacier around 2 o'clock. One day it became more than cool and we had to leave our loads and race to Base Camp before what looked like another bad storm. Fortunately it lasted only a few hours.

In the warm clear weather the mountains on both sides of the glacier shed much of their snow—exposing rock faces uncompromisingly smooth and steep. The great hanging glaciers on Broad Peak, K2, Skyang

Kangri and other giants continued to send down masses of ice and snow. Some of the avalanches were small, plummeting in cascades of fine snow for thousands of feet, apparently dissolving before they hit the glacier. Others were much larger, thundering down from 25,-000 feet with the roar of a thousand fast freight trains, billowing up in great clouds of snow as they struck the level glacier.

On July 1 Petzoldt and I were left in a camp right at the foot of Abruzzi ridge. On this day we had the first serious mishap to our equipment. A four-gallon container of benzine had been left under an overhanging rock on the glacier to protect it from the rays of the sun. But the sun had had another effect. Melting the ice on which the rock was resting, it caused the huge slab to fall over, wrecking the heavy can and losing us almost four gallons of precious fuel. It was a serious blow, for we were light on fuel and could ill afford such a loss. We knew we could get along on what was left by being very economical, but, with no reserve, another accident might necessitate a return before we had finished our work. Moreover we had not yet started any difficult climbing, and the chances of losing a load or damaging it would be much greater higher up.

Captain Streatfeild, who had been with the French Expedition to Gasherbrum I in 1936, said there was a chance that some of the gasoline left by that party might still be at the site of their base camp on the upper Baltoro Glacier. It was only a faint hope, for following their return to Askole most of the coolies had gone back to loot what had been left behind. He was willing to make a try, however, and the next day, taking Ahdoo and two Sherpas, he went down to the Baltoro. If he could not find any gas he planned to send Ahdoo and one of the Sherpas to Askole, seven days' march, to bring up coolies loaded with wood. This could be used at our Base Camp and possibly higher, instead of the now precious liquid fuel. The accident did have some compensation, for we were able to send out mail to our homes and would perhaps receive mail when the wood coolies arrived.

Unlike Base Camp, which was located in a hollow, Camp I, where Petzoldt and I were left, stood in the open beside a jagged cliff of broken ice. From it we could look down over the glacier for many miles. Above, towering only a few miles away, we could see the great shaft of Skyang Kangri with its perpetual snow plume flying from its summit. Across the glacier, but hidden from us by the ice cliff, were the white-specked walls of Broad Peak rising almost 10,000 feet and looking steeper and less accessible even than those of K2 immediately above us.

After the rest of the party had left we climbed to the top of one of the ice towers and watched them threading their way through the maze of crevasses below. It was good to know that they would be back the next day to add their strength to ours. Personally, I felt there was little chance of finding campsites and that all we could accomplish would be to confirm this. Neither of us voiced such thoughts, however, and when we went to bed that night it was with cheerful assurances that luck must surely smile on us now.

We rose late the next morning, for the tent, hidden from the rising sun by the cliff above, was like an icebox. It was a relief to scramble a few feet up the rocky slopes where we could warm our hands and feet. Following the route chosen by Houston and myself a week before, we climbed diagonally up the Abruzzi ridge, planning to cross to its westernmost edge where it appeared more broken. An hour more and we were gingerly crossing the smooth waterworn bed of a minor gully. Below, it shelved out of sight in polished slabs which became a racecourse for the rocks we dislodged. We could hear these long after they went out of sight, the narrow walls of the gully noisily re-echoing the clatter. Our nails gritted and scraped on the smooth rock; above we could see hundreds of boulders so precariously balanced that they looked as though they might come down on us at any moment.

Beyond, we came to a steep snow field which marked the western edge of the ridge. Still we found no place for tents. We sat down to eat lunch, gloomily wondering how long it would take to build tent platforms on the 30° slope where we were. The usual tasty lunch of dried fruits, crackers, cheese and chocolate revived our spirits and soon we were climbing up the lower part of the snow. At its top there might be a level spot before the slope dropped off sheer to the south face. Along its western edge, too, there were many pinnacles, and perhaps we could find lodgment for our tents behind some of these.

We had learned by now to distrust our eyes when they registered angles, so we were not surprised to find the slope grow rapidly steeper. Soon we had to punch handholds as well as footholds in the crusty snow. With memories of the ice slope beneath Savoia Pass fresh in our minds, we feared that higher the snow would turn to ice. It did, but by that time we were so close to the top it did not matter. Cursing, we chopped steps, changing the lead every 50 feet, for the work was exhausting. The rocks on either side had grown less friendly and there seemed even less chance now of finding a place for the tents.

At last, with hearts racing like steam engines, we threw ourselves down on a tiny snow shelf at the top of the slope. A few feet beyond, separated from us by a thin crest of rock, a precipice dropped to the glacier. We could go no farther in that direction. For a few minutes we merely rested and looked around. Nothing we could see or had seen while climbing up the slope gave any hope of a campsite. Above, the rocks rose steep and unbroken, little patches of snow and ice clinging to the apparently vertical faces.

While I was indulging in these dismal observations, Petzoldt crawled around the corner of the crest. He had almost gone the full length of the rope when he gave a shout. There was no mistaking what it meant. There, 30 feet below him, hidden from us before by a corner on the ridge, was a splendid campsite. A pocket in the snow, perhaps 20 feet across, nestled almost level against the rock ridge. It would hold all our tents and would be protected from south and west winds by the wall behind it. We could have hoped for nothing better.

Instantly our attitude toward the mountain changed. With one campsite found we could find others. Above, the climbing looked much more difficult, but we felt somehow we could find a route over it. All the discouragements of those first two weeks suddenly became things of the past.

Not content with handing us one favor, the mountain proceeded to give another in the form of an easier route down. I, cautious and overwhelmed by our good fortune, was willing to go back by our old route, but Petzoldt was not to be stopped. He led me down the crest until, after 200 feet, we stood on broken scree slopes over which load-carrying would be quite simple. Down, down, we dropped, until we had reached the level of the bottom of the snow slope. The route was a good one. Barring a few short stretches which could be made safe by fixed ropes, the whole route could be done by loaded men without even roping together.

Hurrying across the last rocky slopes, we shouted the good news to the others, busy setting up camp. They had moved nearly all the loads to the base of the ridge that day and were prepared to stay there. They were overjoyed and soon we were discussing plans for pushing the attack higher. It was the first time we had felt really encouraged since the icy summit of the mountain shone through the mists almost three weeks before.

Now that we had at least a foothold on the Abruzzi ridge there was no doubt that it should be our choice. Above the site of Camp II the going looked bad. Steeply sloping faces and ridges, filled in between with ice, continued above the easy broken rock to a great tilted snow plateau at 25,000 feet.* This terminated the ridge. Two thousand feet above its upper edge rose the summit. We did not dare think too much about it at the time. To gain this snow plateau was now our goal, for if the 7000 feet of the Abruzzi ridge could be conquered, one of the greatest problems of the mountain would be solved. Even if we got no farther than that, it would be an achievement.

* The sky-line profile of the Abruzzi ridge was measured by hypsometer to be approximately 45°. This was maintained from the glacier (17,700 feet) 7000 feet vertically to the edge of the snow plateau, 3000 feet below the summit. At no point, except close to the glacier, was the angle much lower, and in some places it was considerably steeper, although the general profile did not indicate this. We were unable to make an accurate measurement of the ridge of the summit cone above the snow plateau. It looked a little steeper than the Abruzzi ridge proper.

Chapter XII

The Attack

William P. House

Chapter XII   The Attack

ON the morning of July 3 we set out to establish
our first camp on the mountain. Carrying light
loads, the five sahibs and four remaining Sherpas
mounted the rocky slopes toward the snow pocket found
the day before. About 500 feet above the glacier we
noticed some unusual looking piles of rock. Closer examination proved them to be the remains of the tent

platforms built by the Duke of the Abruzzi when he made his attempt on the ridge in early June, 1909. In spite of almost 30 years' action of frost and avalanches they were in surprisingly good condition. From this camp his guides had climbed up to the col where Houston and I had found parts of his boxes. Above, they had found such difficult going that on the basis of their report the Duke abandoned his efforts on this side of the mountain.

It is interesting to note that we had followed an entirely different route in reaching the site of the Duke's only camp on the ridge. From de Filippi's account he had been able to come directly from his base camp, underneath the south face, and across the lower slopes of the ridge itself. We, on the other hand, had to stay in the middle of the glacier until we were above the base of the ridge, then cut back toward it—a devious route which some of our party had tried to shorten with such unhappy results on the 23rd. The condition of the glacier in 1938 was such that travel was absolutely impossible along the route taken by the Duke. It also looked as though the rock slopes which he had climbed above the glacier would present serious difficulties now.

This suggests that conditions must have been very different in 1909, a fact not surprising if one considers the forces always at work in the mountains. Not only must the glacier have been smoother, and therefore more easily traveled, close to the ridge, but more snow must have lain in the lower gullies to enable his party to climb them so easily. His attack had been made in early June, however, whereas we were a month later, and much snow could have melted in that time.

This coincides with conditions we found on Savoia Pass, where the Duke's party had reached the top with little difficulty—presumably on snow—and we had found steep ice. Furthermore, across the Godwin-Austen Glacier east of Broad Peak lay a great cirque with a notch in it called Sella Pass. This had been reached in 1909, but in 1938 it did not look to us as though any safe route lay over the 2000-foot snow slopes leading to it. Whether these apparent changes were due to the lateness of the year when we visited the region or whether snow conditions have actually changed so markedly in the course of 30 years cannot be definitely decided. Probably both explanations are valid.

We reached the airy perch chosen for Camp II early in the afternoon after a climb of about four hours. We were then at about 19,300 feet, 1600 feet above the glacier.* Later, when the porters had become accus-

* The elevations of camps were determined from corrected barometric readings made by Burdsall and by clinometer readings of surrounding summits of known elevation made by House. These were later computed by Burdsall on the basis of distances on the Survey of India map sheet #52 A. Where there were great discrepancies recourse was had to individual judgments of the distance between camps. Two points of known elevation on the ridge served as bases from which the final elevations of the seven camps were computed. One was a prominent rock wall above Camp IV, triangulated by Streatfeild and Burdsall from the lower Godwin-Austen Glacier as 21,500 feet; the other a 25,234-foot shoulder reached by Petzoldt and Houston on the snow plateau beneath the summit cone. Although the distances between

tomed to the way and we had strung more rope on it, the climb was made more quickly.

Once there, a level place was stamped out in the snow and the Meade tent set up by the industrious Sherpas. Petzoldt and I, on the theory that we were in favor with the mountain sprites, were left, with the customary 10 days' supply of food and fuel, to reconnoiter the next camp. The others returned to the glacier to complete stocking that camp as well as Camp II itself.

The mountain gods now smiled indeed. July 4 dawned an incomparable day. About us rose rank on rank of ice-covered mountain ramparts, yet our eyes could follow only the valleys, for we were still far below most of the ridges that cut us off from the outside world. In the crystal clear atmosphere every detail in those white-streaked walls stood out. The formidable black summit of Teram Kangri, now just peeping over the crest of Windy Gap, looked only a few miles away, yet we knew it was at least fifteen. Above us, as far as we could see, the upper slopes of K2 were free of clouds. It would take real obstacles, we thought, to stop us on this day.

Kicking steps in the softening snow, we skirted the crest of the arête, pausing to look down over the other side to the south face now dark in gloomy shadow. Where the crest ended in almost vertical walls we en-

camps may be somewhat inaccurate, these two checks make the errors small and not cumulative.

CAMP II—MOST SPACIOUS SITE ON ABRUZZI RIDGE

CAMP II FROM ABOVE

BURDSALL

tered a steep, narrow gully up which extended a ribbon of ice. Two hundred feet higher it narrowed to an alley eight feet wide, bounded by vertical rock. Up into its dark maw we climbed, placing our feet and hands gently, for the bed was of loose stones. High up, as through a gunsight, we could see the bright sunshine gleaming on inhospitable slabs of grayish rock.

When we emerged at last into the sun we were cheered, for we saw that by crossing another gully we could reach the easternmost edge of the Abruzzi ridge. We already realized that the precipices on the west side of the ridge were unclimbable and that to make any progress we should need to find easier going near the ice slope on the east side. In half an hour we were on a small col at the edge of the ice slope. Below, we could look directly down on Camp I, 2000 feet lower. We had now crossed the breadth of the ridge a second time and were about 500 feet above the highest point reached by the Duke's guides. We could see why neither they nor Houston and I had been able to go higher there, for the rocks were steeply inclined and very smooth.

Above, the going did not look too difficult. The snow-covered ice was broken by numerous slabs and buttresses of rock and we thought a way could be found on these. A late breakfast was in order, so we stretched out on the warm rock, nibbling chocolate and enjoying the glittering summits all around us. All too soon we had to start up again. By following an erratic arrangement of slabs and soft snow we were able to make fairly good progress for a while. Then we found ourselves forced farther and farther out on the ice slope, away from the main ridge where we had hoped to find space for tents. The down tilted character of the slabs became more evident and we longed for the moral support of some good solid ledges. Toward noon the going became worse as we struck pure ice. From atop the sharp crest of a rocky fang, however, we could see two buttresses a few hundred feet higher whose tops might yield a campsite.

Anxious to reach them without delay, I started to cross a steep ice patch on which a little snow uncertainly adhered. I was well belayed by Petzoldt with the rope, and so cut as few steps as possible, utilizing the snow for footholds. The inevitable happened. I planted one foot in the last tiny patch of snow, which bore most of my weight, and then started sliding. Petzoldt was watching me closely and I felt the rope tighten around my waist. Before I could step back to safety my foothold had gone completely and I was on my back sliding toward the glacier. I had gone only a few feet when the rope pulled me in an arc toward the buttress on which Petzoldt was stationed. Ten feet lower I brought up with a bang against the rock, unhurt but angry with myself for letting such a thing happen. With the rope my companion helped me up to his side where he tried to console me for having been the guinea pig in this futile attempt to save time.

Thoroughly aroused by now, we attacked the ice traverse with fury. Again well belayed by Petzoldt, I cut great steps to the middle of the 55° slope. There, balanced precariously, I hammered a flat-bladed piton into a crack in a protruding ledge. With my rope attached to this I felt safer and after cutting 20 feet more of steps reached a band of rock higher up on the other side. From there I was able to secure Petzoldt while he threaded an extra rope through the piton, fastening it on both sides of the traverse, so it served as a handrail. That done, we climbed higher, using what rocks we could until again we were forced to cut steps 200 feet to the base of one of the higher buttresses. More pitons to safeguard a delicate climb up one of these and we reached the top of the largest. It was only 10 feet wide and 20 feet long—no part of it being level—and sloping off on three sides. Plenty of loose rock lay on it, however, and we knew that platforms could be constructed to make the tents stand level. It had been a hard climb and the last 1000 feet had been very exposed, yet we thought that with additional rope and pitons we could safeguard it for loaded men.

The descent late that afternoon over the dipping slabs and freezing snow convinced us that the route in its present state would be unjustifiably dangerous for porters or even unloaded men. The continuously steep angle and the lack of belays was disturbing, for if a man slipped on that slope it would be very hard for the next man to stop him. Also, descent in bad weather or in some emergency would be fraught with danger. We had been unable to locate any better route, however, and the present one would have to do.

A cheery note and new loads at Camp II informed us that the others had been busy. Houston had spent the day with two Sherpas bringing in the abandoned northeast ridge camp while Bates and Burdsall with two more porters had carried heavy loads up from Camp I. Our complex machine was moving into high gear.

Petzoldt, in a yodel that must have made some new cracks in the glacier, conveyed to those at Camp I that we had been successful in finding a higher campsite. A faint answering halloo from below told us that the news had been received, although at that distance the words were unintelligible.

The next morning, carrying 900 feet of light line and a larger supply of pitons, we started up again, planning to safeguard the difficult places. It was an easy matter to string rope over the vertical pitches. The upper end was either threaded through a piton driven into a crack or tied tightly around a projecting nubbin of rock. If the place was particularly difficult the rope would be knotted every few feet. On the hardest stretches we tied loops into the rope so the laden climber could rest as he pulled himself and his load to the top. In using these fixed ropes the climber grasps the rope in both hands to balance himself and take some weight off his feet, which are making all possible use of natural holds in the rock or ice.

Safeguarding the horizontal traverses was more complicated. First a suitable spot had to be found at each end, to which the rope could be tied. If these were lacking, pitons would be driven in and the rope tied tightly instead. Sometimes it was necessary to drive in additional pitons in the middle of the rope to keep it from sagging. If the ends were in ice, long tubular steel pitons were used instead of the shorter solid ones for rock.

The traverse immediately below the site for Camp III was particularly difficult and we spent several hours extending the ropes we already had placed there so as to give the utmost protection. Right up to the campsite we carried our ropes, making an almost continuous handline for 250 feet.

In addition to the fixed ropes we tied many slings into the slope for use in roping down or for belaying porters. These are simply coils of rope affixed around rocks or through pitons. When the leader of a rope of climbers reaches one, he either ties himself to it and with the added security belays the men coming behind him or loops their rope directly through it. In either case, if a man slips, the strain comes on the sling or piton and the lead man is less likely to be pulled off by the jerk.

These additional safeguards are also valuable for

roping down, for the climbing rope can be looped
through, used for a *rappel,* and then pulled out again
from the bottom. On the way to the mountain we had
taught our porters how to use the *rappel* in anticipation
of just such places. They had grown very skillful at thus
looping the doubled rope around their thighs and backs
and sliding to the bottom with their speed controlled
by the friction of the rope over their clothing.

Early in the afternoon the weather started to turn
bad so we were unable to put the finishing touches to
our work. As we hurried down, thankful for the rope
aids we had just put in, the wind drove up into our
faces, carrying stinging particles of fine snow. Sometimes we had to crouch toward the slope and cover our
faces with our gauntlets when a particularly violent
gust hit us. Spurred on by the wind and cold, we raced
down the slabs as fast as we dared, reaching the tent
to find it quivering and straining at its lashings in spite
of the protection given by the crest behind. As before,
we found new loads and a note congratulating us on
finding a route. Such evidences of thoughtfulness and
appreciation are even more important in the mountains
than at home.

Hurriedly we made preparations for the night, for
the wind was now a gale, thundering up over the south
face. In a few minutes we had piled more snow around
the tent to hold it firm, and had crawled in, shutting
the storm out. In spite of the hammering of the wind

the little Meade tent stood up well. Its construction, with no ridgepoles—only inverted V-poles at each end —gave a maximum of flexibility, allowing it to give to the wind where a more rigidly designed tent might have burst.

In addition to the storm, which might hold up the attack for days, we had a greater worry. Petzoldt had a recurrence of his illness. Even his sleeping bag and all his clothes could not counteract the effect of his chills and as they continued I grew more alarmed. A hot meal of pemmican helped some and he soon went to sleep and was more comfortable. It was still a disturbing situation, for the storm might continue for days and I could do little to help him. We could only hope that the illness would follow its usual course and leave him in a day or so.

My fears were not lessened when I awoke at 2 A. M. to hear his teeth chattering. He was so cold that he could not light the primus. I am afraid I was a very unsympathetic companion when I had to get the stove going and melt some snow to make a hot drink for him. To make matters worse, when I opened the tent door to get the snow, a violent gust blew a bucketful onto the head of my sleeping bag. That brought out some barely muffled remarks about people who get sick at high altitudes and can't get their own hot water.

As had happened several times before, by morning he was feeling all right and, though a trifle weak, insisted that we go up to the site of Camp III again. The weather had improved considerably but blown snow made visibility poor. Anxious to test our route by carrying loads over it, we started out with 25 pounds apiece and extra rope for use on places that were still too difficult.

Higher up we found the ice traverse still insufficiently protected and had to spend considerable time relocating the ropes. I remember in one place trying to enlarge some ice steps with my load on my back and a single finger linked through the head of a piton for balance. Petzoldt, who by now had completely recovered his strength and spirits, unfortunately chose this moment to deliver an enlightening and thoroughly sound discourse on step-cutting, with particular respect to how I might improve my technique. He admitted later that this was a poorly timed joke, for he had not realized I was hanging on by my eyelashes. Anyway he claimed that the blasphemous torrent brought forth by his remarks had melted all the ice on the rope between us and that for the rest of the day it had been much easier to handle. We both agreed that there were safer methods of melting frozen ropes.

During the day the wind had increased again. Just below the campsite we had to leave our loads and scurry for Camp II. The glacier was visible only momentarily through openings in the clouds and generally we could see little farther than a rope's length. It was no time

SUCCESSIVE VIEWS OF AN AVALANCHE ON THE SOUTH WALL OF K2

HOUSE ON RECONNAISSANCE SOUTH OF GODWIN-AUSTEN GLACIER

to be caught on those slabs. By the time we reached the tent the storm had grown so much worse that we decided to descend to the glacier camp.

As we hurried toward the glacier we emerged from the storm zone into quiet. We could still look up and see the clouds hurtling across the cliffs in ragged patches, as though holes had been torn in them by the sharpness of the ridges. Once on the glacier we were puzzled, for we could find no trace of camp. Soon, however, shouts and waving of scarfs farther out on the ice announced its position. Bates, fearing that the storm would deposit snow which might avalanche from the upper slopes, had moved the tents 100 yards out, a wise precaution, although while we were there no avalanches fell.

It was good to see the Captain, who had just returned from the French base camp. The gas tins had, as he feared, been destroyed by the coolies. He had, however, found some tins of meat and vegetables which would be a welcome addition to our camp diet. Following his discovery he had dispatched Kitar and Ahdoo to Askole to bring back coolies loaded with firewood.

It was good to be all together again. Even a few days away from one's companions seems like a long time; and it seemed longer when the moral and physical support of those companions was as much needed as it was on such a mountain. We told them our fears about the route we had chosen and doubts as to what lay above.

They in their turn told of stocking Camp II, further strengthening the glacier camp, and bringing in the outlying caches. The Sherpas, they said, had handled themselves well with loads to Camp II and were impatient to be taken higher on the mountain.

As usual, the reunion was celebrated with such culinary gaiety as our modest pantry permitted. A hot grog was served up and somewhere an excellent fig pudding was found. Later two chess games started and before we knew it Bates launched into a series of his favorite Alaskan sourdough ballads, startling even the Sherpas, who peered from their tents in awe. Petzoldt was in good form again; we were all strong and, even more important, in good spirits. In spite of the uncertainty above Camp III we felt we could still go high on the mountain.

A fine night's sleep in the sheltered quiet of this camp made us eager to get back to Camp II, despite the unfavorable weather. Higher up it was still snowing hard, but it seemed to be letting up and we wanted to establish two men at the next camp as soon as possible. The Captain and Burdsall started off toward Base Camp to bring more rope and fuel. The rest of us, with three Sherpas, carried loads up to Camp II where we settled down to another night of storm.

Pasang and his Sherpas were snugly, if stuffily, packed into their pyramid tent, and to judge from their laughter and songs were very happy, in spite of the fact that nearly all the inexpensive air mattresses which we had purchased for them in Bombay had proved worthless and were little better than ground sheets. They slept quite happily, however, curled up on a layer of deflated mattresses, ropes and sacks, and we envied them their resistance to cold.

That night we had the worst storm experienced so far. Sleep was impossible toward morning, so violently were the tents battered by the wind. One moment they were as tight as drumheads; in another they were suddenly limp, as if exhausted and gaining strength for the next terrific strain. It was not the continued force of the wind that worried us, but the gusts that tore at the tent fabric until it seemed as though no material could possibly stand it. Above the banging of the tents we could hear the gale as it swept across the southern slopes of the mountain, the roar rising at times to the deep pitch of an organ as it tore over the sharp-crested ridge a few feet above the tents. Sometimes there would be moments of quiet when all we could hear was the distant moan of the wind high above our heads. These always presaged more violent activity and we found ourselves unconsciously growing tense in anticipation of the next blast. The temperature that night dropped to 7° F.

Morning brought some quiet, but it was still too dangerous to venture on the slabs above. Bates, Petzoldt and I were content to take the day off, lying in the tents, but Houston, active as ever, took the Sherpas down to the glacier camp to bring up more loads. As we lolled luxuriously in sleeping bags we could not help admiring him, although going out on a day like this seemed carrying virtue too far. Thus we justified ourselves.

In spite of the cramped quarters, for we lived two to a tent, we spent the day comfortably. There were diaries to be brought up to date, food lists to be prepared, and the inevitable expedition letter which should go out with the next mail. Later, when Houston returned, having made a record round trip in three and one half hours, we discussed plans for the future. Since so much depended on weather we could not predict, we could do little more than decide who should be established at Camp III when we reached it. Petzoldt and Houston—a strong team—were agreed on. While they reconnoitered farther, Bates and I, with the Sherpas, would carry up more supplies.

When time lagged on our hands and we were tired of playing chess or reading, it was considered good sport to stir up a debate between Houston and Petzoldt on the use of pitons. The former held that their use mechanized mountain climbing to a point where one might just as well use a cog railway. He had been against their use from the start and had been aghast when he learned that the 10 which he thought sufficient had been augmented by an assortment of 50 purchased on our way through Paris. Slowly, under Petzoldt's pontifical arguments, he was won over to recognizing the protection they gave when natural belays were lacking. Even after they had proved indispensable for safeguarding the route higher up, however, he still condoned their use and referred to them apologetically as "iron ware."

Bates remained a strict neutral, in part for reasons which did not come out until later. A loyal companion of previous trips with Houston in Alaska, he concealed a hideous story which was not divulged until we were well on our way home and the piton issue a thing of the past. It was that once this defender of mountain virtue had carried dynamite and blasting caps to the top of a corniced ridge and had actually tried to safeguard the route below by blowing the cornice off. Such a man indeed we thought would shoot a fox, but while the discussion raged in camp we did not have this valuable evidence. How could a man hide such a black past and argue so sincerely?

On July 9 it was still blowing, but the worst of the storm had passed. Unwilling to lose a day, but still unwilling to expose the relatively untried porters on slabs made more treacherous by the storm, we left them in camp and carried loads ourselves. If we found the route safe, they could start carrying next day. Later, after they had had more practice, we learned to trust Pasang, Phinsoo and Tse Tendrup almost as much as we did one another. They developed into skilled rock-climbers who could use a rope safely and were dependable on almost any kind of going. At that time, however, we were not certain about them and did not take chances, in view of the uncertainty of our route.

On the next day, with the addition of Burdsall and the porters, we carried loads to Camp III, leaving Petzoldt and Houston there to carry on the reconnaissance. They had a real problem, for above, the angle of the rock steepened and ice slopes on either side restricted their movements. We felt guilty at leaving them on such an exposed position, because they had no protection from the wind. Our fears were realized and that night they were treated to the fury of a storm which made all previous ones seem like gentle zephyrs. With the canvas flaps extending outside the tent piled high with rocks and the guy ropes lashed to large boulders, they got through it all right, but it was a bad night.

In spite of the night they had spent, the two started out early next morning to prospect higher. Immediately above them rose a ridge composed of broken rocks loosely frozen together by ice and snow. Several hours of delicate climbing brought them to the base of a great gendarme or pinnacle which blocked the ridge. The south or outside face of this was nearly vertical for 150 feet.

With Houston anchored to a piton driven in at its base, Petzoldt edged up past him into an overhanging crack toward what looked like a good ledge. It was a difficult piece of work, for although the rock here was fairly sound the holds sloped down and the crack overhung. After several attempts he managed to reach the ledge, where he kept a tight rope on Houston as the latter tried to find an easier way around the obstacle. From the ledge they worked over to a narrow sloping shelf which ran around the side of the buttress, meeting an insecure scree slope behind it.

Several hundred feet above this point a wall of reddish-brown rock blocked the route completely. Thinking that this could be turned via a long tilted snow slope to the left, they traversed across a series of down-plunging slabs to the edge of the snow. Here they found the snow adhering precariously to hard ice. It was obviously no choice for a route and they retraced their steps to the top of the gendarme—thereafter dubbed Paul's Gendarme—where they decided Camp IV should be located. A chill wind had sprung up, so they were not sorry to hurry as fast as they could down over the face to the rotten ridge and then to Camp III.

While they were engaged in their difficult task Bates and I, with three Sherpas, were carrying another set of loads up from Camp II. A short distance below the camp Pasang gave a shout and a few moments later several small rocks whizzed by. From then on we kept careful watch; it was obvious that the climbers above were dislodging them. Rock fall here puzzled us, for ordinarily falling rock will not stay on the crest of a ridge but bounce off to either side. As we approached Camp III the stone fire stopped, but we were alarmed to find that the single tent had two large rips in the side toward the mountain—made by rocks which fell directly into camp.

As there were no more stones falling, Petzoldt and Houston apparently realizing the danger, we left Pasang and Tse Tendrup to set up their tent. This inversion of the normal arrangement took place because neither Bates nor I liked taking the Sherpas over the tricky slabs below that camp. There were only a few loads left and we could bring them up with one Sherpa the next day, leaving the other two to help with the carrying to Camp IV.

Before departing we left a note for the two climbers, telling them about the rocks and asking them to stay in camp until we arrived the next morning. At Camp II we found Burdsall, who had brought an extra tent, stoves, fuel, oatmeal and Sherpa food from Camp I. He would now join the Captain at Base Camp. We had found that three Sherpas and four sahibs were the most efficient group for the sort of climbing we had run into, and he kindly agreed to be the necessary link between Base Camp and the climbing party higher up on the mountain. Between trips to Camp II he would work with the Captain, plane table surveying on the Godwin-Austen and Baltoro Glaciers. We said good-by to him next morning, glad to know that the job of liaison was in such good hands.

July 12 proved to be the worst day on the mountain. When Bates and I arrived at Camp III, having relayed the last loads, we found the others dutifully waiting for us. Anxious not to miss a day's carrying, they started up immediately with Pasang and Tse Tendrup to take loads to Camp IV. After the experience of the day before it is hard to see why we decided to do this, for it meant leaving three men exposed to possible rock fall while the others climbed above. Perhaps it was one of the minor effects of altitude that encourages careless-ness and chance-taking. Anyway, while Bates and I, with Phinsoo, began building the tent platforms, the others started up, saying they would be as careful as possible with the loose rock.

It was a serious mistake. When they were 500 feet above, the first rock fell. It came right among us, punc-turing the tent we had just erected. From then on, at infrequent intervals, rocks dropped. Sometimes they fell far to one side; sometimes they flew overhead with a high-pitched hum; sometimes they crashed right into camp, bursting like shrapnel as they hit the slope. There was no escape, for the gullies to either side and below them acted like funnels and caught all the stone fire.

A high wind was blowing so the climbers could not hear our shouts and thought the rocks were bouncing harmlessly out to the sides. At the other end they were not having an easy time. Imagine a slate roof piled high with rocks of all shapes and sizes. Then imagine climbing up this without slipping and without knocking a rock down on the man below you or on a camp 1000 feet lower. Under such conditions the rope itself becomes a hazard and may dislodge stones if not handled very carefully.

By the time the others started down we were wild and talked of the things we would say when they came. Fortunately we had all shared in the decision to send the party up and so we were all to blame. Here was an opportunity for a flare-up which, aggravated by high altitude, could shatter the morale of any expedition— we, thoroughly angry at what looked like inexcusable carelessness, the others outraged at so little appreciation of the hard job they had done in carrying loads to the higher camp.

As they climbed down into camp, already warned by some bitter remarks wafted up to them on the wind, they had the tact to keep quiet, finding their cheery greeting followed by a dead silence. One look at the holes in all three tents was enough to tell them what had happened. Hostile eyes peering through the side of our torn tent indicated that the situation demanded diplomacy.

Fortunately they were equal to it. While we sat and sulked, seeking the most effective way of voicing our great displeasure, they rummaged through the food supplies. A short time later they brought humble offerings of jam, dates, and hot tea hastily conjured out of sun-melted snow. With such companions ill-humor could not last long, and soon we were laughing sheepishly at what we had let ourselves in for. We agreed that hereafter no one should be at Camp III while men climbed above, and as soon as possible it was to be used only as a dump for supplies.

That evening Bates and Houston made a careful check of all food and fuel. They knew almost to the ounce how much pemmican, vegetables, oatmeal, etc., would be needed for so many days' stay at each camp, and our loads had been made up on that basis. It now was necessary to know exactly how much longer our food would last and still give us a margin of safety. Not only must food be taken higher to new camps but some must be left at camps en route for use on the way down. We found that we still had food for almost three weeks. This meant that we had only about ten days of climbing time left, for we always planned on a reserve to see us through a prolonged storm. Moreover, we realized now that descent between camps in any sort of a storm might have very serious consequences. Therefore, we could not risk being caught high up with insufficient food and fuel.

Our main staple now was pemmican, which filled most of our meat requirements. This, cooked for a few minutes in boiling water with dried vegetables and crackers added, made a most nutritious dish. The fat, rice, raisins and dried meat of which it was composed did tend to become a trifle dull, yet our appetites were nearly always good enough to overcome this, and we had smaller quantities of other foods, such as tinned fish and meat, to vary the diet.

Petzoldt's ingenuity at concocting new and tasty dishes was amazing. One of his most successful was "Klim Skardu"—nothing more than Klim, hot water, butter, sugar and salt. Under ordinary circumstances it might not have been relished, but with our ravenous appetites it was in constant demand. It was generally agreed that the flavor closely resembled an oyster stew —alas, lacking in oysters.

Breakfast is perhaps the most interesting, though not the most pleasant, meal at these altitudes. It is interesting in that it requires the ultimate in close co-operation and planning to achieve the relatively simple aims of getting fed and dressed.

To begin with, two sleeping bags just fill a Meade tent. At their head, tucked in between them, the little primus stove is always ready in the morning. The more energetic climber places a small piece of meta underneath the burner, lights it, and, still in his sleeping bag, watches it anxiously. After a few minutes, when the burner seems hot enough, pressure is built up by means of the pump and the burner slowly fed gas. When the flame is steady, a *dekshi* containing either ice or hard-packed snow is placed on it. Usually we stored water in a *dekshi,* wrapping it up carefully to prevent freezing, so it would be available in the morning. The situation from this point on becomes fraught with danger, for if the floor is uneven, as it always is, there is a good chance of knocking the whole business over. This, when it happened, was a great tragedy, for not only was hard-won liquid lost, but sleeping bags and tent were made messy and the long process of melting snow must start again.

While the snow or ice is melting both men usually remain in their bags unless an early start is called for. When the weather is good this period of grace is necessary, for boots, unless slept with, must be put outside in the sun. Becoming damp in the daytime, they invariably freeze at night and have to be thawed out before they can be put on one's feet. When the leather has to be softened over the primus the confusion is vast. High-altitude boots are large enough anyway, but when they are held over a tiny primus which is trying to heat a *dekshi* of water as well, the situation becomes impossible.

When the water has come to a boil part is poured into the ever-ready pint mugs, tea bags are dropped in, sugar and Klim added, and the strength-giving morning brew is drunk. While this is sipped, oatmeal or corn-meal is put in the remaining boiling water and by the time the mugs are empty the cereal is ready to eat. Butter or Klim and sugar are added generously, and all too soon it is finished and breakfast is over.

If the camp is to be moved, the next step is the deflating of the air mattresses. This is done simply by unscrewing the valve. It is the finest way for a man of weak character to get himself out of bed, for in the comfort and warmth of his sleeping bag he can by a simple and irreversible decision let the air out of his mattress. As it subsides—and it is a very weak-minded person indeed who screws up the valve again—the rocks beneath the tent floor, gently at first, then more forcefully, prod him into action.

If camp is to be moved, air mattresses are immediately hung outside the tent to dry off, for they frequently become very wet from melted snow and ice. Sleeping bags also are aired and particular care is given to their mouths where the breath of the sleeper has condensed to ice during the night. Loads for the day are then assembled. By that time the mattresses and bags are dry and can be rolled up into their light covers. The tent is dismantled and rolled up, with the bamboo poles carefully placed in the inside of the bundle; then loads of 30–40 pounds are completed and swung on, the men are roped together, and creakingly the party moves upward.

If camp is not to be moved, the procedure is more simple. *Dekshis* filled with tightly packed snow are placed on the rocks so they will absorb heat from the sun, and snow is piled on the flaps of the tent, so that when the men return in the evening the tiresome and fuel-depleting process of melting snow over the primus will be unnecessary. All the tent openings are tightly tied, guy ropes are checked, and the camp remains safe and snug until ready for use in the afternoon.

With all four sahibs and three porters carrying the next morning, we started up the treacherous ridge. Before doing so we took the precaution of dropping all the tents and covering them and the supplies with flat rocks to save them from injury. Soon it was obvious that no matter how much care was exercised it was impossible to avoid dislodging rocks. Those of us who had suffered from the bombardment of the previous afternoon felt much better disposed and indeed wondered why more rocks had not come down. Except where patches of ice or snow held them tightly together, they were like a house of cards, ready to collapse at the slightest provocation.

Two hours of careful climbing brought us to the base of the gendarme turned two days before. Despite a fixed knotted rope it proved hard to surmount. We were all, except the leader of the first rope, exceedingly thankful to be belayed by a stout climbing rope from above. Even Petzoldt, who had led it originally, admitted that it had not grown easier.

The scramble around to the side and up behind the gendarme took a long time as the rock was shaly and

had a tendency to slide. Somehow the realization that a
few feet below the ground sloped off to a vertical cliff,
ending thousands of feet lower, made the slowly moving rocks ominous. A slip of only a few inches seemed
like the beginning of a slide that inevitably would carry
a man over the cliff. This, however, did not happen,
and after about five hours we reached the site for
Camp IV.

Lunch here was a delightful affair, the more so since
the porters insisted on hurrying through theirs so they
could build the tent platform. Their love of building
things out of rocks was a source of constant amazement
to us. When it came to building tent platforms we were
quite willing to let them indulge themselves to the utmost.

Lunch away from an established camp was usually
the most appreciated of all. In the first place we allowed
ourselves delicacies such as dates, figs, cheese, crackers,
and malted milk tablets, which were not ordinarily included in other meals. Of these the malted milk tablets,
early nicknamed "go quick tablets," were standard and
could be had at any time; the others were saved only
for lunches. Each morning we put a flat tin of chocolate
flavored malted milk tablets in a pocket and munched
them on and off during the day. While resting, it was
customary for one man to pass around his tin politely
to the others with all the decorum which in another

age would have marked the passing around of a snuff-box.

But the pleasantness of lunch—except of course on days of bad weather—came from other sources too. With only half a day's work behind us we generally were not so tired as we were in the late afternoon and our minds were more receptive to impressions and to each other's conversation. Also, there were none of the minor drudgeries that always preceded a more formal meal at camp —no empty primus stoves to fill, no snow to be laboriously scraped into piles for melting, no damp boots to be taken off and tilted precariously against rocks so the last rays of the afternoon sun could partly dry them. Instead of all these and many other bothersome chores, the only problem was to find a comfortable place to sit. The human anatomy is surprisingly well adapted to irregular terrain and even on the sloping ledges we could generally make our posteriors conform comfortably. Often we kept our packs on, for the pack frame makes an admirable back rest, more form fitting even than a deck chair.

If one person were carrying the lunch we waited until he had unpacked it. Then the individual shares were laid out and each individual, taking his, would retire to his nook and try to make the delicacies last as long as possible. As we went higher and became divided into smaller parties, the lunch ingredients were stowed in each person's capacious pockets, to be eaten all at once or spaced out during the day. The Sherpas in the meantime would be huddled together eating their rations, consisting mostly of *chupattis* cooked over their primus at breakfast.

Sitting in the warm sun, with the toils of the ascent temporarily forgotten, we could reflect more cheerfully on our progress. From Camp IV at 21,500 feet, we could look down on the glacier, now 4000 feet below, and recall the many days we had spent on it wondering if we were ever to get higher. Even the huge lateral moraines on the lower Godwin-Austen now looked like narrow roads. We knew from experience, however, that some of them were hundreds of yards wide. The tremendous crevasses that had blocked us below Camp I were now only faint pencil lines.

All too soon our reveries had to end, for the returning party must start down in order to get the slow, tiresome descent over before evening. Bates and I were left behind at this camp to find a route over the reddish-brown cliff that apparently blocked farther progress. We said good-by, hoping that when we saw them next we should have solved this new problem.

For what was left of the short afternoon we studied the forbidding wall above us carefully. It gave little encouragement. Although broken in several places by wide cracks, it was uniformly steep and the strata seemed to slope down even steeper than on other parts of the ridge. After outlining several possibilities, without much conviction, we completed the rock platform started by the porters and soon had the tent in position for the night. As usual the temperature dropped suddenly, this time to 20° F., as soon as we were in the shadow cast by the summit. We sat for a long time outside, muffled in our heaviest clothes, watching the peaks of the Karakoram blaze in the last light of the day. First the lower ones, last the highest, died into dull steel-gray. Only a few golden clouds high in the pale blue sky reassured us that the sun had not died. Soon even they faded into twilight and the deep Himalayan night swallowed up mountains, glaciers and humans alike.

The next morning the early sun shone bright on our tent. In spite of this it was not until nearly 9 that we were ready to leave. Even after steady practice it was a great effort to make an early start, and partly because of the cold we rarely started action until the sun had warmed the tent a little. This otherwise unmixed blessing had only one drawback: the warm rays melted the frost formed on the inside of the tent by our breaths during the night. This dripped down on necks and sleeping bags and did not help tempers in the already trying process of preparing breakfast. The situation, however, could be remedied by beating the tent roof and then retiring hastily inside one's sleeping bag, to emerge only when the moisture had stopped dripping.

Armed with 400 feet of extra rope as well as ice and

rock pitons, we tackled the ice slope that led to the cliff. Like most of the ice we had met on the mountain it was very tough and required many blows of the ice ax to fashion an adequate step. It took more than an hour to reach the base of the cliff, though it was only 75 feet above the tent.

The surface of the rock—here lying at about 80°— had given the impression from Camp IV that it was well broken by cracks and tiny ledges. The ledges turned out to be diminutive indeed and sloping so sharply that they were of little use for anything but friction holds. The cracks were too narrow to insert a finger into and penetrated the rock only an inch or so. We at last decided to try a great slanting gash that led off to the left, which, because it slanted diagonally, partially compensated for the steepness of the cliff. Two other routes we had considered looked no easier and their tops were guarded by 10-foot overhanging snow cornices. It was this choice or none, we thought.

Ten feet from the base of the crack was a tooth of rock three feet high standing a foot away from the cliff. Bates cut large steps for his feet below this, tied himself firmly to it and passed my rope behind it. It was an excellent belay, but would be of little use to me when I got higher in the crack. Traversing from his perch to the crack was tricky. Once there, I was glad to drive a heavy piton in and loop my rope to it. This was the only crack that could be used for such a purpose for the first 50 feet.

While Bates held my rope tight I rested, for the sides of the gash above were smooth and I would need all my strength. With feet and hands gripping both sides, I climbed up 20 feet to where the walls flared outward and became so smooth that I had to put my back against one and feet against the other to hitch myself up a few inches at a time.

It was at this point I discovered that I had neglected to leave my crampons with Bates, for they were in my rucksack, pressing into my back and catching on the rock. This carelessness cost me dear, but after awhile I was able to use feet and hands on both sides of the chimney. A little ledge 40 feet up gave me a timely rest, for any progress under such conditions is exhausting. I remember spending precious strength trying to drive in another piton so I could loop my rope through it and slide down, but the metal only crumpled up after penetrating a half-inch of rock.

I felt I was pretty close to my margin of safety, but there were no piton cracks and I thought anything would be better than climbing down without some protection from above. Bates, who had been unable to hear the comments I had made because he was out of sight and the clatter of little pebbles made too much noise, shouted up that maybe I had better come down. It was a suggestion I certainly would have liked to follow. I could only shout back to let the rope slide through the lower piton easily so as not to catch and throw me off balance.

Another struggle of 15 feet took me beyond where the chimney narrowed to a foot and a half, its back a wall of ice, and placed me on some holds wide enough for my boots. Still another rest and I scrambled over the easier upper part, emerging on a tiny ridge 80 feet above Bates. The whole climb from our tent had taken two and a half hours and I was then less than 150 feet above it.

Bates was by now nearly frozen, having remained in the same position for almost two hours, but there was a delay until I could tie myself onto a rock and belay him. I must admit it gave me a vicarious satisfaction to hear his mutterings as he struggled up between the outward flaring walls. We were all to curse that place more than once afterward.

When he reached the top of the cliff we congratulated each other, for ahead of us easy snow slopes rose for several hundred feet. Hurrying up these, we came to a buttress of black rock beneath which we decided Camp V must be. It was only 500 feet above Camp IV, but search a couple of hundred feet higher revealed only narrow rounded ledges which would not hold tents. We had now reached a point on the ridge at the base of what we called "the great black pyramid." Actually it was the last upswing on the ridge before it ended on the snow plateau at 25,000 feet. This was still over 2000 feet above us and the going did not look easy.

The return to the top of the chimney was a fast one, so we spent much time placing a fixed rope in the whole length of the gully. Bates, who tested it out on the descent, declared it insufficient and after I had followed him I agreed. We were both too tired to do any more that day, so we left it, hoping we would have strength to climb it again the next day.

While we were engaged in this we saw Petzoldt and two porters arrive in camp, deposit their loads and leave again—their light-brown clothing making them almost invisible against the brownish rock. Petzoldt shouted up congratulations and told us that Houston had gone to Camp II for mail and more food. Both of them, with the three Sherpas, would come up the next day to stay. This was good news, for it meant that the attack on the upper part of the ridge could be speeded up. Then they disappeared one by one over the edge of the slope, Petzoldt's great figure remaining the last as he paid out the rope to the porters below.

July 15 was fully as good as the previous day, so we started out with 25-pound loads toward Camp V. The chimney was made easier by tying loops in the fixed rope every foot, but it remained almost as difficult to climb with the fixed rope as without. There were so few footholds that nearly all of one's weight (plus his pack) had to be held by the arms. Pulling hand over hand was exhausting.

When we returned, after leaving the loads at the campsite, we found the rest of the party assembled around the tent at Camp IV. Both Petzoldt and Houston had carried packs weighing more than 50 pounds over the difficult route from Camp III. It was then only noon, so we decided after lunch to go up again with loads and leave Petzoldt and Houston at the next camp to reconnoiter farther. Houston told of a note from Burdsall at Camp II reporting all well with the Captain at Base Camp. He had brought up with him a great bundle of mail. This had been carried from Srinagar by regular mail coolie to Shigar, where it had been picked up by a special mail runner and brought five days' march to Askole. From there it had been brought to Base Camp by Ahdoo, who was escorting the wood coolies. Some of the letters were postmarked in the United States only five weeks previously, having been sent air mail. Burdsall had also reported the arrival at Base Camp of a coolie laden exclusively with eggs, an item of food for which we then all had a great craving. The note confirmed our previous arrangements for 35 coolies to come in on July 26 to take us out. He and the Captain were about to establish, on the Baltoro Glacier, a camp from which they planned to fill in a blank spot on the map just east of Masherbrum peak.

PETZOLDT

CAMP V (22,000 FT.)

CAMP VI
(23,300 FT.)

PETZOLDT

After lunch the four of us started out with food and equipment for Camp V. The Sherpas were left in camp, as getting seven loaded men over the cliff would have taken more time than we had that day. Even four men took long enough, and it was late when Bates and I left Houston and Petzoldt at the upper camp. We planned to return with the Sherpas the next day. In the meantime the reconnaissance pair were to try to locate a route to another camp on the upper part of the ridge.

The descent of the chimney late that afternoon was more trying than usual but in camp below us were bundles of mail which had not been opened at lunch. It took all our self-control to come down slowly and safely, for this was the first mail that had reached us since we left home three months before. Once at camp we exercised even more self-control and completed all the chores for the night before lying on our sleeping bags and devouring our mail. It was like a ray of sunshine to read letters written by family and friends of an outside world. For two months since leaving Srinagar we had been so wrapped up in ourselves and in the problems of the expedition that we had given little thought to what might have been happening outside.

Such isolation from the normal world has both a good and a bad effect. Its good effect is that there is little chance to compare one's present situation with that enjoyed by friends at home. The trials of frozen boots, cold hands, damp socks, balky stoves, melted snow in the tent—all these and many others become an accepted part of one's life in the high mountains, just as do the magnificent scenery, the feeling of accomplishment after a successful day, the companionship of one's partners. It is too easy to compare the disagreeable parts of one's life in the mountains with the comforts of civilization—good food, warm beds, reasonable physical security; but as long as these are kept in the background it is much easier for the individual to accept the hardships and stresses to which he is being subjected.

There is no doubt in my mind that it is the petty inconveniences and discomforts and the uncertainty that exercise most of the influence on a mountain climber's adjustment or lack of adjustment to the unnatural environment which he craves. The actual physical and mental effects of high altitude and the conflicts of personalities also exert a strong influence, but they are in a different category and may be termed the background on which the minor influences are superimposed.

In so far as the climber can avoid comparisons which by their vividness make him dissatisfied with his environment, he has a good chance of satisfactorily adjusting himself. When he begins to think too much of these comparisons, the resulting dissatisfaction may make him acutely unhappy and a complete loss to his party. That is what I term the bad effect of too close contact with the outside world.

On the other hand, there are beneficial effects which may outweigh the bad ones suggested above. One is very likely, when trying to climb a mountain which approaches his limits of strength and morale, to lose all perspective. Failure to find a route on a given day, loss of time because of bad weather, even such a minor incident as the loss of a spoon or a cherished article of clothing can assume an importance all out of proportion to its actual significance. A few days of frustration may seem a real catastrophe, whereas if they could be viewed with some perspective they would be nothing more than temporary delays, like the breaking down of one's car or missing a train. As difficulties and reverses pile up, they may have the same effect as obstacles that are actually insurmountable.

During such crises news from the outside world has a tranquilizing effect. Other people are living their lives, meeting frustration, overcoming obstacles which to them are fully as important as any met in the mountains. This realization, brought home by letters or other outside contact, is like a dash of cold water, bringing the mountain climber out of his self-centered world into the world of reality where billions of others are facing the problems and uncertainties of life too. This, I think, is a strong argument for the use of radio on expeditions or at least for adequate postal contacts. If the above makes any sense it is that the mountain climber, however strange his field of endeavor, is essentially no different in his reactions from the billions of his brethren who are content to meet life on level ground.

For whatever reason, Bates and I both felt greatly cheered by the letters we read in our little tent at 22,500 feet. We read them and reread them countless times, putting them away carefully at last to be saved and enjoyed again. I for one vowed that no friend of mine on a protracted expedition should go without some word from me.

Things were going much better than we had expected, more than compensating for the discouragements of reconnaissance. We had established five camps over difficult terrain, were acclimating well, were still congenial, and although the end of food and time was in sight, going well. How high we would get we did not know. The summit was very far away but there was still hope. Behind that was a consciousness that many once serious obstacles lay below us. Perhaps those ahead might be overcome in the same way.

Chapter XIII

Last Camps

Charles S. Houston, M.D.

Chapter XIII   Last Camps

O N Saturday the 16th, Petzoldt and I ambitiously
started the primus at 5 o'clock, hoping to get
away early. But at 7 when we finally started, a cold wind
and threatening snow drove us back to lie in our tents
for an hour. Then the sun broke through the clouds
and we started off again. From previous inspection we
felt that the right side of the buttress above Camp V

was more hopeful than the steep snow gully, the beginning of which was just visible to the left.

I led off and traversed a steep snow-covered ice slope where crampons were necessary, but we were soon forced to climb directly up the right side of the buttress. The rock was very exposed and flaky, and in addition covered with powder snow, which made for considerable anxiety on the part of the leader and the second man. We found ourselves barely 200 feet above camp after several hours of hard work. To our great disappointment such difficult climbing clearly made this no route for supporting higher camps, and we turned back.

After the usual luncheon, our spirits rose again, and shortly after noon we turned to the left side of the ridge where we worked up a steep snow gully. Here the snow was very deep and fell away out of sight in the depths below, giving the climbing party an eerie feeling of insecurity. Fortunately, the snow soon led to the top of the buttress, and we climbed easily for several hundred feet. Paul's almost uncanny ability to smell out the best route several yards in advance was a great help, but we soon reached very nasty broken rock which gave rise to considerable profanity from the second man as small stones were knocked down on him. We persevered and came to a tiny nook at the foot of another large gendarme which seemed to be as difficult as the one above Camp V.

It was then 4 o'clock and the weather was getting

stormy, so we turned back to camp, where we found Bates and House with the three Sherpas cosily ensconced in the tents it had taken them all afternoon to pitch. We all crowded into one small tent to devour a supper cooked by Paul which almost surpassed his previous culinary efforts. After supper some renditions from the Oxford Book of English Verse sent us off to our sleeping bags in a very contented mood.

The wind rose steadily all evening and we fell asleep to the ominous flapping of the tents. The outlook for morning was gloomy, and we woke at 5 to find ourselves completely surrounded by mist. Breakfast was started to the inevitable drip, drip, drip of frost melting on the inside of the roof. One of the *dekshis,* knocked over by a blowing tent wall, drenched someone's sleeping bag. The waiter, carrying breakfast to the other tent, almost froze his hands in the wind. All in all it was a nasty morning.

At 8 the weather had improved slightly and we decided to push on to Camp VI carrying our sleeping bags. The support party planned to start several hours later and establish one tent with food at Camp VI, while Petzoldt and I made an attempt to go still higher. We started off bundled in windproof suits, mittens, and helmets. Once out of the shelter of the ridge we felt the full force of the wind, which, laden with cloud and snow, howled through the rocks. Immediately beards frosted over and hands and feet became numb. We realized the imminent danger of frostbite, and, fearing that we soon might not be able to find our way back through the storm, returned to camp. The others, who had evidently been worried about us, came from their tents with hot drinks, and Pasang greeted us with, "Just like Nanga Parbat, sahibs," and then proceeded to pull off boots and rub frozen feet into consciousness.

We spent the rest of the day encouraging our spirits with continuous feasting. Lunch began as usual and was continued with small tidbits until time for tea. Tea in turn was prolonged into high tea, and finally into supper. Then, after long conferences, comparisons of this and previous weather, and general optimistic imaginings, we found it necessary to take a small sustaining snack to see us through the night. Even with that, when we turned in about 8 o'clock, our spirits were very low. The wind was increasing in violence, blowing heavy clouds from the west. Driven snow froze on the tents and the temperature was steadily falling. Our snug sleeping bags were very welcome.

To our surprise, Monday the 18th was one of the most perfect days we had yet seen. Every peak about us stood out brilliantly clear, topped with purple and pink in the early morning light. The wind had disappeared, the new snow had been mostly blown from the rocks, and, best of all, the morning's sun warmed our tents rapidly. In this calm weather breakfast was pleasant to prepare, and Petzoldt and I got away before 8, carrying our sleepers and a light lunch. We reached the perch which was to serve for Camp VI well before noon and left our loads. Petzoldt then started off to the left of the buttress and almost immediately was stopped by steep snow-covered slabs. After an hour of futile attempts to find some route over which these could be crossed, we turned back and tackled the right side. This seemed on first inspection to be even more severe, but I found a chimney about 20 feet straight up which was climbed with some difficulty. At the top of this an airy traverse, still on the right side of the ridge, was secured by several pitons and brought us to a platform barely 200 feet above the campsite.

The support party arrived about this time with tents, food, and the usual imprecations about falling rock. They had been subjected to occasional bombardments of small fragments, although the larger stones had fallen clear of them on either side of the ridge. As Petzoldt and I worked still higher, Bates and House, at first incredulous about the possibilities for pitching two tents, or even one, on the narrow shelf, set to work to achieve the impossible. The Sherpas, with their natural zest for masonry, constructed three dubious platforms and set up one tent for the reconnoitering party. The group then returned to Camp V, planning to bring up the final loads next day.

Petzoldt and I meanwhile were finding some trouble with the route above. In several places fixed ropes were necessary, and the ice in the gullies at either side of the ridge very effectively kept us on its crest. About 500 feet above camp, Paul lost a mitten, which blew over the edge and vanished in a second. This was serious, for to lose irretrievably so vital a protection makes one fully realize the narrow margin between warm hands and frostbite. About us the downy cloud which seemed always to hang in this part of Abruzzi ridge was dank and clammy but we reached a point from which we could see easy going for several hundred yards before starting back toward camp. The blessed support party had blown up air mattresses, laid out sleeping bags, and even melted a few precious spoonfuls of water. Tea was soon ready and, during the usual pemmican supper, plans were laid for morning.

The night was cold and very beautiful. For the first time we noticed a full moon, which gave the high peaks about us a rare, ethereal glory, but the night was too cold to admire for long our superb surroundings. In the morning, the weather was partially clear, though thick, dark clouds appeared to the east. This was unusual, for generally the clouds appeared in the west and south. We wondered if the long anticipated break in our good weather were upon us. Fortunately, about 9 o'clock the west wind sprang up and for several hours we could see the battle of the winds with great rolling masses of mist sweeping over Windy Gap, there to be met by a stronger wind from Kashmir which drove them back into Turkestan. The sun warmed the rocks and the day became very comfortable.

Soon Petzoldt and I had passed our high point reached the day before and were well on our way up the famous Black Pyramid which caps Abruzzi ridge. This was to be the crux of the climb for, ever since our first examination of it, we felt that the last thousand feet leading onto the great snow shoulder was by far the most difficult and inaccessible stretch of all. We were very excited, but the severity of the rock work kept our minds completely on the business at hand. Petzoldt again skillfully anticipated the best route several minutes before we reached it, and by noon we came to a steep snow gully which we had studied from below and up which Paul had predicted our route would lead to the top of the Pyramid.

For an exhausting half hour we kicked steps up the narrowing gully, and were finally forced to traverse out to the right onto perilous looking slopes. More pitons were used, their protection being very welcome. A slip on these slopes would have landed us in Camp I after a rapid but by no means comfortable journey. Shortly after noon we shook hands at the top of the Black Pyramid at an altitude of approximately 24,500 feet. Abruzzi ridge had been conquered and we had found a route to the snow fields of the 25,000-foot shoulder.

The exhilaration of that moment was not due entirely to our altitude. Most of the Karakoram was in

view before us. Far to the southwest the white cone of
Nanga Parbat rose high above the snow peaks about
it. Broad Peak, graceful as ever, seemed near enough to
touch across the glacier below. Masherbrum, farther to
the west, was clear and beautiful. We wondered whether
its summit had been reached by our friends on the British party. Still we had no view into the Shaksgam to the
north. That was to come later.

After a restful cigarette, which seemed especially
welcome at these high altitudes, we turned again to our
task. Above us was a steep, high slope spotted with
patches of powder snow. To our left a brief rock ridge
fell away into nothing, and on the right, above a great
cliff, was a small slope leading to a broken icefall which
came from the 25,000-foot shoulder. The last seemed
the easiest and safest route, and we began to cut steps
for a horizontal traverse toward the icefall. The pure
green ice fell away sharply to an awful abyss below, for
it lay at an angle of $45°$. It is possible that this ice could
have been formed by wind or pressure, but in the face
of existing theories we think it more likely that melting
of the snow must take place even as high as 24,500 feet.
An hour's work was needed to cut some 80 steps, and
to drive two ice pitons to secure our passage; we then
landed in the middle of a great icefall formed of blocks
and towers of firmly packed snow tumbled from the
summit of K2. We puzzled a way through this maze to
find ourselves on a $30°$ snow slope with clear sailing

ahead. Up this we plodded, going slower and slower, and being reminded more and more of our advanced altitude. Around 3 o'clock we emerged at the top of the snow slope 300 feet below the long-sought 25,347-foot point.

Here at last was one landmark whose altitude we knew precisely from previous triangulations, and which had been the focal point of our eyes for many weeks. Alas, the summit was still out of sight above us. Between us and the face of the cone stretched another small slope whose gentle curve hid the final rock pyramid from our anxious gaze. It was too late to go farther, so Paul took photographs of our magnificent surroundings as we turned back toward Camp VI. When we arrived, we found the support party stubbornly, though not comfortably, established in three precariously pitched tents. They too had their tale to tell, for they had carried 35-pound loads up from Camp V over the loose stones below. The Sherpas and Bates and House had labored all afternoon in this restricted space, chopping away rocks frozen in the ice and building up braced but sloping platforms for the two other tents.

We now felt further removed from the common world than ever before, for our tiny campsite clung insecurely to the steep slabs, and the nearest level ground which we could see was some 7000 feet below us on the Godwin-Austen Glacier. Life at home, with its complications, petty annoyances, hopes and struggles, seemed futile and very, very far away. And yet our thoughts were frequently with our friends and families. We all felt that could we only be home for a few days, our energies and enthusiasm would be greatly strengthened, and we could attack the last few thousand feet with renewed vigor. Our nearest contact with home consisted of letters which we could be writing, but, alas, never seemed to do.

After dinner came a council of war, by far the most serious and decisive of the many we had had. With us in Camp VI we had perhaps 10 days of food and fuel. Several camps below were well stocked, so that we could retreat without taking food or tents with us. Above us we were certain at least two more camps would be necessary were we to reach the summit. This meant that each camp would need at least 7 days of food, and several days must be consumed in establishing them. Our margin of safety was getting very slim. Should we push on higher as fast as possible, hoping that our brilliant weather would continue? Or should we play the conservative game and retreat in full marching order? The latter was undoubtedly the wiser move, but somehow, having worked so long and gone so far, we felt that a small chance must be taken.

The big question was the weather. If we were sure the good weather would continue, we would be quite safe to go higher for two more camps, returning only when our food was almost exhausted. With good

THE ICE
TRAVERSE
JUST BELOW
CAMP VII

PETZOLDT

MASHERBRUM
FROM NEAR
CAMP VII

weather and without mishap, we felt that we could reach the summit. On the other hand, if a storm should break in two or three days, we would have no alternative but to wait until the weather cleared again.

The mere thought of climbing down in storm over our route, which had been difficult enough under perfect conditions, was horrifying. In storm or even after fresh snow, we would be in serious trouble on House's Chimney, on Petzoldt's Gendarme, and on the slopes below Camp III. The long delays required for safe assurance of each climber would mean certain frostbite if we retreated in a storm. No, there was no alternative. We must go down in good weather.

Therefore, we must either turn back before the storm broke or else be prepared to wait until the storm had exhausted its fury. That there was to be a storm in the near future seemed probable. We had had two weeks of almost uninterrupted clear weather at a time in the season when all authorities agreed the weather was bound to change, and for the last two days the cloud bank over Turkestan had grown ominously larger. A storm was certainly to be expected, but how severe it would be was a question that time alone could solve. All our previous storms had lasted only three to five days, but the French Expedition in 1936 had lain in their tents for two solid weeks of snow and wind. It was becoming increasingly evident that we could advance at most but one camp higher.

Our first objective had been the establishment of a safe and direct route to the summit. Our second objective far overshadowed the first—to bring the entire party home unscathed. We felt that in reaching the great snow field below the summit cone we had well completed our first objective. Abruzzi ridge, though far from an easy route, was a direct one, and, if discretion was used, a safe way to the summit.

After several hours of discussion, we finally decided that we would still be within our margin of safety if two men were established as high as possible with three days of food, with the understanding that they would return immediately should bad weather threaten. Those two could climb in one day as high on the summit cone as time and strength would allow before returning to Camp VI and beginning the retreat. It was a difficult decision. We all felt its gravity but agreed that it was the only one which could be made, a compromise between our vaulting ambitions and safety.

Who then were to be the two chosen? The whole group had made plans as a committee; each man was in perfect condition, and each man equally able to carry the burden of the final climb. But Petzoldt and I had reconnoitered the route, and the few extra days of high altitude had presumably acclimatized us slightly better. Accordingly House and Bates volunteered to establish camp for us, and return to Camp VI while we two went higher. No one slept soundly that night, for we all

realized that our adventure was drawing to a close, and
that the high goal which we had set ourselves was to be
unattained.

On the morning of the 20th we had again perfect
weather, confirming our decision of the previous evening. Above us the sky was a dark inky blue, a sky of
very high altitude. Far to the west a tiny cloud bank
kissed the top of Nanga Parbat. There was no wind—
our weather was still holding. Four loads were made,
one for each sahib, for the Sherpas, we felt, had reached
the limits of their climbing ability. Just before we left,
the indomitable Pasang begged to be taken, and we
could not resist his smile or his spirit, so our loads were
lightened to make a fifth pack. We did not consider the
other two Sherpas, stalwart though they had been,
capable of going higher over the increasingly difficult
route. We left them to drowse in the sun.

House and Petzoldt started first on one rope, while
Bates, Pasang and I followed closely. Our spirits were
high, but a curious lethargy lay over the party. Perhaps
it was a feeling of defeat, a regret at nearing the end of
our climb, or perhaps altitude was beginning to take
toll. Bates was complaining of stomach trouble, his first
mishap on the entire trip. Our loads were light, under
20 pounds, but progress was very slow.

Not until afternoon did we reach the top of the snow
gully with its tricky ledge leading higher to the top of
the Black Pyramid, where we snatched a quick lunch,

rubbing our feet, which had been numbed by the straps of our climbing irons. Attempts were made to melt some snow on the warm rocks, for we did not carry water on these climbs. The ideal combination, long since worked out, of fruit drops wrapped in snow, did not seem very satisfying to our dry mouths.

Not until 3 o'clock did the entire party reach the top of the Pyramid, and the beginning of the traverse across the 45° ice slope where Petzoldt had cut steps and fixed the pitons in the ice to secure the passage. We found that the sun had melted the ice around the iron spikes, which dangled on the rope, while water filled the holes they had occupied. If House, Bates, and Pasang were to return to Camp VI before dark, they must start at once, so they shed their loads at the beginning of the traverse. This was to be the highest point they reached, about 24,700 feet, and both Petzoldt and I realized what a sacrifice they were making by allowing us to be the two who continued the attack. But there was no time for sentimentalizing. The other three started down and, after a difficult but uneventful passage, arrived in camp just before dark. Petzoldt and I took on extra pounds and relayed the entire camp across the ice traverse, digging in our tent in the deep snow on the far side of the icefall.

The minute the setting sun left us, we became conscious of the intense cold of high altitude, a cold that seemed almost liquid and entered our very bones. We huddled into the tent and the stove was assembled, when to our horror we discovered that the match supply had been left in Camp VI. This was a catastrophe. In my pocket I found four safety matches and five strike-anywhere matches, all of dubious value. The latter, brought all the way from New York, carefully dried in the sun at many of the lower camps, had persistently failed to function well above 20,000 feet, and only with extreme care and preparatory rubbings with grease did they even glow. The safety matches, on the other hand, were made in Kashmir and were very fragile.

Petzoldt struck the first one. It fizzled—and went out. I tried one of the safety matches. It broke off at the head. Petzoldt, in desperation, seized a strike-anywhere match and struck it almost casually. It burst into flame and the stove was lighted.

Only six matches were left, so after supper we melted a great supply of water for the morning. The pot then was wrapped in all our clothing and put under our feet, a device which we had before found effective in preventing water from freezing. We cursed ourselves for forgetting to bring extra matches, and my diary notes say, "This neglect must have been an evidence of altitude effect." Everything else was complete, and as we snuggled into our warm sleepers, each of us wondered about the coming morning.

"I think the weather looks settled," said Paul.

"I'm sure of it," I replied, feeling all the while that

the clouds had looked rather ominous, and wondering if he had the same doubts.

"If only the wind holds off, the cold won't be too bad."

We each thought for a moment about numb fingers and toes on other mornings before the sun reached us.

"Are those matches safe?" from Paul.

"They're here in my sleeper."

"We'd be out of luck with no matches."

Silence.

"Well, tomorrow's the big day. Let's get some sleep."

Chapter XIV
Five Miles High
Charles S. Houston, M.D.

Chapter XIV   Five Miles High

IN the morning we did not stir until the rising sun warmed the tent. It was a perfect day. Three matches were used before one finally lighted our stove and assured us of a warm breakfast. Three matches remained.

We left our tent in order for the return of the two exhausted climbers we were sure to be that evening, and finally donned our climbing irons in the cold, wind-less morning. Our four Shetland sweaters, flannel shirts and the windproof suits with two pairs of light wool mittens and ski gauntlets barely sufficed to keep us from frostbite, even though there was no wind.

Separated by 60 feet of light alpine rope, we began the final stage of the climb. Two hours of steady effort brought us to the point reached two days before, where we rested and took more photographs of the inimitable scenery below. The cloud bank over Turkestan had vanished, but the west wind was still holding its own. Nanga Parbat was clear and we seemed assured of at least one more beautiful day.

Above the shoulder, we were again forced to the east, where we struggled up gentle snow slopes of pe-culiarly variable consistency. For 100 feet the sharp spikes of our climbing irons barely dented the icy crust. Over the next stretch we waded up to our knees in powder snow, and then came patches of frost feathers. These strange structures are formed by winds of high velocity and low temperature which pile masses of fine powder snow into fantastic drifts, some of them hun-dreds of feet long, three or four feet deep, and several feet wide. When one steps on these drifts, a great piece many yards long may break off and slide away; conse-quently one must approach them with circumspection.

On the whole, however, we found the going not too difficult, but gradually, as we were forced more and more toward the east, the snow became deeper and more powdery in the lee of the true shoulder. Progress grew more labored. Soon we came to the foot of a veritable cliff 50–60 feet high, the upper lip of a great crack in the snowfield. It was hopeless to attack this, so we continued along to the east, finally finding a steep narrow snow bridge which led to the upper level.

This was very shaky, and only after some difficulty were we able safely to reach the higher slope, where we floundered in soft powder snow up to our hips. The altitude was beginning to tell. Petzoldt was feeling strong and moving rapidly, but I had a curious weakness in my legs, so that every upward step was an effort requiring several breaths. And yet my mind seemed very clear and active. By 1 o'clock we had reached the top of the great snow field; barely 300 yards away across a gently sloping snow shoulder rose the final cone.

At first glance it seemed difficult, but more detailed inspection convinced us that it was a direct route from the snow field to the summit. Between us and the base of the summit pyramid, however, lay several hundred yards of snow shoulder covered with ice fragments which clearly were remnants of avalanches coming from the great ice cliffs below the summit. We had seen from below such masses of ice break off, and were we to be caught by such a fall, there would be no question of our fate. The distance over which we would be exposed was quite small, however, and there were no difficulties to prevent us from crossing rapidly. Still, it was a hazard, and one which future expeditions must bear in mind. We lunched briefly and rested with almost the whole of the Karakoram well below us. Then we took off the rope and coiled it to dry in the sun while we went a little farther.

Petzoldt, being the fresher, started off sturdily and in a few minutes was out of danger from icefall at the base of the summit cone. I could see him ahead of me working steadily upward, pausing now and then to take bearings. My progress was ludicrously slow. Every inch I gained in altitude was an effort. My legs were so weak I was forced to rest every five or six steps, and soon fatigue made me forget all danger from above. I struggled on— why I do not know, for it was foolish to try to gain a few more feet, and yet something within drove me to go as high as I possibly could. Various thoughts flashed through my mind. Had I ever been so tired before? Would I be less tired with another day of acclimatization at this altitude? Could Bob or Bill have done better?

At last, at the base of the final cone, I could go no farther. Petzoldt was 150 feet above me, working on the rock, as I sat down against a huge boulder. I had reached my limit. Soon I turned back and staggered down to where we had left the rope on the outer end of the shoulder, well beyond reach of avalanches. There I lay in the sun and rested. Petzoldt had stopped and was working in the rocks.

After 15 or 20 minutes of complete rest I counted my pulse. It was 135, whereas normally at sea level it is 50. I thought of all sorts of notes to write in the little book I carried, but somehow had not the mental energy to put them down. Mingled with a deep and heartfelt regret at abandoning the attack, when success seemed within our grasp, was a sense of relief that at last the hard struggle was over and we were free to return to Base Camp and home, with the realization of our job incomplete but nevertheless well done. I tried to look ahead years into the future so as to cement firmly in my mind recollections of these great moments on our mighty peak. There were other emotions too deep to be expressed. I felt that all my previous life had reached a climax in these last hours of intense struggle against nature, and yet nature had been very indulgent. She had scarcely bothered to turn against us the full force of her elements. Indeed, she had favored us with perfect weather and not too difficult conditions, preferring to let our puny bodies exhaust themselves in the rarefied atmosphere. How small indeed we were to struggle so desperately to reach one point on the earth's surface, a point which had been so real a goal to us for many months! I believe in those minutes at 26,000 feet on K2, I reached depths of feeling which I can never reach again.

My musings were interrupted by a shout from Petzoldt who struggled down and collapsed beside me. He too was very tired, though much fresher than I. We had come up from Camp V very rapidly. There had been only three nights of acclimatization above that camp, and we had been working almost continuously under difficult conditions for the past two weeks. He told me after a brief rest that he had found at the very base of the summit pyramid a large flat space which he felt would be an ideal site for a final camp. From what he had seen of the rocks above this platform the climbing would not be so difficult as the Black Pyramid at the top of Abruzzi ridge. He had spent some time in examining it, and was convinced, as was I, that a direct and not too difficult way led from our resting place directly to the top of the mountain. At a little over 26,000 feet he had fixed his camera in the rocks and with the point of his ice ax tripped the shutter and taken a self-portrait, which later turned out to be excellent.

There was no question but that our work was done, and we turned to descend at 4 o'clock with mingled emotions. The whole world was deathly still; not even the clatter of rock falls broke the calm. All the peaks about us seemed breathlessly awaiting our descent. We trudged down to Camp VII in a deepening twilight. About us the mountains turned first pink, then lavender, then purple. We reached camp safely, exhausted and cold, but curiously content.

Our first thought was tea. With infinite care we

waxed one of the matches, dried it as much as possible, and struck it. It fizzled and went out. A safety match broke off at the head. Paul in a gesture of bravado struck our last one. It lit and we were assured of our warm supper. Too tired for much talk, we melted water for the morning, snuggled in our sleeping bags, and drowsed off to a dreamless sleep.

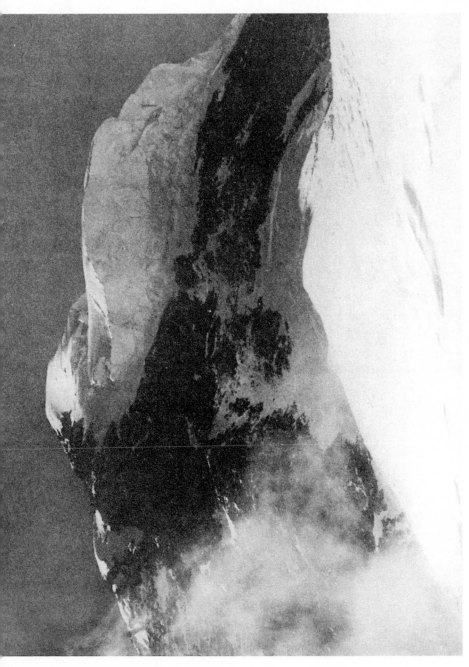

LOOKING

TOWARD THE
SUMMIT
FROM
25,700 FEET

PETZOLDT

ROUTE ON ABRUZZI RIDGE FROM CAMP IV TO HIGH POINT REACHED

Chapter XV

The Retreat

Charles S. Houston, M.D.

Chapter XV   The Retreat

WE slept heavily that night, and in the morning, although there were high clouds in the sky, the weather was still clear and windless. Both of us were disgusted at cold water, crackers and jam for breakfast, but we managed to gulp enough to sustain us for the trip down and rolled up our sleeping bags. There was some discussion as to whether we should leave intact our last stronghold on the mountain, but we finally decided to retreat in full order, and took everything with us across the ice traverse to the top of the Black Pyramid. There we lashed our crampons and a primus stove to one of the pitons we had driven in the rock and started the long, difficult descent to camp. A light, cold wind was blowing up from the south, cold enough to make us fully appreciate how serious even a moderate wind could be. Several hours later, with a last clatter of stones and loud shouts, we descended on the others in a rush.

One look at our faces told the story, but there were many details to be filled in. Bates and House had spent the day before in camp writing letters and diaries, their thoughts several thousand feet higher with us. Their relief at our safe return was obvious. We told them the whole story and were gratified by their congratulations. The Sherpas were equally generous. When, in our broken Hindustani, we told Pasang that we had failed to reach the top, he turned and spoke rapidly to the others. Later we found that he had formed a firm conviction at that moment that K2 could not be climbed, "because the sahibs had not climbed it."

There was no time to be lost. We broke camp rapidly, left a few odds and ends of food firmly tied to the rocks in a duffel bag, and with all our equipment continued down toward Base Camp. The descent was not difficult and we reached Camp V in mid-afternoon, paused there to eat a few of the delicacies which had been left in the cache, and hurried on to Camp IV. The descent of House's Chimney was fully as severe as we had expected. It was not until dark that all of us assembled on the tent platforms built the week before, which now seemed almost spacious after the restricted quarters at Camp VI. When it actually came to climbing down with our heavy loads, we realized that we had not overestimated the difficulties of the descent, and we were glad indeed to have fine weather.

Supper was a gala affair. Somehow one tin of kippered herring had been left at Camp IV, and we had our fill of this unusual treat. The Sherpas were given their share and camp was very happy that evening. The tension and nervous strain of the attack were wearing off and we felt that we were almost safely home again.

Early next morning, we continued the retreat. The high clouds had grown thicker and there was an ominous ring around the sun, which we photographed from all angles, as if to justify our abandonment of the attack. Petzoldt's Gendarme took several hours and we almost lost a load in lowering our packs. Once below this, however, we felt that our last serious difficulty was past. On the glacier below us we now saw three tiny figures moving up to Camp I, and shouted ourselves hoarse, even rolling great boulders down, hoping that they would see us and realize that the attack was over. The figures continued and were lost in the maze of cracks at the foot of the ridge, until soon we saw two tiny tents spring up.

Camp III was reached by noon and after lunch two of us recut the steps across the gully and started down the steep snow slope to prepare the way. We found, to our dismay, that the firm snow had changed to loose granulated spring snow over ice, wet and totally unreliable. Even with several hundred feet of rope securing the first man, it was a precarious business to reach the rocks below, and finally we were forced to slide our packs down the fixed rope on an involved and very unsatisfactory system of pullies. The climbing party came down ignominiously on their bottoms. As the last man reached the rocks, Pasang gave a shout and we looked up in time to see a large boulder hurtling down from high above us. Men leaped in all directions to take cover under projecting rocks, and with a deafening crash the missile burst into fragments in our midst. It was a near escape, for several small, jagged splinters grazed us. Pasang announced that we owed our safety to the snow men, who he said had told him to look up at that moment. Snow men, or no snow men, we were grateful for our escape, feeling that K2 had loosed a parting salvo at us.

We continued on, finding the route completely altered. The snow and ice, which had covered the rock on our ascent, were melting fast. Little rivulets flowed everywhere. Our steps had vanished and we were forced to work our way down the water-smoothed, outward sloping slabs with great care. The afternoon sun grew oppressive and we began to feel the fatigue that comes with the release of nervous tension. On the saddle below the slabs we left our climbing ropes and turned for a last look at the way above us. The route had seemed so difficult, almost impossible, on our first inspection from this point, and now that it had been successfully worked out, it seemed almost easy.

One by one our weary party trickled down the gullies and across the rock traverse to reach Camp II and supper. Once again we filled ourselves with the luxuries left in camp and retired early. The weather, though still clear, was deteriorating. We hoped that we would not be forced to spend the next day stormbound in camp.

Curiously enough, our descent to Camp II, where the air was far richer in oxygen than that we had been used to in the higher camps, gave us by far the most tiring and exhausting day we had had. Climbers have noticed before that coming down from high altitudes to lower ones has a distinctly fatiguing effect which cannot all be caused by release of nervous tension. Whatever the cause, however, we slept to a late hour the next morning, when the weather was definitely cloudy.

No one was very ambitious to start. Breakfast dragged on for hours, with each man sampling different combinations which ranged from honey and oatmeal to sardines and jam. Then we decided that, if we waited long enough, the other party, which surely must have heard us the day before, might come up to help us down.

Sure enough, about 9 o'clock three figures left Camp I and started out. We sat restlessly in camp until noon, when Burdsall, followed by two grinning Sherpas, appeared at the top of the rock chimney leading to Camp II. His relief at finding us all safe was very evident and he seemed delighted that we had climbed so high, rather than depressed that we had not made the top. The Captain, he explained, had a touch of fever, but was coming up to Camp I that day to meet us.

Burdsall had heard our shouts and had seen the avalanches we had sent down, but had not been able to locate us among the rocks. He had been on his way to Windy Gap for more photographs but, realizing that we must be on our way down, had abandoned the idea and come up to help us. It was a grand experience to see him again, to hear his news, and to tell our own. The Sherpas were having a huddle with their stalwart climbers and one by one they too came over to shake our hands and express what we thought must be congratulations.

After a while we managed to drag ourselves away from our last mountain camp and start down to the glacier. I was the last to leave Camp II and looked back on it with real regret. How high and far advanced, how precarious and isolated it had seemed when first we

BURDSALL

BASE CAMP AGAIN

STREATFEILD SURVEYING NEAR GASHERBRUM I

pitched our tents in the cosy hollow. And now that the climb was over, this little snow shoulder seemed only next door to Base Camp. Here we had weathered windy days, our emotions had wavered from high hopes to deep despair, and now we were leaving it, perhaps forever.

On the way down to Camp I, we found the route had changed. All the snow had disappeared. The loose scree and gravel were worse than before, and in one of the gullies the ropes we had fixed had been broken and torn away by rock slides. We had some difficulty crossing the smooth slabs, but finally reached the ledge above Camp I where we took a last look at the tent sites built 30 years before by the Duke of the Abruzzi. We wondered whether the spirits of his great expedition might be lurking about those tent platforms watching our retreat.

Shortly afterward we staggered into Camp I and there found the Captain, in his red windproof suit, grinning from ear to ear, happiness written all over his face. The party was united again, all well, all happy. The Captain with great foresight had prepared huge pots of steaming cocoa, and again we talked continuously with our mouths full. First came tales of the higher camps, of the storms, of the difficulties on the rocks, and of our last climb. Questions flew back and forth, but there was hardly time to hear much from Burdsall and the Captain.

We packed up light loads and started for Base Camp. The Captain and I swung off ahead at a good clip, which did not last long, and the others drifted along behind. The glacier route had changed surprisingly little, save that most of the frozen lakes and rivers had melted and we fell in knee-deep many times. Late in the afternoon the party straggled into Base Camp to be warmly greeted by Ghaffar Sheikh, Ahdoo, and the coolie, who seemed almost as glad to see us safely back as we were to be with them. Then we appreciated the frugality which at Camp I three weeks previously had preserved full half of the bottle of Hudson Bay Demerara Rum already mentioned. This potent spirit, brought from Fairbanks, Alaska, to New York by my father, had made the arduous journey to Base Camp wrapped carefully in sweaters and underwear, and was now serving its intended purpose to the full. Two tablespoonfuls of this 150-proof nectar in a mug of hot water and sugar almost restored our weary bodies.

We looked at each other curiously, for the first time realizing the strain and tension which were apparent on our sun-blackened and bearded faces. During our three weeks above Base Camp our arms and legs had grown very thin, but not till now did we realize how much weight we had lost. None of us could do more than lie happily on the warm dry rocks of Base Camp, enjoying to the full the flatness and the roominess of that previously desolate rock. No one who has not spent weeks

living on steep slopes where home is a six by four platform precariously perched on a sliding base can savor to
the full the joy of returning to a land where there is
room to move about freely, where boots, cups, air mattresses do not slide away into an abyss when put aside,
and where one can walk about at ease without being
roped to another man. For over two weeks we had never
gone more than 10 feet from camp without being roped
together.

Here was running water in large amounts, and we
could drink again from streams and not from scanty
remnants in a dirty pot with bits of lint and feathers
and gravel in the bottom of it. Base Camp, indeed,
seemed heaven, and our party was a joyous and understanding one. In the evening the Sherpas were treated
to a taste of our small supply of spirits, and far into the
night we heard them singing and talking.

At bedtime came another treat—the joy of having an
entire tent for oneself and one's possessions. Each tent,
which had been so cramped two months previously,
now seemed as big as a cathedral; and the pleasure of
tossing about freely without one's companion saying,
"Take your feet out of my face," was a major pleasure.
We slept long and soundly, lulled by trickling water, a
sound we had not heard at night for many weeks.

Being waked in the morning by the familiar sound
of Ghaffar Sheikh's police whistle was now a pleasure
for the first time, and we assembled for breakfast with

real appreciation. There was an omelet of a dozen eggs, a great luxury after many eggless mornings. We had no dishes to wash and water was to be had in abundance. After eating we lolled happily around the Base Camp in the sunlight, sharing our experiences with each other. Bates had a brilliant idea and disappeared shortly to hold a consultation with Ghaffar Sheikh. In half an hour we heard shouts of glee and looked out to find him reveling in the Captain's bathtub full of hot water. The idea was contagious and gallons and gallons of icy glacier water were heated with the last of our gasoline. What a pleasure to shed our woolens for the first time in three weeks, to scrub all over with warm, soapy water, and to put on our low-altitude clothes.

Petzoldt relaxed on an air mattress and read *Blackwood's Magazine*. Burdsall gathered up the butterfly net, his field glasses and notebooks and started off determinedly in search of those butterflies which we had promised to collect for a museum at home. The idea of finding any butterflies at 16,000 feet was a funny one, and he returned empty handed in a short while. We then gave the net to the Sherpas, who considered this a great honor and an exciting novelty and pursued each other about the rocky moraines with shrieks of glee. They returned with two spiders and a torn net. The spiders were religiously added to our scientific collection, which now consisted of two dead birds found by Burdsall, a number of weary looking flowers collected as high as 18,500 feet, some notebooks of undecipherable altitude figures, and an unused blood counting chamber. The Captain, however, had calculated a great many triangulation figures from which he was later able to correct and add to the existing map. This survey work was really valuable and proved to be our only scientific accomplishment.

There was sporadic photography during the day. The Sherpas settled down to a curious game, played with stones and bits of wood on a board somewhat like a chessboard. They succeeded in losing large numbers of fruit drops and cigarettes to each other, and perhaps it was fortunate that none of us learned to play. About 3 o'clock the Captain remarked, "Wouldn't it be lucky if the coolies arrived this afternoon?" He had hardly spoken when as if by signal we heard loud shouts, and many ragged figures clattered over the stones into camp. When the coolies left us on June 12 we had given them 45 stones, telling them to throw one away each day and return for us when all were gone. Making due allowance for carelessness and accidents of children's games, we hoped they would come within a week of July 26. To have them arrive almost on the date seemed incredible.

The influx of new faces brought new life. As each of us looked about to greet his old friends, Karim appeared with his cheery, "Good morning, sar. Thank you, sar." Hussein Ali and all the others were there grinning from ear to ear, but alas, there was no mail. The mail had not arrived in Askole when the coolies left, so we would have to restrain our impatience for another week.

The afternoon passed quickly in a flurry of packing, sorting, and discarding. Many things were thrown away in a great rubbish heap, but after we realized that the pile grew no larger, we examined the packs of our coolies and found that they were treasuring each scrap of paper, each old tin can, each broken shoe lace. All our discards had to be reassembled and taken far from camp and dropped into a deep crack, for otherwise their loads would have been too heavy to carry. Before supper we again heard the familiar arguments, shouts and screams which signified that the Captain was assigning packs, but now the sound was welcome rather than annoying. We dined in state, not wisely but too well, for the blessed coolies had brought four weakly protesting chickens, a multitude of eggs, and some battered onions.

We spent the evening quietly and sadly. Each one of us stole off at intervals to stand alone a short distance from camp drinking in for the last time the majesty and beauty of our surroundings. Our eyes as well as our thoughts turned to the high summit above us, now wreathed in thin, swirling mists. After so many weeks of hopes and fears, of hard work, of disappointment and success, we hated to leave the barren waste of the glacier.

Chapter XVI

Ice and Angles

Richard L. Burdsall

Chapter XVI   Ice and Angles

LOOKING out of the tent ventilator at dawn on July 12, I was surprised to see blue sky instead of the storm which had threatened and actually begun last evening. Today Bates and House were to move up to Camp III with Phinsoo. In order to save weight, Bates' air mattress had been taken up the day before, so he and I had slept on one placed crossways. It was not bad, but we agreed that a hard-working climber is entitled to the luxury of a whole air mattress, especially as ours were short anyway.

Pempa and I had not descended far below Camp II when he cried out "Captain Sahib," and sure enough down on the glacier were three figures ascending from the Base Camp. While we lunched at Camp I, I apprized the Captain of the situation above. With one more set of loads from the Base, the four sahibs with their three Sherpas would be equipped to go as high as time and high-altitude supplies would permit, provided that bad weather or the mountain itself did not stop them. Meanwhile there were two things we could do—first, try to find out a little more about the northeast ridge, for the benefit of future parties should the present route prove impossible; second, do some survey work which the Captain had been asked to do by the Survey of India.

I tore open and scanned a few of the letters he had brought. The latest from home was dated May 24, and how good it was to read that all were well! But we must get on down the glacier, and the trip to Base Camp was made at a rapid pace. Not finding fuel at the French camp, he had sent Ahdoo and Kitar to Askole. They met Ghaffar Sheikh just starting back, so the shikari returned to town with them for more coolies. They brought 10 (8 to carry firewood), and the stack of this fine cedar, cut at Paiju, gave the Base Camp a most comfortable appearance. Our coolie, Sultana, was missing, a bad foot having kept him in Askole, and Ahdoo was reduced to the hardship of cooking for himself as well as for us.

When it grew too dark to continue reading the letters over again, the Captain entertained me with tales of his experiences during the past year while engaged in guerrilla warfare in Waziristan. He told of the many problems involved, and of road work and other projects being carried out in an endeavor to change the customs of wild tribesmen, who have always been wont to eke out a meager living by raids upon the inhabitants of richer lowland countries.

With supplies for the climbers and for our trip to the northeast, we returned with the three Sherpas to Camp I. Shouts were heard above and our porters soon spied the climbers above Camp III. Just before dark as we lay in our sleeping bags came the swish of pinions low over the tent, undoubtedly the passage of a raven, for we had seen these great birds almost daily. What could they live on in this waste of rock and ice? A few insects were about, but not enough to nourish a raven. Life here must be hard for any creature, yet I saw a mouse at the Base Camp and the delicate tracks of others on the snow near it. One day while Bates and I were resting on the way up to Camp II we watched a huge lammergeier soaring over the glacier below. What could it be looking for? Perhaps, like two Englishmen whom Ghaffar Sheikh had met at Urdukas, it had just come up to see the mountains.

Early next morning, July 14, there was shouting from above and we made out two men descending from Camp III; they looked like House and Phinsoo. We discussed climbing to Camp II, but there were only three loads to carry up, so we lazily decided to send them and a note with the Sherpas, saying that, if we could do nothing more to help, we would go to the northeast spur. Each seated on a cracker box with a fuel drum for a table, we enjoyed a game of chess, disturbed from time to time by the distant whir of a rock coming down from K2. The Sherpas returned with a damaged Meade tent, reported that it was "Bara Sahib" (Houston) and Tse Tendrup we had seen, and handed us the following letter:

Dear Capt & Dick
Had hoped you would come up today for there is much to talk over.
(1) Route from III to IV is quite hard—worse than II to III. Climbing it one has to knock down stones, and we have put big holes in 3 tents, the worst of which we are sending down, and taking the Meade from II. On account of this danger we are leaving nothing at III, but taking all up to IV, so it is necessary that II should have at least one tent & food etc.
(2) Camp IV is at the base of the big red buttress which is level with the base of the pyramid. Bob & Bill are reconnoitering to V today, and we shall move

all the Sherpas and us up there tomorrow. Then Paul
& I will establish V & look for a route to VI. The
climbing has been throughout very hard, but we
have 15 days' food for all & should be able to last a
storm.

(3) We are all set for anything now—all well & fit, &
only wish we had more time. If the weather holds as it
has, we shall go to the last gasp, and will not be at the
base until July 26. Unless we come down earlier you
might send up to I and II all the available carrying
power on July 25 or 26 as we will try to make only
one relay down. We will go as long as we can before
stopping. Gas is very plentiful as is all food.

(4) We're keeping the bottle & sending down the
large can, because we need all the bottles (for gas).

(5) We will not count on a sleeper at Camp I [II]
and are sending it down, for it is much more vital
to have 2 Woods at I.

(6) We will count on gas, *some food, and 2 sleepers*
at I, no tent or stove. O.K.?

Nothing more except very very best luck to you on
N.E. We'll be very careful, and unless passage is impossible will reach Base on nite of 26th.

Will be damn glad to see you one of these days &
hope all goes well.

Chas.

During our day at Camp I, I kept a log of all avalanches from 8:15 A. M. to 7:30 P. M. and recorded 19,
an average of 1 every 35 minutes; 15 of these were from
Broad Peak, most of them coming down the northeast
side. The log stops at 7:30, for ordinary avalanches or

cracking of the glacier near the tents no longer awakened us, but we *were* aroused by a large fall of snow and rock ten minutes before midnight.

With camp gear and food for a week, rather heavy loads, we left with our three Sherpas, Sonam, Pempa and Kitar, and traveled northward, working out a new route along the eastern side to avoid *serac* falls from K2, which come almost across the Godwin-Austen Glacier at some points. A mile above Camp I the glacier was humped as it came over a rise and was broken by enormous crevasses running clear across, their western ends being curved toward the south. Considerable zigzagging was required to get across these, but we finally won through to the smooth snow of the upper glacier. We stopped at the foot of the northeast spur where the Captain and Houston had camped before.

This was where Houston had later heard the spirit voice or "snow man." Now we heard it too—a weird call, half human in quality, coming from away up on the ice ridge. The Sherpas nodded gravely but did not seem unduly alarmed. What could it be? A black bird soared over the ridge but disappeared too high to be identified. I had suspected a raven, but the call was too high pitched; it may have been a chough, though far be it from me to pit this slight evidence against the many reports which make the existence of the "snow man" almost as certain as that of the sea serpent.

Tonight the moon was nearly full, with Jupiter close by, and the brighter stars burned steadily. Skyang Kangri and other mountains stood pale and wan in the unearthly light, while away up above a cloud floated a cold white apparition, the summit of K2. Back in the comfort of my sleeping bag, I lay dreaming of that awe-inspiring sight outside, one I shall see in my dreams in years to come.

July 16 was cloudy. We packed up our Meade tent and supplies and started up with the Sherpas, all of us carrying light loads, our aim being to pitch a camp about 1200 feet up the spur and let the Sherpas return to their tent on the glacier. Next day we would climb as high as possible, perhaps even reach the 22,379-foot pinnacle and so obtain a view of the knife arête to discover whether the towers can be turned to the north. Our route would lead up a snow gully at the very end of the spur, up which Houston and the Captain had easily kicked steps on June 26. We found the snow hard and, not having crampons, were forced to cut steps. Higher up it turned to ice so, after climbing 200–300 feet, we came to the conclusion that it would hardly be safe to send the Sherpas down alone and reluctantly turned back, bad weather strengthening our decision. When we reached camp it was snowing and the ridge toward which we had climbed was hidden; but it was still early, so we decided to go up to Windy Gap at the head of the Godwin-Austen, taking only Kitar with us on the rope as an extra precaution against falling into a crevasse.

The climb was longer than we had anticipated, but easy, the only obstacle being a covered *bergschrund.* The pass itself was a sharp ridge of bare rock. Here we stood on the continental divide which separates the Indus Basin from that of the Yarkand River. The north side of the pass is steep and would be very difficult to reach from the Skyang Lungpa Glacier which lay thousands of feet below us. The tops of the mountains rising on the other side of this glacier were hidden, their bases alone being visible. As we looked back down the Godwin-Austen, Masherbrum 25 miles to the southwest presented a splendid sight rising above the mountains at the lower end of the valley, framed on the right by the walls of K2 and on the left by those of Broad Peak. On a clear day the view from Windy Gap must be glorious, and we lingered for an hour vainly waiting for the clouds to lift from K2.

Back at camp we studied the summit cone through field glasses as it became partially unveiled. The left or southern edge never cleared but the right one did and appeared to us unclimbable. If this is true, the northeast route, even if the knife ridge could be traversed, would lead to an unfavorable position on the shoulder. Unless the ridge could be crossed and the ascent made on the north face, there would have to be a traverse to the south edge of the shoulder, beneath the enormous, hanging ice fields of the summit cone. This passage seemed to us unjustifiable.

Snow fell during the night and in the morning only the lower portions of the surrounding mountains could be seen. Had it been clear we would have climbed up to the pass again for photographs, but in this weather decided to return to Base Camp lest another day be wasted. Wands, placed on the way up, enabled us to get through the crevassed area easily and mid-afternoon found us at our destination. The lower part of the glacier was melting rapidly and there were many pools and streams of running water. At Camp I we picked up the damaged Meade tent and now set Ahdoo and Ghaffar Sheikh to work with needles and thread mending it, a task which they accomplished quickly and neatly.

A day was devoted to preparation for the survey trip. In a crack of the cliff at the base of The Angelus, I placed a minimum registering thermometer of the United States Weather Bureau pattern, taking a photo and sketch of the location to present to the next expedition to visit K2.

July 19 dawned clear and mild, the temperature being 40°F. at 7 o'clock. With our three Sherpas we went down to Concordia, where we selected a campsite beside a little stream, and after lunch I climbed a crest of the moraine and took a complete round of photographs. Seated on a large rock I drank in the stupendous panorama, feeling like an art lover who sees for the first time the great original works whose reproductions he has studied. Sit with me for a moment here in the heart of the Great Karakoram, under a cloudless sky, surrounded by some of the world's highest mountains.

Ridges of snow and rock moraine extend northward for six miles up the Godwin-Austen Glacier to K2, perfectly framed at the head of the valley. At the right of its base the upper Godwin-Austen flows in, a mass of ice pinnacles, while from the left comes the end of the Savoia Glacier. The pyramid of K2 rises boldly against the clear blue sky; down its face the de Filippi Glacier tumbles, while the rest of the surface is equally divided between stern, bare rock and snow-filled gullies and terraces. The slanting afternoon light throws into strong relief the complex multitude of ridges. To the extreme right is the reddish buttress at whose base Camp IV is situated. It is only a start on the climb, and now, better than ever before, we see how great is the task of scaling the thousands of feet above this high camp.

At the left of K2, connected by a ridge, rises the immaculate snowy cone of The Angelus, its left edge shining in the sunlight, its summit rising half as high as K2. To the right is the rounded dome of Broad Peak with a long broken ridge sloping southward. From the end of this a glacier comes down toward us in two icefalls, separated by a jagged cone of gray marble. The ridges and cliffs above are also of marble. Continuing to the right, we see, due east, a dark rock mountain with a rounded peak at the right and a sharp marble one at the left. To the right of this rises a snow-clad mountain with three summits, the middle one like a clenched fist pointing upward, the thumb projecting beyond the knuckles. These mountains hide the higher Gasherbrum peaks beyond them. A needle of rock, rising from a ridge, is directly in front of the snowy Golden Throne, but leaves one arm of that great white chair in view. Bride Peak and other mountains to the south are also entirely covered with snow.

The upper Baltoro Glacier stretches away toward them, a vast waste of hills of rock, some dark and some light-gray marble, while in between masses of snow and ice gleam dully. Beyond it a great expanse of snow rises to the Kondus Saddle, with a curious flat-topped knob on the sky line. To the right is Chogolisa or Bride Peak, with a broad summit, the right side being higher. The river of ice flowing in between Bride and Mitre Peaks is the Vigne Glacier. Mitre Peak is black schist with a precipitous snowfield at its wedge-shaped summit. The Baltoro Glacier, coming from the south, sweeps around its base and out to the west. Looking down this tremendous reach of moraine, we see it lined on both sides with needles and peaks of rock, partly snow covered, and at the end, 25 miles away, the splendid pinnacles of the Paiju Peaks, now turning a hazy blue as the sun descends. Hard by at the northwest towers a black mass, with white marble rising from its top, giving it the name Marble Peak. A striking formation, it marks the junction of the Godwin-Austen Glacier with the Baltoro. Up the left side of the Godwin-Austen are snow and rock peaks, and we are back again to the climax of the panorama, the snow-white Angelus and the great majestic pyramid of K2.

The Captain called me to come down to camp for supper. I left reluctantly, yet gladly too, for I was hungry and the Captain is a good cook. As we ate our fried salmon, onions and stewed apricots, the sun dropped behind Marble Peak and the temperature dropped with it so that we needed sweaters at once; and as soon as the meal was over and dishes washed, we were glad to enter the tent and get into our sleeping bags. The Captain had furnished a few current, or past current, periodicals for the expedition, and now he read his always popular *Blackwood's Magazine,* which I had finished, while I looked over an ancient copy of his *Weekly London Times* and read about the new road being built from Mandalay to Yunnanfu.

Another cloudless day favored the start of our survey work. The Captain's object was to fix the location and measure the altitudes of some high mountains in the region southwest of Mitre Peak. To do this it would be necessary to take observations from widely separated points or "stations," and for today's work we had to cross Concordia. If a city of stone skyscrapers were

totally demolished by an earthquake, the resulting hills
of rock, though smaller, might bear some resemblance
to the terrain we were traveling over. The debris however would be more stable, for on a glacier the rocks
rest on ice and are often ready to slide with the weight
of a foot; in fact they sometimes slide of their own ac-
cord. There were odd stones of different colors, green,
yellow, red, many glistening with particles of mica, and
we picked up a few fragments of beautiful rose quartz.
A stream blocked our way and we had to follow it until
we came to a snow bridge. These glacial streams are of
beautiful clear water, with ice sides often deeply un-
dercut. About three miles from camp a position was
reached which gave a clear view up the Vigne Glacier
to the unknown peaks, so the Captain set up his plane
table and took the required sights, while I entered the
data in his notebook.

The plane table is simply a drawing board mounted
on a tripod, with adjusting screws, by which it can be
leveled. On the table is tacked a work sheet, in our case
a Survey of India map of the region. When the table has
been exactly oriented, by a somewhat technical procedure a point can be fixed on the map which will be
the true location of the table. By means of the alidade, a
ruler having vertical strips at each end with slits to sight
through (some have telescopes), a line can now be
drawn on the map to show the direction of any object
sighted—an unknown mountain top for example. Later,

with the table set up at another station, a line can be drawn from that point toward the same mountain, and the intersection of the two lines will fix its location. By scaling on the map the distance to the mountain and measuring, by means of an instrument placed on the table, the vertical angle to the summit, its altitude above the table can be computed. The altitude of the table is found by scaling the distances and measuring the vertical angles to peaks whose altitudes are already known. Thus a new mountain is placed upon the map and its elevation above sea level determined.

On the way back to camp we found the stream twice as large as in the morning, but fortunately the snow bridge was still intact.

Another clear day enabled us to complete the survey by traveling four miles westward down the Baltoro to points from which we could look through gaps to the unknown peaks. Three stations were established during the day and it was 4 o'clock when two tired surveyors got back to their tiny green tent, almost lost among a million boulders.

Our Sherpas arrived early next morning and we returned to Base Camp, working two survey stations on the way. There had been no news from the climbers. During our three days at Concordia we had scanned the mountain many times through field glasses, hoping to pick up moving specks on some high snow field, but it was in vain and we could only speculate on their progress.

"Do you think there is any chance of their making it?"

"I don't see how they can possibly do it; and yet it will take a lot to stop them."

If the weather remained clear I wanted to go to the upper Godwin-Austen again to take some clear photos of K2 from the northeast. The Captain wanted to work on his survey data, so we decided that I would take Sonam and Pempa to Camp I the next day, and, not having loads to carry, perhaps be able to reach Windy Gap before having to return. The Captain and Kitar would come up to Camp I and on the 25th we would all climb to Camp II and help pack the loads down. The Captain was afraid the others might abandon some of the tents and *dekshis* (cooking pots) on the mountain, which would deprive us of luxury and epicurean delights on the return journey.

July 23 dawned clear, but soon clouds formed around the summits of K2 and Broad Peak, auguring ill for the morrow. When I reached Camp I with the two Sherpas, we heard shouts from above on the mountain, and at frequent intervals a rock would come down with a loud whir like a gigantic bumblebee. Through the glasses I could occasionally see one as it appeared against a patch of snow away up above Camp III, and could follow its descent in tremendous thousand-foot bounds until it came to rest, usually in a snow gully a quarter of a mile away. They made a sickening sound in their leaps through the air, and loud crashes as they struck ribs of rock on the way down.

The stones showed that the climbers were descending from Camp IV, but it was some time before the first man appeared on the rocks to the left of Camp III. They came at intervals until finally all seven were accounted for, starting down from Camp III. I could hardly wait to hear their story, and of course decided to climb to meet them next day, instead of going toward Windy Gap. I shared my field glasses with the Sherpas and we took turns following their progress down the mountain. The route is visible from Camp III to the col about halfway down to Camp II. Soon after 4 o'clock a shout announced the arrival of the first at Camp II. We could see him on the snow ridge there and greeted him with answering yells.

Next morning we got an early start for Camp II, leaving a note for the Captain. Pempa's eyes were troubling him a little, due to too long use of my field glasses yesterday, but the dull overcast weather favored him, all the mountains being hidden. The condition of the route had changed greatly since our last descent over it 11 days before. The snow in the lower gullies had hardened so that it was necessary to cut steps in places; much of the snow had gone from the upper part, making it easier in some spots and more difficult in others; a length of fixed rope which had stretched across some slabs had been cut in two by a falling rock. It began to snow a little as we climbed the last gully and swung over the rib of rock above Camp II.

How fine it was to look down into the camp and see everybody safe and well! We shook hands all around, Sherpas and sahibs, and in answer to my eager question they replied that they had reached 26,000 feet.

"You know that rock cliff below the final snow cone?" explained Petzoldt, "Well we were on that."

K2 was still unconquered, but they had forced a route to the top of the Abruzzi ridge and to the base of the summit cone, a wonderful achievement!

Chapter XVII
Return to Plenty
Richard L. Burdsall

Chapter XVII   Return to Plenty

WE were up before dawn on a cold, raw morning, July 26. Clouds hid the surrounding mountains and a chilly wind sped our departure as we climbed out of the shallow depression on the moraine, leaving the site of our Base Camp as bleak and inhospitable as we had found it. Movement of the glacier would soon destroy all traces of our occupancy.

We were traveling light and there were no long faces as we chose our route down a central stretch of ice, broken into rough little paths. Secret thoughts of what might have been would return to haunt us, but now our minds were drawn toward a sunnier clime. Drunk with unaccustomed oxygen, the men who had come down from the heights felt somewhat queer as their bodies and numbed toes began to readjust themselves.

After a few miles we were forced off the ice onto the rocks. At Concordia we paused hoping for a farewell view, but K2 had wrapped her mantle of cloud about her and gave us only a few glimpses as she drew it tighter. She was as indifferent to our going as she had been to our arrival six weeks before.

On the bare moraine we picked up a Forrest snow finch (*Leucosticte nemoricola altaica.*) The little body was dried and well preserved. It now lies in state in a steel case of the Museum of Natural History in New York. Surface melting of the Godwin-Austen Glacier had revealed the remains of numerous birds. Two could be identified, the foot of a coot and the wing of a pintail duck, both picked up between Camp I and the Base Camp. These brave migrants had perished on their journey across the high divide to nesting lakes on the northern plains.

Lunch was a welcome rest and the march afterward seemed long. The Captain had been surveying on the north side of the glacier and now found himself with his two Sherpas cut off from us by a large glacial stream. After vainly trying to cross at several points, he managed it in this way: A climbing rope was thrown across and made fast around a big rock on his side and a great lump of ice on ours. He made a loop of rope to sit in and clipped it by a karabiner to the suspended rope. To his waist he tied a rope thrown over from our side, and another which he gave his Sherpas to pay out as we hauled him over. The rope sagged but he managed to keep clear of the icy water and was quickly over. The Sherpas had demurred, but after seeing it done, they pulled the karabiner back and followed in turn. The performance was as good as a circus to our grinning Baltis who formed a gallery on the bank above.

We camped here and after the tents were pitched we sat gazing up the Biange Glacier toward the famous Muztagh Tower. Parts of it broke through the clouds from time to time, enthralling us with hidden grandeur.

As we turned in for the night we chuckled over an amusing incident. Houston had discarded a little bag of what looked like powdered milk. The Sherpas found it and put some in their tea, when a bitter taste caused them to rush up in alarm asking if they had been poisoned. Investigation proved that they had used some of Petzoldt's tooth powder!

We were up again at 5 and away at 6. In an hour or two we had to recross the Captain's stream, now larger and flowing in a deep gorge with walls and bed of blue ice. It was spanned by a bridge melted to a thin shell, which the coolies did not like and crossed as if walking on eggshells.

For a while we followed down a ridge of light-colored moraine, the best traveling on the whole Baltoro Glacier, passing once more the fleet of ice ships, evidently becalmed here all summer.

House had planned to enrich science with a collection of butterflies. We had seen two at 20,000 feet, near Windy Gap, and several near the Base Camp, but our nets had been wielded in vain. Now the Sherpas were given a try, Sonam and Pempa grinning as they trudged along each carrying a net. In the afternoon they came upon Ahdoo laughing at them; he had captured the first butterfly in his hat.

The moraine here broke up into a horrible maze of hills, troughs and holes where we passed three glacier tables with rocks 20–30 feet long. After hours of toil we heaved sighs of relief as we descended from the moraine and climbed onto the grass at Urdukas. Here were flowers—dandelions, buttercups, fireweed, purple asters and many others. The Captain, who had arrived earlier, had seen two ibex. Red finches flew about, and during supper we saw on a near-by rock a little animal which was probably a cony.

When we walked upon grass, after weeks on rock and snow, we had somewhat the feeling of a sailor who sets foot on firm land after a long and stormy voyage. One

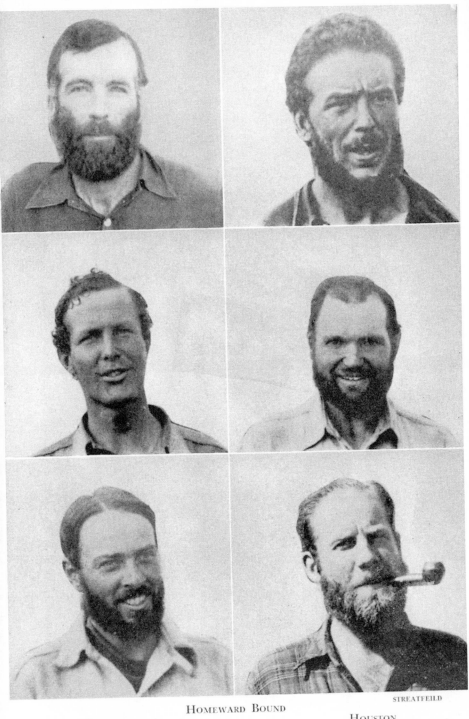

HOMEWARD BOUND

STREATFEILD
HOUSE
BATES

HOUSTON
BURDSALL
PETZOLDT

STILL UNCONQUERED

reward of such an expedition is the ability it gives one
to find enjoyment in the simplest things of life, those
which we take for granted to such an extent that we
lose the faculty of deriving pleasure from them. As we
lay in delightful relaxation on the grass, the little living
things about us seemed to welcome us back to a normal
existence.

Among them were house flies, which were trouble-
some for the first time. There had been a very few at
Base Camp and we even saw one near the northeast
spur. Their altitude record was surpassed by a flea that
got up to Camp II. It seemed unwilling to go higher for
with three ungrateful hops it left the arm of the sahib
who had carried it up. I trust it found its way out of the
tent and with more jumps and glissades reached the
glacier safely. Braver mountaineers were the little black
spiders that seemed very much at home at high altitudes on K2.

With light hearts we left Urdukas, for a double
march would take us off the unpleasant glacier. Its surface had changed and some of us were glad to follow
sturdy Rose Ali who led the column of coolies back
over the intricate route by which they had come. At
one point access to the south bank was blocked by an
ice cliff which had collapsed. Sahibs and coolies carefully picked their way around great blocks, some of
which tilted precariously above their heads. After an
exhausting journey up and down the hills of rock we at

last descended the snout of the glacier and stood on the river plain. We paused to look back with satisfaction at the black wall of ice and rock stretching for two miles across the valley.

Two more weary miles brought us to our camping place at Paiju. At Urdukas we had come to our first grass; here we came to the first trees, and it was very pleasant to sit beneath them drinking our tea. The Biaho, swollen by melting ice and snow, had flooded most of the area and covered several bags of *atta* which the coolies had left there. Fortunately they were able to fish out the sodden mass and no one went hungry.

A morning's fast march brought us to Bardumal, our camping place on the way in, where we now stopped for a lunch glorified by tea. Our somewhat precarious route had led along a clay cliff, high above the river. A photo of our porters rounding a shoulder, when compared with a photo taken at the same point by the French Expedition, shows the surprising permanence of this clay. Stones imbedded in it had not fallen out during the interval of two years.

The Dumordo River, flowing down from the Punmah Glacier, which we had forded with some difficulty on the way in, was now several times wider and deeper. This necessitated a rough, three-mile trip up its valley to a rope bridge. From our campsite, before reaching the bridge, we looked back across the Biaho to Mango Gusor dominating the valley, with its white tooth rising 8000 feet above us. Our return trip was being made with a peace of mind sometimes lacking on our journey in, when we were fearful of delays; we could smile at these feelings today as we passed Gurrah, the scene of a strike by our porters. The bridge next morning was not difficult and we were soon back to the Biaho River again, passing through a cold rainstorm on the way.

"Good road, Master," said Ghaffar Sheikh, pointing to a cliff whose base was lapped by waves of the dark-gray river. One would have said that no route could exist there; but he was right, for the strata dipped inward, forming many little ledges, which, though narrow, gave good footing and safe handholds. Soon we were on the dead moraine of the Biafo Glacier. From a pool I flushed a white-tailed sandpiper, which flew up with shrill whistles. A flock of large swifts flew by, probably the Alpine swift. We had to climb up onto the snout of the glacier to get across the river flowing out from under it. While eating lunch beyond, we watched a pair of crag martins nesting on a cliff above, possibly a second brood.

The remainder of the march was a pleasant walk with rapidly increasing signs of civilization—irrigation canals, fields of grain, crows and magpies and house sparrows. Passing two old forts, we entered Askole, where our wild appearance terrified the women and children; they fled before us in great alarm, leaving an almost empty street through which we paraded to our former camping place. Somewhat reassured, the people now gathered about and stood looking at us from the other side of the thorn-topped wall. Askole, which on the way in had impressed us as the most remote little village on earth, now seemed like a veritable metropolis. We found mail and other good things, including a sheep, the first fresh meat we had tasted in weeks.

As Houston had stopped here with Petzoldt for three days in May, the town had become a real medical center. Learning of our return, the people had come for miles to receive treatment. Many of their ailments were beyond the power of pills or minor surgery, but no one was turned away and all received what help he could give them. Who knows but it proved far more effective than seemed possible?

At Askole we crossed the Braldu on our last and longest rope bridge, a span of over 100 yards, and left the river to take advantage of a short cut over the Skoro La (16,644 feet), a pass blocked by snow earlier in the season. On our long climb out of the valley we paused frequently to look back over Askole and the end of the Biafo Glacier, which we had crossed the day before. After lunch we came to a high shepherds' village, picturesque among huge boulders. We continued for several miles along rolling slopes covered with lovely flowers and camped early beside a spring. The three Kashmiri and two of the sahibs spent a bad night because of a digestive revolution variously blamed on bad meat, bad water, and bad eggs, but probably due to too much good eating.

August 1 dawned raw and cloudy. Our route—the path had ended—lay along a grass slope, then onto moraine deposited by three small glaciers. The mountain tops were hidden in cloud and it began to snow hard. It was well that Rose Ali knew the way and led us up the proper glacier. The climb to the pass was long and rather steep. It seemed strange to be crossing crevasses again, for we thought we had finished with glacier work. The pass was spectacular, a sharp rock crest between two huge gendarmes. The last few feet were bare of snow, though flakes were still falling.

Looking down the other side, we saw a steep rock slope descending to a gorge, with a stream leading into a narrow crooked valley. Away in the distance was the Shigar River, with trees on the far side indicating a village. The slope was white with snow part way down, but below was green grass which looked most inviting.

Our lunch in the shelter of a huge rock was rudely interrupted by a near catastrophe. The coolies, following us down from the pass, dislodged a boulder weighing half a ton, which came bounding down the gully beside us. At the last moment, instead of passing clear, it took a bound in our direction, crushing the pack frame from which Tse Tendrup had just removed the lunch. Had the coolies come a few minutes earlier we should have been without our food.

After this interlude we scrambled down 4000 feet of steep grass slope. While resting on a shoulder I watched two huge vultures, Himalayan griffons, soar by, turning their naked heads from side to side. Here we found quantities of wild rhubarb and gathered a supply which proved excellent. Later we camped on the floor of the nullah. We had descended 5000 feet from the pass, and agreed that this long steep climb would make a crossing of the Skoro La in the opposite direction much more difficult.

A fine morning found us on our way before 6 o'clock. The path was a little rough and tried our patience by climbing a considerable distance before dropping steeply into the Skoro Nullah. There followed a lovely trip down this narrow gorge whose cool depth protected us from the sun's heat. We had to cross the stream many times, the passages becoming more difficult as the volume of water increased. Finally we came out into open country and found ourselves in the Shigar Valley, back on our old road.

The walk down to Shigar along a lane shaded by great poplars was delightful. Apricot trees were loaded with delicious fruit and despite Ahdoo's warning we were tempted to eat too many. To the Sherpas each tree presented a golden opportunity and they stuffed themselves and their pockets to the bursting point; but soon even their limit was reached and they were forced to pass on with puzzled, longing looks, unable to profit further from this abundance. Everywhere natives were harvesting the apricots, shaking the trees and gathering them in large baskets. In all the little villages, the flat roofs of houses were piled with the drying fruit, which is an important article of food. Apricots and their kernels, which are used for flavoring, are the principal exports from Baltistan.

Everywhere wheat fields were yellow; some of the grain had been cut and was being threshed on hard clay floors. From four to seven black oxen were bound side by side and driven around a stake in the center. On other floors, following this operation, men were tossing the wheat into the air with long-handled forks to let the wind blow the chaff away. A young English-speaking revenue officer, whom I met later, told me that local appraisers have to list the size of each field and the crop grown. His duty was to check up on these men to see that they were impartial.

We reached Shigar at 1:30 and camped once more on the polo field. While we were eagerly reading letters from home which we found awaiting us, the fine old Munshi arrived with his little son and the young Rajah of Shigar. Two servants followed, bearing platters of apricots. These were placed on the ground and we all sat around enjoying them and carrying on a limited conversation with the Munshi, who knew a few words of English. The Captain returned with two missionaries, the first white men we had seen for months. General Frost of the Indian Army (retired) and Dr. Gilbert, a young medical man, were both enthusiastic evangelists. We found them charming company.

The Munshi fulfilled a hope we had been cherishing for weeks by again inviting us all to his house for tea. It came up to our highest expectations and despite our feasting on apricots most of the day we did full justice to the cinnamon tea, thin cakes of sugar cooked in fat, and other delicacies. We could hardly stagger back to camp and Ahdoo's call to supper did not receive the usual enthusiastic response.

After starting the coolies off with the kit next morning, we went down to the river where we had engaged two *zoks* for the voyage down to Skardu. At 7:30 we shoved off, the Captain, Bates and Petzoldt on one *zok;* Houston, House and I on the other. Each had a crew of four Baltis, armed with poles for paddles. The current was swift and there were stretches of rapids with grand waves. In calmer places our men blew up some of the leaky skins by untying the binding at the end of a leg and applying lung power. We succeeded in working up a very mild rivalry between our crews, vagaries of the current favoring first one, then the other. The last part of the trip was a crossing of the Indus, the men paddling wildly with their miserable poles. We were practically beaten when an eddy carried our opponents out into the river again and stranded them on a reef. We landed victorious and gave them many helpful suggestions as to wading ashore! The voyage had lasted two hours.

The men immediately commenced taking the rafts apart to carry them back to Shigar. The *zok* is a queer and ancient craft, but for its purpose quite efficient. The hire of each *zok* with its crew of four men cost us 8½ rupees or $3.15.

The current of the Indus had carried us downstream, so we had a walk of about two miles to the Skardu resthouse where we arrived soon after ten. The choukidar prepared tea and brought us some apricots, muskmelons, and large cucumbers. Our coolies arrived and were paid off. We were sorry to see some of them depart, especially Rose Ali and Hassein, who had been with us all the way from Base Camp.

The Tehsildar invited us to tea in his garden, with his brother and the Lieutenant from the garrison of the fort also present. It was delightful to sit at the long, shaded table, surrounded by zinnias, dahlias and other flowers raised from seed procured in Bombay. Two servants wearing red turbans waved cloths above our heads to keep away the flies. With the tea we had apricots, enormous mulberries and *pecors*. The latter are made of a piece of vegetable—potato, onion, or spinach —dipped in whole-wheat flour and fried, so that the finished morsel has a hard brown shell and is eaten like a candy.

The Tehsildar was a high caste Brahmin, and full of the lore and legends of the country which he loved. He was an energetic little man and told us he had set out 100,000 trees during his three-year term of office. This term was just ending and he would be transferred to Jammu in two weeks. The Wazir, whom we had met on the way in, had already gone and his successor had not yet arrived.

Yesterday the Tehsildar had climbed a near-by mountain to investigate an accidental shooting in which a boy had killed his companion while hunting ibex. He told us there had been only one other killing during his term of office, that time a murder for which the guilty man was hanged at Srinagar. The Tehsildar was a sportsman and had shot ibex, sharpu, bears, wolves, martins and snow leopards, all in the vicinity of Skardu. After tea we adjourned to a tennis court where Bates defeated the Tehsildar in a hard-fought match, and I was beaten by a young trader from Yarkand. It was a novel setting for tennis, with plenty of solemn-faced servants to chase the balls.

On the next morning, August 4, we left Skardu for the six-day journey over the Deosai Plateau to Srinagar. We had 10 pack horses, a riding pony for each of us, and one for Ghaffar Sheikh, with a good group of horse wallahs from Skardu and Satpura.

Two miles south of Skardu, across the Deosai River from our road, was a Buddhist monument, a boulder

20 feet high with the sun shining brightly on the carvings of its eastern face. I crossed the river and climbed the steep bank to examine it. A seated figure of the Buddha was cut in low relief with right hand extended in the teaching attitude. Around it were carved 20 small seated figures, and on each side a large standing one. At the bottom were rather lengthy inscriptions in Tibetan characters. This monument is a relic of the time when all this country was Buddhist, before the conversion of the natives to Mohammedanism.

After climbing a boulder-strewn slope the trail became a well-constructed road like that along the Indus, and led to a beautiful lake a mile and a half in length, upon whose green waters the mountains cast deep purple shadows. Beside it was an ancient stone fortification probably used to defend Skardu from the south. Beyond the lake the road disappeared onto an area of round stones which extended a couple of miles to the pleasant village of Satpura, where I overtook the others eating lunch, surrounded by smiling natives.

Leaving Satpura, famous for its good porters, we started to climb in earnest, the trail zigzagging steeply. Our stocky ponies took it willingly, but we frequently walked to relieve them. Five hours of steady ascent carried us above timber line to a beautiful valley carpeted with grass and flowers. Behind us we could see the distant Shigar Valley with its green trees and barren walls, and beyond that a vast expanse of high mountains.

We camped just below a snow-rimmed pass at the edge of the plateau. All about us were pony caravans from Srinagar, carrying salt, rice, sugar, cloth, and other staples to Skardu. A trader with two coolies, bound for Srinagar, had some articles made of "Shigar jade," a sort of green soapstone, and we purchased a few bowls. Though we paid his asking price, he seemed loath to sell, feeling perhaps that it would make his journey to Srinagar less worth-while.

In the chill of early morning we climbed over the pass, walking to keep warm, and were soon dropping down into one of the shallow valleys which make up the Deosai Plateau. We seemed to be in a sort of saucer, ringed by mountain tops with patches of snow on them. As we rounded a shoulder, a clear view opened out to the west, where Nanga Parbat rose shining white against a blue sky. With field glasses we examined the tremendous southern face and could distinguish Rakiot Peak rising from the middle of the snowy northern ridge. The climbing route lay on the other side, but we could see the approximate location of the "Silbersattel," the plateau above it, and the summit cone, which looked very steep indeed. Again we wondered how the German Expedition was faring.

The plateau was covered with coarse grass and stones. Wild flowers grew in profusion—blue poppies, yellow snapdragons, a dainty little white flower with cleft petals, looking at first glance like a tiny daisy, and many others. On this vast plain "full many a flower is born to blush unseen"; yet not entirely so, for as I look back now my mind's eye pictures the whole plateau sprinkled with these lovely blossoms.

Larks were abundant, running on the ground before us, while along the crystal streams which we forded were numerous Hodgeson's yellow-headed wagtails. We camped on a gentle hillside, with tents flapping in a strong breeze. Near by were marmots, big tawny rodents much larger than our American woodchucks. Their whistles were loud and harsh, but they were quite tame, often allowing us to approach within 50 feet before diving into their burrows.

Next morning we continued across this spacious upland, riding and walking alternately. A broad gap in the hills gave us another splendid view of Nanga Parbat, the "Naked Mountain." We climbed slowly for several hours, finally reaching a rocky pass with a patch of snow. Almost on the pass were two deep-green lakes. After lunch on the other side we dropped down into a valley of the "Little Deosai." Following this for several miles, we climbed out of it across the Chota Burzil Pass and then went down a steep trail. Passing through a forest of small white birches—apparently bowed down by snows, for each tree grew out horizontally a few feet before turning upward—we emerged on the Gilgit Road about half a mile below the Burzil Bungalow. This is the road which most of the Nanga Parbat expeditions have used. To us it seemed like a boulevard, for it was 8 or 10 feet wide with substantial wooden bridges. There was also a telegraph line.

We camped just above Minimarg, a little village of ungainly log houses below a hillside with a fine stand of evergreens. Next day our road led down the valley of the Kishanganga. On our right were open rolling meadows, on our left the river of clear water, now rushing down narrow gorges, now lingering in deep, green pools. Across the river a heavily forested mountainside was a pleasing contrast to the barren country over which we had been traveling. One of the pools in the river tempted Bates and Houston to a cool plunge which frightened myriads of trout. Here we made tea and had our mid-morning lunch. Among the flowers along the roadside were large white columbines with blue throats. From the woods came the clear notes of the Himalayan whistling thrush, a blue-black bird with a yellow bill, resembling the English blackbird.

The Sherpas were unusually slow and quiet. Questioning brought out the fact that in an orgy at Minimarg the night before they had consumed a whole sheep! Late in the afternoon we came to Gurais, a village of log houses scattered for several miles along the valley. The roofs consisted of wooden slabs running from ridge to eaves, giving a rough ungainly appearance. We crossed the Kishanganga on a fine suspension bridge with cables of steel instead of woven willow withes, and continued for a few miles below the town to a grove of enormous cottonwoods. A more beautiful camping place would be hard to imagine. Soft grass carpeted the glades between giant trees, while fallen trunks four feet in diameter separated the cooking area and formed a dining alcove.

Through the wood flowed a clear, cold stream which was filled with trout. Houston and Bates cut some poles and fished with bent pins tied onto mending thread, while Phinsoo, using a heavy tent pole, was just as unsuccessful. After dinner we sat and talked while moonbeams filtered through the trees transforming our park into a fairy wood.

Learning that there was to be a long hard climb next day, the Sherpas, with Ghaffar Sheikh acting as their agent, hired three horses on which to take turns riding. Poor horsemen, but proud of themselves and determined to get their money's worth, they kept whipping their steeds into an uncomfortable trot; they clung to their saddles with pack frames banging against their backs as they disappeared shrieking around the bends. At frequent intervals we would overtake one who had dismounted to retrieve his hat, to smoke a cigarette, or to wait for another Sherpa to come along and take his turn on horseback.

For several miles our way lay through wooded parkland along the Kishanganga, then left the river to ascend a long side valley to the Tragbal Pass (11,586 feet).

We passed two camel trains on their way from Srinagar back to Gilgit. One associates these large creatures with desert country and it was quite surprising to meet them striding along a forest trail. The road led upward through stands of huge deodars and spruce, with some growths of blue pine and white birch.

Rising above tree line we had a splendid view back over the wooded valley. It was still a long way to the summit. Near the top we came upon a great flock of sheep, two thousand or more. We were told that they are driven up here in the spring to fatten during the summer on this high country.

The pass was filled with cloud, preventing a hoped-for view of Nanga Parbat. A few miles down the other side we pitched our last camp on a grassy shoulder. Below us lay Wular Lake and the Vale of Kashmir, spread out in a great carpet of misty greens. Above the haze, which added to the Vale's allure, were hundreds of kites and vultures, soaring in slow, majestic circles. The trees began 100 feet below us and 1000 feet farther a tiny lake showed the location of the Tragbal Bungalow. Behind us was a grassy hollow dotted with grazing *dzos*, its outline framing more distant hills, while off to the southeast rose Haramukh, the mountain from which K2 was first triangulated.

We spent the afternoon lolling in the hot sun and talking quietly of all that had happened during our three months' journey. After dinner, as we looked down into the deepening haze, we spoke a little sadly of our return to civilization, sorry to be quitting our happy nomad life. Long after dark we crawled into the tents and lay on our sleeping bags, each with his own thoughts of the past and future gradually dissolving into sleep.

On August 9 the police whistle called us for the last time when Ghaffar Sheikh made his round of the tents with "Good morning, five o'clock." We breakfasted in the growing daylight and left at 6. Our men and horses went by road while we dropped straight down on rocky paths through the woods, descending 3000 feet in an hour and a half. Then we passed through the outskirts of a village with fields of tall ripe maize to a bridge a few miles above Bandipura. Crossing the river, we found a grassy spot in the shade of some trees to await the arrival of our lorry which had been ordered by wire to meet us at 2 o'clock.

A barber made his appearance with hundreds of chits which he insisted on our reading. One by one they added to his praises until we realized that if these recommendations could be credited we had at our disposal the services of a truly remarkable barber, undoubtedly the best in Kashmir, if not in the whole of India. A chair was placed in the shade of a tree, Ahdoo heated some water, and the good man set to work on our tousled locks and scraggly beards, causing such a transformation that upon their arrival a little later our grinning Sherpas hardly recognized their sahibs. They apparently approved, for they also had their hair cut while we engaged in a half-hearted ball game, using a small food bag filled with sand.

With the lorry came a surprise, ordered by the Captain, a basket containing bottles of beer on ice and a luscious pink cake. Some of the beer was shared with the Sherpas while we fell ravenously upon the cake. We paid our horse wallahs and bade farewell to their head man, a giant, good-natured fellow with a deep-voiced, *"Bo-da-cha, sahib, bo-da-cha."* (Very good, Sir, very good.) They set out for Bandipura hoping to pick up some freight to carry back to Skardu.

Then 6 sahibs, 6 Sherpas, 3 Kashmiri, and 10 pony loads of kit were piled in and onto the little Chevrolet lorry. When, a mile down the road, we overtook our horses, they broke away from the men and stampeded in all directions; probably they had never seen an automobile before. One ran snorting ahead of us for a mile or more before finding sanctuary with other horses in a field and allowing us to pass. We continued on our rough ride, with frequent stops to refill the boiling radiator, until we came at last to the outskirts of Srinagar, where many vendors sat along the roadside with trays of melons, grapes, apples, plums, and all sorts of delicious looking fruit. Soon we were embroiled in the bustling city traffic, with its jingling tonga bells and tooting automobile horns and unaccustomed crowds of people.

We proceeded to a houseboat engaged for us on the Jhelum River, where a high tea officially closed the expedition. *The Royal Family* was a magnificent craft and as we sat in the dining room, served by the mangi and his little uniformed son, consuming pounds of fruit and dozens of little cakes, we agreed that civilization had some charms after all.

In the evening we sat on the upper deck, with cooling drinks, watching the lights of the town and the small boats passing by, and talked till midnight. The Captain must fly at once to England. Petzoldt would remain in India for a while. The rest of us planned to go up through the Khyber Pass and journey homeward across Afghanistan and Iran.

Behind us were unforgettable days—days on the march, and days on the peak, whose memories we would not exchange for anything. No harm had come to us or to any of our helpers. In a few days we must say farewell to our Kashmiri and our faithful little Sherpas. We would often think of them in the days to come, and also at times of certain stalwart figures and swarthy faces back in the little villages of Baltistan. Later we sahibs too must part to go our separate ways, but we knew that our bond of friendship would last as long as life itself. And perhaps deep in the mind of each was the wistful, doubtful, almost unhoped-for wish that some day we might go out again together, with conquest as our single aim, and climb once more those rocky, icebound slopes which rise to the lofty summit of K2.

Appendix I

EXPEDITIONS TO THE KARAKORAM

Richard L. Burdsall

The date, leader and principal accomplishments of each expedition are given. References are made to periodicals, and by numbers to the list of books at the end. Abbreviations: AJ. = Alpine Journal; GJ. = Geographical Journal; HJ. = Himalayan Journal; Riv. = Rivista Mensile del Club Alpino Italiano; Zft. = Zeitschrift des Deutschen und Österreichischen Alpenvereins.

1856–7	A. Schlagintweit	E. Muztagh Pass (about 18,045 ft.) HJ. VI (1934) p. 147; 15.
1887	Younghusband	Muztagh Pass (17,789 ft.) after crossing Asia. AJ. XIV (1889); GJ. 1930, p. 522; 21.
1889	Younghusband	Explored source of Oprang (Shaksgam); discovered Saltoro Pass; Indira Col (20,866 ft.); 21.
1892	Martin Conway	Explored Hispar, Biafo and Baltoro Glaciers; crossed Nushik La; climbed Pioneer Peak (22,600 ft.) AJ. XVI p. 413; 1; 6; 9.
1899	Bullock-Workman	Explored Biafo Glacier; climbed Koser Gunge (21,000 ft.) and in region of Skoro La. AJ. XIX p. 623; AJ. XX p. 13; 2.

1902 O. Eckenstein	Attempted K2, reaching 21,-400 ft. on northeast spur. Zft. 35 (1904) p. 88; 12.
1902 Bullock-Workman	Explored Chogo Lungma Glacier. AJ. XXII p. 16; 3.
1903 Bullock-Workman	Explored Chogo Lungma Glacier; climbed Mt. Chogo (21,-506 ft.) and Lungma (22,573 ft.); attempted Pyramid Peak (24,492 ft.), reaching 23,390 ft. AJ. XXII p. 494; 3.
1903 Ferber and Honigman	Muztagh Pass. GJ. 1907, p. 630; Zft. 36 (1905) p. 113.
1908 Bullock-Workman	Explored Hispar Glacier. Riv. 1934 p. 651; 4.
1909 Duke of Abruzzi	Attempted K2, reaching 21,-870 ft. at Savoia Pass; attempted Skyang Kangri [Staircase Peak] (24,750 ft.), reaching 21,-650 ft.; attempted Chogolisa I [Bride Peak] (25,110 ft.) reaching 24,600 ft. AJ. XXV pp. 107 and 331; 10.
1909 T. G. Longstaff	Saltoro Pass; Kgyong La; Chulung La; discovered Siachen Glacier. AJ. XXXIV p. 413; AJ. XXXV (1911) pp. 38 and 485; GJ. XXXV (1910) p. 622; 5.
1911 Bullock-Workman	Explored between the Baltoro and Siachen Glaciers. AJ.

	XXXII p. 141; Riv. 1934 p. 651; 5.
1912 Bullock-Workman	Explored Siachen Glacier; Indira Col (20,866 ft.). AJ. XXXII p. 141; GJ. 1914, p. 117; 5.
1913–14 Filipo de Filippi	Explored Rimo Glacier and near sources of Shyok and Yarkand rivers. AJ. XXXVII p. 397; 11.
1922 C. Visser	Explored Saser Muztagh. AJ. XXXV p. 75; 19.
1925 C. Visser	Explored Hunza Valley and Batura Glacier; GJ. 1926 17; 19.
1926 Kenneth Mason	Explored the Shaksgam Valley. GJ. 1927 pp. 289 and 342; 13.
1927 Montagnier	Explored Gujerab Glacier. AJ. 1918 p. 252; GJ. LXXI p. 513.
1929 Duke of Spoleto	Explored Baltoro Glacier and Shaksgam Valley; climbed Cheri Chor (17,881 ft.) GJ. 1930 pp. 385 and 402; 14.
1929 C. Visser	Explored Siachen Glacier and Saser Muztagh; Karakoram Pass; Shyok Valley. HJ. III (1931) p. 13; Die Alpen 1930 p. 201; Die Alpen 1931 p. 281; 18; 19.

1930 G. Dainelli — Lolle Italia (about 20,000 ft.) (Teram CSher); Rimo Glacier. HJ. IV (1932) p. 46; 7.

1933 Gregory and Auden — Topographical expedition to Biafo Glacier. HJ. VI (1934) p. 67.

1934 Dyhrenfurth — Climbed Baltoro Kangri [Golden Throne] (23,990 ft.) and Queen Mary Peak (24,350 ft.) and attempted Gasherbrum I [Hidden Peak]. HJ. VIII (1936) p. 107; Riv. 1936 p. 337; Die Alpen 1935, p. 67; Der Bergsteiger 1935, p. 193; 8.

1935 C. Visser — Explored Shaksgam Valley.

1935 J. Waller — Attempted Peak 36 (25,400 ft.), reaching 24,500 ft. AJ. XLVII (1935) p. 282; HJ. VII (1936) p. 14; HJ. IX (1937) p. 127.

1936 H. de Ségogne — Attempted Gasherbrum I [Hidden Peak] (26,470 ft.) reaching about 22,960 ft. HJ. IX (1937) p. 100; La Montagne 1936, p. 43; Alpinism 1936, p. 317; La Montagne 1937, p. 5; 16.

1937 E. Shipton — Explored Shaksgam. AJ. L p. 256

1938 J. Waller — Attempted Masherbrum (25,660 ft.) reaching about 25,000 ft. on face between southeast and east ridges. HJ. XI (1939).

1. Bruce, C. G.: *Twenty Years in the Himalaya*. London 1910.
2. Bullock-Workman, Dr. F. and Mrs. W. Hunter-Workman: *In the Ice World of Himalaya*. London 1900.
3. —— *Ice-Bound Heights of the Mustagh*. London 1908.
4. —— *The Call of the Snowy Hispar*, London 1910.
5. —— *Two Summers in the Ice-Wilds of Eastern Karakoram*. London 1917.
6. Conway, W. M.: *Climbing and Exploration in the Karakoram-Himalayas*. London 1894.
7. Dainelli, G.: *Buddhists and Glaciers of Western Tibet*. London 1933.
8. Dyhrenfurth, G. O.: *Dämon Himalaya*. Basel 1935.
9. Eckenstein, O.: *The Karakorams and Kashmir*. London 1896.
10. Filippi, F. de.: *Karakoram and Western Himalaya*. London 1912.
11. —— *The Italian Expedition to the Himalaya, Karakoram and Eastern Turkestan 1913–14*. London 1932.
12. Guillarmod, J. J.: *Six mois dans l'Himalaya, le Karakorum et l'Hindu-Kush*. Neuchâtel 1909.
13. Mason, Kenneth: *Exploration of the Shaksgam Valley and Aghil Range, 1926. Records of the Survey of India*. Vol. XXII. Dehra Dun 1928.
14. Savoia-Aosta, Aimone di, Duca di Spoleto, and Prof. A. Desio: *La spedizione geografica italiana al Karakoram*. Milano-Roma 1936.
15. Schlagintweit, B. H.: *Results of a Scientific Mission to India and High Asia undertaken between the Years 1854 and 1858*. London 1861–1866.
16. Ségogne, H. de.: *Himalayan Assault*, by the French Himalayan Expedition 1936. Translated into English

by Nea Morin. London 1938.

17. Shipton, E.: *Blank on the Map*. London 1938.
18. Visser, C.: *Zwischen Kara-Korum und Hindukusch.* Leipzig 1928.
19. —— *Durch Asiens Hochgebirge (Himalaya, Karakoram, Aghil und K'un-lun).* Frauenfeld-Leipzig 1935.
20. Visser, C. and Jenny Visser-Hooft: *Wissenschaftliche Ergebnisse der Niederländischen Expeditionen in den Karakorum und die angrenzende Gebiete 1922, 1925 u. 1929–30.* Leipzig 1935.
21. Younghusband, F. E.: *The Heart of a Continent.* London 1896.

Appendix II

SUMMARY OF EXPEDITION ACTIVITIES

Charles S. Houston

April 12 Party leaves New York

  27 Houston leaves New York

May 9 Rawalpindi: Entire party assembles for first time

  13 Departure from Srinagar after three busy days

APPROACH

DATE		MILES	
May	16	60	We cross the Zoji La (11,600 ft) at midnight
	17	88	Dras: First day in Baltistan
	19	120	Kharal
	22	168	Tolti: We see a native polo game
	25–26	241	Skardu: Capital of Baltistan. We cross the Indus
	27–29	279	Yuno: Our coolies strike
June	3–5	323	Askole: Petzoldt is sick for three days
	8	343	Urdukas: Our first camp alongside the Baltoro Glacier
	12	362	Base Camp at last: Coolies sent back to Askole to return in 45 days

RECONNAISSANCE AND ATTACK

June   13 Base Camp: Snow
          14 First camp on Savoia Glacier
               Bates and Streatfeild return to Base
          15 Second camp established in storm
               Bates and Streatfeild go towards Concordia and back
          16 House and Houston established below Savoia Pass
               Bates and Streatfeild pack to base of Abruzzi Ridge
          17 First attempt on Savoia Pass by House and Houston fails
               Houston and Burdsall return to Base
               Bates and Streatfeild start for the Northeast Ridge
June   18 Snow: House and Petzoldt return to Base
          19 Entire party assembles at Base
               House and Petzoldt return to Savoia Pass camp in snow
          20 Second defeat on Savoia Pass due to fresh snow
          21 Entire party moves up to camp on Godwin-Austen Glacier at foot of Abruzzi Ridge
          22 Bates, Burdsall and Houston examine Northeast Ridge from several sides
               House and Petzoldt climb southern wall of valley to look across at Abruzzi Ridge
          23 All return to Base
               House and Houston reconnoitre to nearly 19,-000 ft. on Abruzzi Ridge and return to Base

June   24 Bates and House camp near Savoia Pass for
            third attempt
            Houston and Streatfeild return to camp be-
            neath Abruzzi Ridge
        25 Bates and House are turned back on rock rib
            east of Savoia Pass
            Houston and Streatfeild climb to 20,000 ft on
            Northeast Ridge and return
        26 Storm
        27 All return to Base in storm
        28 Storm
        29 Entire party carries loads to Camp I at foot of
            Abruzzi Ridge and returns to Base in snow
        30 Second pack to Camp I in clearing weather
July   1 House and Petzoldt are established at Camp I
            while others return to Base
            One tin of gasoline is lost
         2 House and Petzoldt reconnoitre to Camp II
            Others move up to Camp I
         3 Entire party packs to Camp II establishing
            House and Petzoldt there
            Streatfeild starts for Concordia and Gasher-
            brum
         4 House and Petzoldt reconnoitre to Camp III
            Bates and Burdsall and Sherpas pack loads to
            Camp II
            Houston and two Sherpas bring down loads
            from Northeast Camp
            Streatfeild goes from Concordia to Gasher-
            brum and back
July   5 House and Petzoldt pack to Camp III
            Bates, Burdsall and Houston pack to Camp II

Streatfeild comes up to Base from Concordia

July   6   House and Petzoldt descend to Camp I after
strengthening route to Camp III
Burdsall and Houston with Sherpas go to Base
returning to Camp I with loads
Streatfeild arrives at Camp I having found no
gasoline

7   Four men move up to Camp II
Streatfeild and one Sherpa pack to Camp II
and return to Camp I
Burdsall and Sherpas go to Base returning
with loads

8   Storm
Houston and Sherpas go down to Camp I and
bring up loads
Burdsall moves up to Camp II

9   Four men pack to Camp III

10   Houston and Petzoldt are established in Camp
III by others who return to Camp II
Streatfeild goes to Base to meet coolies from
Askole

11   Houston and Petzoldt reconnoitre to Camp IV
Bates and House carry loads to Camp III leav-
ing two Sherpas camped there
Burdsall and Streatfeild fetch loads from Camp
I to Camp II
Twelve coolies arrive at Base Camp with wood
and mail

12   Bates and House and one more Sherpa move
up to Camp III
Streatfeild and Burdsall go down to Base

July   12   Houston and Petzoldt carry loads to Camp IV
        13   Bates and House established in Camp IV by
              others
              Burdsall and Streatfeild move up again to
              Camp I with mail—the first in six weeks
        14   Bates and House reconnoitre to Camp V
              Petzoldt and Sherpas carry loads to Camp IV
              Houston descends to Camp II to bring up
              supplies and mail sent up to Camp II with
              Sherpas
        15   Bates and House carry loads to Camp V
              Houston and Petzoldt move from Camp III
              to IV with three Sherpas and later go on to
              Camp V
              Burdsall and Streatfeild move to camp at foot
              of Northeast Ridge
        16   Houston and Petzoldt reconnoitre to Camp
              VI
              Bates and House with three Sherpas move up
              to Camp V
              Burdsall and Streatfeild climb to 20,000 ft. on
              Northeast Ridge turn back and go up to
              Windy Gap
        17   Storm holds mountain party in camp
              Burdsall and Streatfeild return to Base from
              Northeast
July   18   Houston and Petzoldt pack to Camp VI and
              reconnoitre above
              Bates and House with Sherpas set up one tent
              at Camp VI and return to Camp V
        19   Houston and Petzoldt climb Black Pyramid

and return to Camp VI

July   19   Bates and House with Sherpas move up to
                Camp VI
                Burdsall and Streatfeild go down to Concor-
                dia

          20   Four climbers and Pasang Kikuli carry loads
                to top of Black Pyramid establishing Houston
                and Petzoldt there in Camp VII while others
                return to Camp VI
                Burdsall and Streatfeild survey about Con-
                cordia

          21   Houston and Petzoldt climb to base of sum-
                mit cone at 26,000 ft and return to Camp VII

          22   Houston and Petzoldt return to Camp VI
                Entire party descends with kit to Camp IV
                Burdsall and Streatfeild return to Base from
                Concordia

          23   Party descends to Camp II
                Clouds come in over summit
                Burdsall goes up to Camp I

          24   Burdsall climbs to Camp II to help party
                down
                Streatfeild goes to Camp I from Base
                Entire party reunited and descends to Base

          25   Rest day at Base with baths
                Coolies arrive a day early

          26   We leave K2 and start home
                Thin high clouds on all the summits

          30   Askole again   ·

August   2   We cross the Skoro La in a blinding snow
                storm

           3   Skardu

August 5–6   We cross the Plains of the Deosai
       7–9   Along the Gilgit Road
        10   Srinagar: Journey's End

*   *   *   *

	HEIGHT (In feet)
Base Camp	16,600
Camp I	17,700
Camp II	19,300
Camp III	20,700
Camp IV	21,500
Camp V	22,000
Camp VI	23,300
Camp VII	24,700

Appendix III

EQUIPMENT

Charles S. Houston, M.D.

CLOTHING

Woolens: Duncan. Four sweaters, two underwear per man. Turtle-neck sweaters, long underwear, natural very lightweight, loose-weave woolens. Excellent.

Mittens and Socks: Lawrie. Six pairs Herdwick brushed-wool socks, in two different sizes to fit one over the other, marked with different colored tape. Do not shrink, very warm, best climbing sock we know. Four lightweight Shetland mittens. Excellent.

Windproof Suits: Flint. Double thickness Grenfell parka and trousers separate. Absolutely windproof, very tough, built to measure. One of best items we had.

Gauntlets: Osborne. Soft buckskin mitt with canvas cuff. Leather is soft enough so mitt can be used on difficult rock safely. Very warm, dries rapidly.

Boots: Lawrie. Unlined Mark VIII with nailing to taste. One of finest boots for alpine climbing made; leather is nonfreezing and very good. The toe is not deep enough, and the sole not wide enough to wear comfortably over socks needed at high altitude. If this is corrected, and if boot is fitted by Lawrie personally, or by cobbler here over desired number of socks, then this boot will be very good. We do not know any other boot as good even with these faults. Paul Bauer has a boot made in Munich, with the sole built on a slight curve to avoid the inevitable crease over the toe. P. Allain in Paris also has a good boot.

Shoes: Personal. Each man has individual taste for the long hard walk in. Majority preferred a low, rubber-soled shoe. Must be chosen with great care and thoroughly broken in before trip starts. Sneakers are good. Metal arch-supporters recommended.

Rain Capes: Camp and Sports. Rambler model, light and tough, and waterproof; built to shelter pack also. Useful even if one never sees rain.

Miscellaneous: Wool scarf for high altitudes. Face mask of cloth or light leather very useful against high winds in upper camps. Soft-felt hat is more comfortable than solar topi and just as good. Many handkerchiefs, large and preferably silk. Insoles, felt or better sea-weed (Osborne), very important against sweating of feet. Pajamas worn by most of us as high as 16,000 ft. Polo shirt, shorts, long stockings, light ski-jacket for march to base camp.

CLIMBING KIT

Pack-frames: Camp and Sports. Light (1.5 lbs.), of duraluminum, Everest model. Very necessary for carrying boxes, bags, etc. For Sherpa porters and sahibs.

Crampons: Lawrie. Stainless steel. Eckenstein model with two-strap binding simple to do and undo, and does not bind the toes too tightly.

Pitons: P. Allain. Iron or duraluminum; by far the best and lightest we know. The duraluminum ones did *not* break in cold weather under sudden strain.

Karabiners: Lawrie. Small tapered ones with small filed

edge on opening jaw to facilitate quick use.

Goggles: Hamblin. Everest model of Crookes glass. Pale-golden color, very comfortable to wear and absolutely safe. Head strap not as good as frame and glass. Can be made to prescription at extra cost. Best mountain goggle we know.

Rope: Beale. Latest and best is halfway between Alpine line and Alpine rope: very strong, soft and safe. For fixed rope we used ⅜" hemp bought in Bombay, 1700 ft.

Willow Wands: Personal. ¼" x 36" dowels. Paint one end black for 6–8" to aid visibility. Essential for marking route along crevassed glacier in case of storm.

Snowshoes: Camp and Sports. Duraluminum frames about 18" oval, with rawhide lacing. Too flexible, not very good, need much improvement, then would be valuable even on steep slopes.

CAMPING KIT

Tents: Burns. Meade model, called Yak tent, has V-poles at each end, holds two men and stove, very simple to pitch. Of excellent cloth and design, waterproof, and will not tear even in very high wind. A splendid tent especially where campsites are small and need to be built up.

Tents: Abercrombie. Pyramid tent, with center pole, one guy rope, no wall, holds three or four men. Easy to pitch on hard terrain. Not perfected as yet; needs changes.

Tents: Woods. Standard Logan. Best tent for base camp or any level ground. Spacious and stands wind well. Needs waterproofing.

Sleeping-bags: Burns. Two bags: inner of eiderdown, lined with soft flannel; outer of live goose down. Total weight 7.5 lbs. Both bags tapered, inner with good design hood. We were never cold. Bag is a little too short for a tall man, should be a little wider for the average man. Made to order costing about $45 for eider in inner bag, $35 for goose in both (almost as good). The most satisfactory bag we know for warm light sleeping.

Mattresses: Abercrombie. Half length air mattress. Very tough, weighing about 4 lbs. Lasts two seasons at least. Where sleep is as important as it is at high altitude we feel extra weight is worth it. Lighter, cheaper mattresses puncture too easily, leak.

Snow-shovels: Beale. Bernina model, of aluminum, with short handle, detachable. Better than model that attaches to ice ax. Very light and strong.

Stoves: Condrupp. Primus stove model No. 221 L. Burners adjusted for any specified altitude by maker. Benzine can be bought in India; gasoline is as good. We had no trouble as high as we used them, 24,700 ft. Get set of extra parts and spare cleaners. Don't use ethyl gas. Funnels to fill stove must be bought at home.

Fuel: Benzine or gasoline; brand recommended by Condrupp can be bought anywhere and is good. Use Meta, solid fuel, to start stove; much better than alcohol or gasoline. Strike-anywhere matches are not good above 16,000 ft.: take box-matches, also small friction-top tins for carrying above base. Take about four times as many as you think necessary, as coolies are crazy for them.

Containers: Camp and Sports. Aluminum water bottles, with screw tops, holding 1 qt. Ideal for carrying gas on mountain, strong, light and leak-proof. On way to base use 2-gal. tins; 4-gal. is too heavy. Take at least two qt. bottles for every camp anticipated.

Packing: Abercrombie. 18" duffles for personal kit. 9" duffles for food, etc. 15, 10, 5, 1 lb. paraffin bags for carrying cereals, sugar, fruit, etc., are essential; these fit neatly into duffles (9"). Best and safest way to carry perishable food. Large sacks to carry 50 lbs. of coolie food, etc., can be made in Kashmir: make at least twice as many as needed for food, as porters need some to carry their clothing unless others are provided. Plywood boxes (3 thickness) 10" x 12" x 24" can be cut at home and assembled in Srinagar. Re-enforce with ½" strips inside and tin edging. Hinge and lock for lid. If well made these are better and far lighter than local yakdan.

Kitchen: Local. Aluminum dekshi made in Srinagar is cheapest, best and lightest heating cookset we know. Take at least two for every camp anticipated. On mountain we used pint cup and spoon per man. On way in add light plate, fork. Sherpas need same. For march in take several empty 4-gal. gas tins with handles fitted to knocked out tops. On mountain use collapsible light canvas buckets made by Camp and Sports.

Hardware: New York. 50 and 100-lb. scales essential. Several dozen assorted copper rivets. Pliers, good screwdriver, one or two spools wire and tape. One ball heavy twine and several hundred feet clothesline. Four light flashlights, and few extra batteries. One dozen long-burning candles and collapsible lantern (Lawrie). Two light steel cash-boxes for carrying coolie pay. Several hundred waterproof tags (Dennison) to tie on food-bags. Small notebooks and pencils for listing at base camp and notes. Sewing kit with much thread. Steel mirror. One wash basin.

PORTER OUTFITS

Woolens: Camp and Sports. Two pair wool underdrawers, 2 pair undershirts, 3 turtle-neck sweaters. Windproof suits or khaki jacqua very good. Balaclava wool helmet. Ski gauntlet and mitts of best wool. Socks should be numerous: suggest six pair ordinary cheap wool pair for march in and on mountain, then at least four pair of best quality to be given out at base camp for mountain. Sherpa wears out socks very fast, needs as many as sahib. Boots: Lawrie. Make on Ghurka last to fit wide short Sherpa foot. Suggest 3 size 7, 3 size 8 and 1-2 size 9. Many extra laces, and grease to suit. Ordinary mountain goggles, two pairs apiece. All coolies have to be given goggles on Baltoro, so get 80–100 cheap Japanese pairs in Srinagar. Porter sleeping-bags made by Burns, double bags, lined or unlined, with good down, costing about $15–$20. Our Sherpas never complained. Mattresses desirable, but not essential. Take good ones, if any, as Sherpas burst the cheap ones rapidly.

FIRMS DEALT WITH:

David T. Abercrombie, 311 Broadway, New York City.

Arthur Beale, 194 Shaftsbury Avenue, London.

Robert Burns, Hanover Mill, London Road, Manchester, England.

Camp and Sports, 21 New Gate Street, London.

Condrupp, 77 Fore Street, London.

Mrs. C. Duncan, New Road, Scalloway, Shetland Isles.

Theodore Hamblin, 15 Wigmore Street, London.

Howard Flint, 38 Maddox Street, London.

Robert Lawrie, Bryanston Street, Marble Arch, London.

Asa Osborne, 8 High Street, Boston, Mass.

Appendix IV

FINANCIAL

Richard L. Burdsall

The total cost of the expedition, including traveling expenses of five men from New York to India and return, was $9434.03, made up as follows:

	Rupees	Dollars	
Equipment			$2620.73
Food			364.24
Travel			3803.80
Freight			387.07
Expenses in Field (3 months)	Rupees	Dollars	
Coolies	1513– 4	567.47	
Pack Horses	549–10	206.11	
Riding Horses	71–14	26.95	
Food and wood for Sahibs	277–15	104.23	
Food for Sherpas & Kashmiris	214– 8	80.44	
Rest Houses	30–14	11.58	
Baksheesh	69– 5	25.99	
Misc.	298–15	112.10	
	3026– 5	1134.87	1134.87
Sherpas (six)	1074– 0		402.75
Kashmiris (three)	440– 0		165.00
Cables, telegrams, postage, stationery			58.28
Photography			430.63
Misc.			66.66
			9434.03

Expenditures were made in the following currencies:

Dollars				4084.44
Pounds Sterling	£374– 0– 4	Average rate $4.99		1866.34
French Francs	3018.35	"	" .0321	96.89
Indian Rupees	9030–5	"	" .375	3386.36
				9434.03

Equipment: Minimum quantity but best quality obtainable; nearly 70% (in value) came from England.

Food: 40 lbs. pemmican from Denmark, 60 lbs. butter and 43½ lbs. Cheddar cheese from England, 20 lbs. Tobler's chocolate (for variety), from France, 10 lbs. tinned meat from India; remainder of food from America. This item does not include food purchased in field.

Travel: Transatlantic 3rd Class; railroad Cherbourg to Marseilles, steamer Marseilles to Bombay, railroad Bombay to Rawalpindi, all 2nd Class. This item includes hotels (2 days in Paris, 1 night in Rawalpindi, 4 days in Srinagar), meals, tips, a week on a houseboat after return to Srinagar, and Houston's airplane trip from London to Karachi, India.

Expenses in Field: Includes everything spent during the 31-day trip from Srinagar to the Base Camp, 43 days at the mountain, and 15-day return journey to Srinagar. Through the kindness of the Kashmir Government we were able to purchase in Srinagar two drafts on the Treasury in Skardu, one for 1500 Rupees ($462.50) which we cashed on the way in, and one for 1000 Rupees ($375.00) which we cashed coming out. Paper money was not of much use beyond Skardu, so we left this town with 75 lbs. (1½ porter loads) of Rupees and eight, two, and one anna pieces.

Coolies: Our food and equipment weighed about 4000

lbs. and when horses could not be used we required 75 porters, who received from one-half to one Rupee per day, depending upon the length and difficulty of the stage. On leaving Askole the number of porters had to be increased to 95 in order to carry their own food for the 8-day trip to the Base Camp and 5-day return. The extra food porters were sent back as the flour was consumed.

Pack Horses: They carried 150 to 160 lbs. (3 coolie loads) so 25 horses were sufficient. Costing 1 to 1½ Rupees per day, including driver, they were cheaper than porters.

Riding Horses: Few were used on the journey to the mountain, but returning we all rode on the six-day trip over the Deosai.

Food and Wood for Sahibs: Sheep (7 to 10 Rupees, $2.65 to $3.75 each), chickens (about 12 annas, $.28 each), eggs (5 annas, $.12 per doz., we took 23 dozen from Askole), rice, and flour were purchased on the journey.

Food for Sherpas & Kashmiris: Tsamba (barley flour), *atta* (wheat flour) and tea were supplied to the Sherpas; also some of our own food when on the mountain. A money allowance for food was given to the Kashmiris.

Rest Houses: We preferred our tents and used bungalows only at the larger towns.

Sherpas: This item includes traveling expenses for the six Sherpas from Darjeeling to Srinagar and return, totaling 285 Rupees ($107).

Kashmiris: Covers wages and *baksheesh* for our Shikari, cook, and coolie.

Photography: Includes the purchase of one 16 mm. movie camera and exposure meter, movie film, and developing, etc.

Appendix V

FOOD

Robert H. Bates

If you ever look over your diary of a former expedition, you will be surprised at the frequency with which food is mentioned. And yet if you recollect the actual trip itself, you will recall that food of one sort or another was almost always under discussion. There were the days of blizzard when, lying in sleeping bags, you all pondered what you would most like to have for dinner; and, as that was impossible, what you would certainly have when the expedition staged its reunion banquet the following winter.

Because of this tremendous emphasis on food, the commissary of any expedition must expect strange laments, such as one I remember on a crevassed Alaskan glacier a few years ago, when the chap behind me suddenly remarked, "Gee, I wish I had a cucumber!" But cucumbers and truffles and champagne cannot be carried on a light, mobile expedition which wishes to limit its food to less than two pounds a man per day. This is forcefully brought home when one realizes that the average expeditionary will eat three times as much at any given meal in the mountains as he eats at home—provided he gets the chance.

Our food lists for the Karakoram were based on the food used by Bradford Washburn in four journeys to Alaska or the Yukon; and on the lists of expeditions to Foraker, Waddington, Minya Konka and Nanda Devi. As there were members of these various expeditions on the Karakoram undertaking, the commissary felt that many of his problems were solved.

During the 30-day trip from Srinagar to the mountain and the 14-day return journey, we bought meat (chickens or sheep) and eggs most of the time. Occasionally we got a few poor vegetables, but for our other supplies we had to depend on the expedition stores.

A typical breakfast on the march consisted of tea, dried fruit, cereal and eggs. On the mountain the eggs (except at Base Camp), and sometimes the fruit, were lacking. For lunch we had crackers or *chupattis* (native unleavened bread) with butter, cheese or sardines, chocolate or malted milk, and sometimes dried fruit or dates, supplemented on rare occasions by hard-boiled eggs or jam. Supper usually consisted of soup, meat, dried vegetables, crackers and tea. On the march from Srinagar, curries, *pilaus* and other native dishes were often the whole meal, while at the higher camps pemmican and biscuits composed the menu.

The amounts taken for the six-man team for three months follow:

50 lbs. of quick oatmeal (25 lbs. iron ration).

20 lbs. Maltex.

10 lbs. corn meal.

10 lbs. Cream of Wheat.

We found oatmeal the easiest cereal to cook at high altitudes, but Maltex the most popular when it could be thoroughly cooked. Variety of cereals for a long trip cannot be too great.

50 lbs. American dried apricots.

20 lbs. Baltistan dried apricots.

20 lbs. dried apples.

20 lbs. confectionized prunes.

15 lbs. seedless raisins.

10 lbs. stoned dates.

10 lbs. dried peaches.

5 lbs. figs.

The apricots from John Leonard, Cupertino, Cal., were especially good to eat raw. The Balti apricots had an entirely different flavor and when cooked were delicious. The pitted prunes (Mrs. Bee Ritchie, Sunnyvale, Cal.) became slightly fermented but required no cooking and came in very handy at the high camps. Pitted dates of the same firm are also good. The dried peaches were bought in the United States and proved too difficult to cook thoroughly.

48 lbs. Danish pemmican.

10 lbs. sardines.

5 lbs. tuna.

5 lbs. salmon.

9 lbs. chicken.

6 lbs. corned beef hash.

10 lbs. beefsteak and onions.

18 lbs. dried beef (6-lb. tins).

Pemmican (Danske Vin et Konserves Fabriken, Copenhagen) is excellent if one does not try to live on it alone. It should be saved for the high camps where cooking is difficult. There it is priceless. Tins of beefsteak and onions are delicious but too heavy for their food value, unless for occasional variety. Dried beef is good at any camp. It has extremely high food value and goes well, cooked or uncooked, with almost anything else. We deeply regretted losing part of our supply through a punctured tin.

10 lbs. raspberry jam.

10 lbs. strawberry jam.

10 lbs. honey.

5 lbs. apple jelly.

5 lbs. currant jelly.

Kashmir honey is recommended, but small pressure top tins should be found if possible. Jam is especially important in cold weather. We should have had more for the march to the mountain.

20 lbs. dried baked beans.

12 lbs. dried corn.

8 lbs. dried beets.

8 lbs. dried mixed vegetables.

4 lbs. dried cabbage.

4 lbs. dried sweet potatoes.

2 lbs. dried carrots.

Mrs. J. F. Kelly, 20 Barker Rd., Pittsfield, Mass., cannot be too highly recommended for her dried vegetables. Her corn and beets are especially good. We found that the beans and beets were the only vegetables we could cook high on the mountain; some thought the beans caused slight indigestion because they were not thoroughly cooked at high camps. The corn, carrots, sweet potatoes and mixed vegetables, while excellent below, took too long to cook at over 18,000 ft.

40 lbs. Cheddar cheese (in 10-lb. tins from England).

10 lbs. Gruyère (in small, tinfoil-wrapped sections).

The cheese was very popular. Gruyère is expensive, but it is good high-camp food and is always welcome. The big Cheddar cheeses were just the thing to make tea and crackers a success at Base Camp and below.

50 lbs. *atta*.

80 lbs. crackers (National Biscuit Co. Hard Bread).

The *atta* (wheat flour) was made into *chupattis* at Base

Camp and below. The crackers were a sort of hardtack, not too hard, yet not friable. They were consistently popular and solved the cracker problem uncommonly well.

   108 Maggi soup cubes.

   36 cans Knorr bouillon and soup.

The Knorr bouillon was very good. We found also that Maggi soup cubes mix well with pemmican.

   50 lbs. Javatex chocolate.

   20 lbs. Toblerone chocolate.

   10 lbs. Epicure chocolate.

   60 lbs. Horlick's Malted Milk tablets.

   400 rolls Beechnut and Life Saver fruit drops.

Good chocolate is always important on any expedition. Walter Baker Co.'s Javatex, specially made for tropical climates, survived the heat well and was always popular, though Toblerone was perhaps the favorite. We used some of our chocolate for iron rations. Horlick's Malted Milk, put up in pressure-top tins, is extremely good. The tablets were soon known as "Go Quicks" and tablets and tins were always in demand. Fruit drops were handy on the thirsty march from Srinagar. Beechnut drops seem to stand up better under intense heat.

   5 lbs. tea.

   1000 tea balls.

   6 lbs. Whitman's Instantaneous Chocolate.

   38 lbs. Klim (dried milk).

At one time we were drinking nearly 2 qts. of tea apiece a day. Incidentally, tea balls prevent squabbles about how dark the tea should be. Klim, of course, can be used to advantage in almost any cooking operation.

   60 lbs. butter.   3 tins pepper.

   30 lbs. rice.   2 tins cinnamon.

15 lbs. macaroni.	2 pks. jello.
12 lbs. hominy.	2 lbs. kipper.
10 lbs. pecans.	2 tins powdered gravy.
10 lbs. salt.	

As far as I know, the perfect tinned butter to withstand tropical heat has not been found. Rice is always good when it can be easily cooked. Pecans make good iron rations and save cooking at high camps. Hominy goes well as a vegetable at supper. Boned kippers are always well received. On another expedition I would take 15 lbs. Our salt was so frequently "borrowed" by natives or by our Kashmir cook that in the end we had to get some from the Sherpas.

1 qt. Hudson Bay Rum.
1 qt. Jamaica Rum.

All hands agreed that a little more alcohol would have been very welcome.

One of the most difficult problems concerning expedition food is how much sugar to take. Some climbers believe that above snowline one should take at least 2 lbs. of *total sugar* per man per day. Others use only ⅛ lb. per man per day, plus sugar from dates, jam, etc. We had only about ⅓ lb. of pure sugar per man per day, plus some sugar in fruits, chocolate, jam, malted milk, etc. It would have been better had we taken at least ½ lb. of pure sugar apiece per day.

180 lbs. white sugar.

Sherpa food is a problem in itself. The porters eat roughly about 2 lbs. of *atta* or *tsamba* (barley flour) per day. They also drink much tea—with as much or little sugar as you allow them. Below snowline they like rice and *dhali* (curry powder).

These are random notes about the food of the Karakoram

Expedition. Each item could be discussed in great detail, but the important fact is that, although we had no added vitamins, the food kept us in good condition *and we had no mountain sickness at all.* On a future trip, however, I would take along additional food for stocking camps, and would also add a little to the bulk. A minority of one or two members thought the rations too slim. We all felt that almost every camp on K2 should be stocked to hold out against at least a ten-day storm. If you have seven or eight camps, this means taking a large supply of additional food which probably will never be eaten.

The writer hopes that more mountaineers will publish their ideas on expedition food.*

* For recent discussion of expedition food see the controversy between Tilman and Odell in *The Geographical Journal,* December, 1938; *Himalayan Assault,* London, Methuen & Co., 1938; or Dr. Teasdale's article in *The Himalayan Journal* for 1939.

Appendix VI

TRANSPORT

Capt. N. R. Streatfeild

Transport for an expedition to the Karakoram is often difficult to obtain unless word of the group's requirements has been sent on in advance. Arrangements for the American Alpine Club party were made as follows: The Government Transport Contractor at Srinagar collected ponies for the rough journey over the Zoji La to Dras; from Dras to Skardu, transport was requested of the Tehsildar of Kargil; while from Skardu to Askole and thence to Base Camp the Tehsildar of Skardu was asked to have coolies ready on specified dates.

On May 13 the expedition left Nedou's Hotel early in the morning and were driven 18 miles to Woyil Bridge. Here 24 ponies were selected from a large collection and loaded for the 5-day stage to Dras. So early in the year the ponies are in poor condition and find the snow on the Zoji La extremely trying; however, they landed us in Dras in the prescribed time and all was well. The Zoji La is not officially open for pony transport until June, so we were forced to pay the exorbitant rate of twelve rupees per pony for the march. After June 1 the official rates come into force and only about half the above has to be paid.

At Dras we found ponies waiting to take our kit the two marches to Kharal; these we paid at the rate of one anna per pony per mile. From Kharal along the Indus Valley to

Skardu the problem of transport is easily solved: by a system known as "Res" the government details certain villages each to supply coolies for a one-day march. Thus one is forced to change coolies each evening on arrival in camp. The rates are very cheap—half an anna per coolie-mile.

At Skardu we found the efficient Tehsildar ready with all we required. From here to Yuno (two marches) all went well, but the coolies then began to demand exorbitant rates of pay and it was necessary to enlist the help of the Tehsildar at Skardu to obtain the number we required at a reasonable rate. As soon as one penetrates beyond the regular trade route to Skardu the rates begin to rise, and we were paying one anna per coolie-mile from Yuno to Askole.

Now came the work of enlisting the 75 coolies to carry our kit from Askole—the last village up the Braldu River—to the Base Camp. It is a journey of eight marches which necessitate not only coolies to carry one's own belongings but additional coolies to carry food for the other coolies! The men in these parts being extremely independent and self-opinioned, the best rates we were able to arrange were one rupee per coolie per day plus two annas food allowance. The men of Askole are naturally indolent, so it is difficult to cover many miles each day: after the first day's march the whole contingent went on strike and refused to proceed farther unless we offered them still higher wages and promised them shorter hours! The strike, however, was soon quelled by telling the ringleaders to go home, as we had decided to carry our own belongings; we also reminded them that there would be no pay for the work already carried out.

The Base Camp was reached without further trouble and

the coolies all paid off and sent back to their homes. A proportion were told to come back on a specified date to carry for us on the return journey.

Such are the whims of the oriental that the journey home is always easier and cheaper to arrange. The coolies we had detailed, with the addition of a certain number of other hopefuls, reached Base Camp a day sooner than we had anticipated. Full of rejoicing, possibly for our safety, they carried our belongings to Askole, for one rupee per day, in five days instead of the eight taken on the outward journey. Most of them then insisted on accompanying us to Skardu. We saved two more days on this portion of the march by crossing the Skoro La (16,700 ft.) in place of following the tortuous course of the river. The last march to Skardu was performed in style on a *zok*—a raft made from inflated goat skins: these rafts are floated down the river and carry one along at about eight miles an hour if the current is strong.

From Skardu another short-cut was taken by crossing the high and barren Deosai Plain to Bandipur. This took us six days and our transport consisted of ponies for which we paid at the rate of one anna per pony per mile. At Bandipur a lorry was awaiting us and we completed the 30 miles into Srinagar in style.

Our six Sherpa Porters were recruited in Darjeeling through the Local Representative of the Himalayan Club. They were sent the one thousand miles to Rawalpindi by train and we collected them there before leaving for Srinagar. In addition to their food and clothing, these cheerful little men were paid at the rate of about ten annas per day below the snow-line, and one rupee above it. More valuable and loyal companions it would be difficult to find.

Much assistance in the collection and management of the coolies and ponies was given by our shikari, by name Ghaffar Sheikh, a rogue who always had a smile on his face and a joke on his tongue.

Appendix VII

K2 WEATHER

William P. House

It seems almost presumptuous to present the meager meteorological observations of the 1938 Karakoram Expedition in anything as definite as an appendix. The truth is, what meteorological data was obtained was of a distinctly lay character. In that light it is presented, not as scientific findings from which sound conclusions can be drawn, but as a record of the weather as it affected a party engaged primarily in getting as high as possible on K2 and therefore limited in extra equipment and in the energy and time that could be expended in collecting data. Weather in the Karakoram is still so little known that perhaps even these amateurish observations will be of some value in correlating the data obtained by previous expeditions and in developing a clearer picture of atmospheric conditions in this little-known range.

Situated as it is north of the main range of the Himalaya, separated from that by the Indus Valley, the Karakoram apparently creates its own climate. As in many other high, isolated mountain ranges, the weather is largely independent of that of the surrounding country. Unlike Mt. Everest, Kanchenjunga, Nanga Parbat and other great Himalayan Peaks, the interior of the Karakoram does not appear to be affected by the monsoon—a factor of great importance to the mountain climber. Rather, Karakoram weather seems to resemble Alpine weather; the change of seasons is characterized not by sudden drastic and complete changes, but by gradual transitionary changes. The experience of previous expeditions shows no uniformity in the date of summer passing into fall, for instance. Some expeditions have found good weather early in the season—in late April and May; others have found excellent weather as late as August. Although some groups have reported breaks in the weather apparently as complete as on Everest and other monsoon-controlled mountains, these almost invariably marked the end of the party's stay in the region. In other words, these changes may have been of short duration followed by alternate periods of clear weather and bad.

The uncertain nature of the weather—characterized by sudden changes lasting only a few days—was the most striking weather feature in the Karakoram in June and July of 1938. Frequently the morning dawned absolutely clear and remained so until noon. Then light clouds formed and a few hours later perhaps a full-fledged storm developed. Often the weather the next morning improved and the day ended fair.

The worst storms in general seemed to come from the south and southwest, although clouds frequently blew in from the east. This was particularly noticeable while we were on the mountain. Wind directions recorded three times a day were almost invariably from the southwest (when there was wind at all) for almost a month from June 27 on. This is not surprising since it corresponds with the direction of some of the main valleys and the axis of several passes to the south of K2. Had observations been made high up on the west side of K2 it is possible wind might have come preponderantly from the northwest. The only justification for advancing this is that from both sides of the Abruzzi Ridge the wind was always in the same direction—counter clockwise around the mountain.

Winds were very high on several occasions—always from the southwest. Except on the K2 Glacier, where there was generally a down glacier wind in the afternoon, high winds never occurred without snow and low visibility.

The major storms were usually presaged by one or more days of cloudy or unsettled weather. What appeared to be a major storm approaching as retreat from the high camps was begun, gave several days' warning: first in a persistent rim of clouds on the southwest horizon, then in a similar rim to the east and south. For three days these came closer. Finally on the fourth the peaks around K2 flew banners and storm clouds of all descriptions. Fish-shaped clouds flew from several of the peaks and elsewhere in the sky were long, freight-train-like strings of clouds. Only on the fifth day when we were back at Base Camp did the upper part of K2 appear to be completely in clouds. During the next day and the march out the clouds remained on all the peaks down to about 18,000 ft. Ten days after leaving Base Camp the region around K2 appeared to be still in clouds. This observation was made from about 13,000 ft. on the edge of the Deosai Plains above Skardu. What we had been able to see of the interior of the range during that time suggested continued storms. Our crossing of the Skoro La (16,700 ft.) was in a storm which seemed confined to the N or K2 side of the pass. Whether the apparent continued stormy weather would have been serious enough to prevent climbing, there is no way of telling. It is possible that in character it was no different from what had been experienced on K2—namely a succession of good and bad days. From the generally low observation points in the valleys it is quite possible that the clouds which seemed to be covering the whole of the interior of the Karakoram were only on the tops of the outer, lower peaks and did not represent a continuous storm at all. This would fit in with what was often observed from K2, namely clouds on surrounding outer mountains, but good weather on K2 itself.

It seems safer, therefore, not to regard it as a definite break in the weather, but rather as a temporary break which might have been followed by stretches of good weather such as were experienced on K2 during June and July.

In general temperatures were surprisingly high. The lowest temperature recorded by the maximum and minimum thermometer from Base Camp to Camp VI was 1° F.* Above Base Camp, both on the Abruzzi Ridge and on the Savoia and Godwin-Austen Glaciers, the minimum temperatures averaged around 10° F. Six A. M. and eight P. M. temperatures were generally well below freezing but were not always consistent with changes in altitude, as can be seen by the chart.

Temperatures taken at 2:00 P. M. were generally above freezing. On only five days on the entire trip were they below freezing. The coldest recorded at this hour was 24° F. Three of these days were too bad for traveling. They were the only days directly lost through bad weather. Many other days would undoubtedly have been too bad for traveling above the glacier—particularly during the first two weeks—but as all observations at the time were made from the glacier they do not indicate it.

---

* It is interesting to note that the 1939 American Expedition to the Karakoram found that the thermometer left near Base Camp by Burdsall in 1938 had registered a minimum of only –3½° F. during the interim.

From comparisons of the relatively low night temperatures recorded during the first two weeks (June 13–July 1) with the temperatures recorded at greater altitudes in the next few weeks it would appear that the season grew warmer from the time we arrived at Base Camp. That is, the night temperatures between 17,000 ft. and 19,000 ft. in late June were in some cases higher than night temperatures above 20,000 ft. in July.

On the basis of temperatures as well as number of clear days, the month of July in 1938 offered the best climbing weather. June, to judge from the bad weather at low elevations, would have been poor at best. August might have remained fine. Of the other months—May, September and October—our observations, limited as they are, can shed no light.

NOTE: All temperatures were recorded from a maximum and minimum thermometer—actual readings being made at 6:00 A. M., 2:00 P. M. and 8:00 P. M. Unfortunately, the minimum temperatures were not recorded regularly enough to be of much value in correlating them with actual temperatures.

For night and morning readings as well as for minimum readings the thermometer was generally hung on the outside of the tent, clear of the fabric and openings, 3 ft. above the ground. It is possible that some errors may have been present due to body heat from the tent. The stoves were never going at those hours.

Afternoon temperatures were taken usually with the thermometer 3 ft. above the ground in the shade—either on a rock or the tent.